C000016494

the fan

the fan

HUNTER DAVIES

POMONA

A POMONA BOOK P-003

Mad in England!

Published by Pomona 2003

1 3 5 7 9 8 6 4 2

Copyright © Hunter Davies 1996–2003

Hunter Davies has asserted his right under the Copyright, Designs and Patents Act
1988 to be identified as the author of this work.

All rights reserved. Without limiting the rights under copyright reserved above, no
part of this publication may be reproduced, stored in or introduced into a retrieval
system, or transmitted, in any form or by any means (electronic,
mechanical, photocopying, recording or otherwise) without the prior written
permission of both the copyright owner and the above publisher of this book.
Any infringement will result in delivery of an Eddie Stobart lorry
direct into your living room during *Sky Sports Extra*.

Pomona Books
P.O. Box 50, Hebden Bridge, West Yorkshire HX7 8WA, England, UK
www.pomonasounds.co.uk

Distributed in the UK by Turnaround Publisher Services Ltd,
Unit 3, Olympia Trading Estate, Coburg Road, London N22 6TZ

A CIP catalogue record for this book
is available from the British Library

ISBN 1-904590-02-0

Cover photography by David Walker

Set in 10 on 13pt Granjon
Typeset by Christian Brett

Printed and bound by Biddles, Guildford

CONTENTS

INTRODUCTION

WHAT A LOT HAS HAPPENED IN THE LAST SEVEN YEARS. A change of Government in Britain, wars in Kosova, Afghanistan and Iraq, Princess Diana died and I wrote 223 columns about football for the *New Statesman*. Am I saying that football matters just as much as politics and deaths? No, not quite. But where I've been sitting, with the remote control in one hand and my season ticket in the other, life does seem to have been revolving round football these last few years. As it has done for millions of others. And what changes in football we have witnessed.

Hundreds of foreign players have arrived in Britain to dominate the Premiership, something we have never seen before in our football history; several England managers have come and gone, mostly gone, leaving us with a foreign manager, another first for British football: Sky TV has acquired even more power over football, able to arrange kick-offs to suit themselves, leaving us with fewer and fewer Saturday games; Manchester United pulled away from the pack but hold on, not far behind has come Arsenal, so now we have two teams rising well about the rest; Spurs have been brilliantly consistent, one of those really reliable teams which so many people find themselves supporting, the very model of mid-table mediocrity; all Premiership players can now be millionaires, if they can be bothered to get out bed or the night clubs in time; David Beckham has gone from baddie to icon and along the way has delighted us with 35 new hair styles—and that was just last year; young Wayne Rooney, fresh out of nappies, has arrived, hold the back pages; programmes have gone glossy, shot up in price but real Bovril is very had to find; England have won bugger all, though they did beat Germany in Munich; English football, as of this moment in time, as has been well documented, despite everything, is more popular, more successful than it ever has been with waiting lists for tickets at all the big clubs.

I've been reflecting and reacting to some of these changes and arrivals in the *New Statesman* since 1996, which often surprises people. The *New Statesman* having a football column, that's the main surprise. People don't expect to find such an animal lurking there, in the undergrowth, amidst the intellectual pastures of politics and literature. Its existence indicates how much football has grown to be part of our general, mainstream, everyday culture, followed by all brows, all classes, all ages and sexes. The broadsheet newspapers now give more space to football than they have ever done, often more than the tabloids, with more stats, more in-depth reporting and reflection.

I've been writing about football for almost 40 years, and have produced seven football books. In the past I also did match reports and interviewed players, but now I mainly write as a fan, as some- one who goes along to the match, pays for his ticket and his pie. It means I can write what I like. With match reports or interviews, clubs can ban you, if you upset them, withdraw favours or access. So you have to tred carefully. Writing for myself, unloading my thoughts and reactions after a weekend of watching football, I don't have to worry about keeping in with the football authorities or any club. I can also use bad language, eff and blind, should I find it slipping out in moments of stress or fury or just laziness, which I couldn't possibly do were I writing in the *Daily Mail* or even *The Sunday Times*.

In writing a weekly column, which normally appears about a week after the events, I don't have to bother with facts and figures, blow by blow description of games, who scored what and when, nor do I have to discuss what Sky delights in calling 'talking points' which usually means dodgy off-side decisions, disputed penalties or off-the-ball incidents, which are usually very boring, always transient, fill acres of space for one day, and then immediately get forgotten.

I like to think my concerns are the concerns of ordinary fans not those of sub-editors who never go to a game, never leave their desks, but have to think up startling headlines every day and create or fuel controversies.

My team is Tottenham Hotspur, but don't let that put you off. Although following them, would put anyone off. When I did a book many years ago called *The Glory Game*, which was about a year with Spurs, the publishers did worry that only a very small segment of North London would be interested. I tried to reassure them that really, it could be any team, the inside of a top professional club any-where in England, or Britain, or Europe, but I feared they might be right. Football fans do tend to be rather myopic, seeing their own team as the only team in the universe.

I've never felt this. Over the years, I have also gone to watch Arsenal, as I like to have a match to go to every Saturday afternoon. When in Lakeland, where we now live half the year, I go to see Carlisle United, my home town team. Football is what I love. I want to see a good game, good players, or players trying hard. And if I can't find one in the flesh these days, there's usually a live one on television, sometimes two or three a day, sometimes every night of the week. Life is so good at present for football fans. So many oppor-tunities to overdose, over indulge, gorge on the goodies.

It was Ian Hargraves, when editor of the *New Statesman*, who suggested I might write a footer column, even though he himself was not a football fan — just a good editor, seeing how life and readers were moving on. Peter Wilby took over as editor, and kept my column going, which was nice, and he does happen to be a foot-ball fan, a supporter of Leicester City. Well done on getting back in the Premiership. My thanks to the magazine for permission to reproduce a selection of my pieces.

The actual selection has been done by Mark Hodkinson of Pomona. I had never though about it, didn't see a collection in them, but it was the fact that they are in a way dateless, not reports of actual matches, which made Mark want to present them to a wider public. He also liked the fact that the columns are set in the context of my own life, with domestic and family and work details butting in from time to time, which of course happens with all football fans. We might be blind and stupid, obsessive and one tracked when it comes to sitting down and watching football, but we also have another life, of a sort, going on in the background, and sometimes the foreground. Over the seven years, that's been changing as well.

Mark, so it turns out, has been reading the columns since they began, in Hebden Bridge in West Yorks, then photocopying and passing them on to his football following chums. Probably illegal these days, under copyright conventions. The *New Statesman*, it has to be admitted, does have a rather restricted, specialist readership, and probably sells few copies in Hebden Bridge or West Yorks. He saw a collection as a perfect bedside book for football fans everywhere, to dip in and out of, whatever teams they might support. I hope he's right.

But I agree with his basic thinking. All football fans are united in the same community, able to communicate with fellow followers, of all ages and countries, even when we don't speak the same language. After all, it is a very simple game. And most football fans do react to it very simply…

Hunter Davies
Loweswater, Summer 2003

1996–97 SEASON

*The power of Sky and
some suggested changes*

ENGLAND'S VICTORY OVER GEORGIA WAS A TRIUMPH FOR CABLE TELEVISION AND INNER STRENGTH

15 NOVEMBER 1996

I WAS ALL AGAINST SKY TV WHEN IT CAME ALONG, gobbling up our game, corrupting clubs with its millions, imposing stupid changes, creating new conditions just to suit the TV schedules. Such as matches starting at dopey times in the middle of the week, not at three on Saturday afternoon as nature intended. I didn't approve. Didn't get a dish. No one in our street got a dish, certainly not. What kind of street do you think this is?

Then these jokers started digging up the pavements, digging around in my prejudices, and cable arrived, corrupting me with its special offers, and the result was, well, I got it, didn't I? I keep it in the corner of the room I call my office, but haven't told anyone in the street. I find that if you watch with the curtains closed, nobody can possibly know.

Last Saturday she went off for her West End fix, taking in Blake and Rubens at the National Portrait Gallery, and a matinée at the

National Theatre. I said don't worry about me, pet, I'll be busy in my room. You've got culture. I've got logistics, psychology, geography, economics, oh, all sorts.

The dressing rooms in the Premier League are absolutely chocker these days. All those interpreters for a start, who have to be ever on hand to translate really hard words such as parrot, moon and gutted for our foreign players. Then there's a whole host of counsellors waiting to hold trembling hands, should any of our home-grown players recovering from alcohol, drugs, gambling, wife-beating and missing penalties need to share. Flying tea cups at half-time, which I have personally witnessed in one of our top foot-ball club's dressing rooms, just doesn't happen any more. There isn't the space. So, that was a logistical problem to ponder.

Psychologically, how would Gazza cope? Hard one that. Not to mention Adams and Southgate, after what they've been through. As for the geographical problem, where exactly is Georgia and if it's 12 o'clock here, what time is it there?

Then economics. How come Kinkladze can buy his old football club when he's only playing for Man City? And if the average Georgian wage is £150 a year, which someone on Sky TV said, or £40 a week, according to the *Independent*, how can they get people to pay £6 for a ticket'

At 11 o'clock, I settled down to wonder and to work, oh yes. I had the TV on, but vee vee low. I am now converted to Sky and am pleased that its millions have had one good effect, namely bringing all those foreign players to raise the standard of our native game, and I think Andy Gray is first class — love his graphics and board games — but I still get caught, and pissed off, because it will start coverage of live matches an hour before kick-off.

So I got some work done, while watching out of the corner of my eye. I groaned when I spotted that Ray "very much so" Wilkins was out there, about to bore for England with his square comments. But I managed a loyal glow each time I spotted a draped Unionjack, showing that supporters from some of our famous clubs, such as Yeovil Town and Thetford, had trailed all the way to Georgia. You what? How did they manage, on £150 a week?

I caught some inane racist observations in the studio, left over from the dark ages, alleging that being Latins, the Georgians would bottle it if they got behind. Yes, there are still so-called football experts who believe Britain is alone in having a never-say-die spirit. You'd have thought being regularly stuffed by Germany, not to mention Brazil, Norway and the US, would have shown this theory to be utter bollocks.

At 12 o'clock prompt the doorbell rang. Oh no. Has she come back for something? Could it be Jehovah's Witnesses? Neither. It was Derek, my neighbour who is an architect. I know your secret, he said. I've spotted the cable on the wall. Unless you let me in to watch with you I'm telling everyone.

The lads done well, thanks to two bits of luck — ie, the two goals. At half-time we opened some Beaujolais. That's one advantage of a lunchtime game. A bit gross to drink at four on a Sunday afternoon, Sky's usual time. At the end we agreed Batty was man of the match and opened another bottle.

I decided Hoddle likes Hinchcliffe in the team because they look alike. They've got the same jaw line. He likes Southgate because he's clearly intelligent, like Hoddle, but that's more worrying. Intelligence can be a troubling quality in football. Think of Steve Coppell, the economics-graduate manager. Worried himself into resigning.

Gazza has GBH rather than IQ worries. He was not himself. But was he ever? It's been said his peak was at Spurs, but I didn't notice. He used to make me scream, not salivate, throwing himself around like a mad cow, frothing and shaking, unbalancing the team, browbeating others into passing to him when he was in a rotten position. He at least kept his head. Ditto Ince, ditto Batty. Our Glenn is having a calming effect all round.

It was all so calm and sensible that there was nobody or nothing to stir the blood and I was longing for McManaman to come on. Instead we got Ian Wright. I like watching Wright at Arsenal. He plays better for Arsenal than Sheringham does for Spurs, yet the opposite happens when they play for England. Explain that one, Glenn. Le Tissier suffers in the same way. So did Glenn himself, come to think of it.

We forget it now, but Hoddle never reached a peak with England, always being less than the sum of his many parts. We also forget what a girl's blouse he could appear as a player: too nice, too soft, never dominating. I was sure he would never make it as a manager. In my mind he was another Martin Peters, someone with a brilliant football brain, but not tough enough. I was wrong. Just shows you. Never categorise from exteriors. Quiet inner strength is what matters, not outward physical aggression. Is it Jesus that's brought it out, giving him a solid centre in his life? I don't think so. Just self-confidence, allied to strong views, good sense, decent values.

How did the game go, she said when she came home, culture-crammed. Any goals? Just two, I said, but it was really all about moral philosophy. French moral philosophy, she said, judging by the Georges Duboeuf wine bottles.

TO BE (AT THE MATCH),
OR NOT TO BE (BECAUSE OF TV)?
A MODERN SOLILOQUY

6 DECEMBER 1996

LIVE OR TELEVISED, REAL OR FILMED, BEING THERE IN THE flesh or sitting watching at home? I remember an argument I had many, years ago with Trevor Nunn, which went on till the early hours, after I'd said I couldn't believe such a talented, creative, energetic young person would want to waste his life on boring old stage stuff—especially boring old Shakespeare, whose only claim to interest is that he got to the clichés first—when he could be making films or TV, getting across his message to the masses, working in a modern and creative medium capable of reaching millions. Looking back, he obviously didn't listen. In the main he has stuck to the stage. Though who could have imagined he would reach millions, and make millions, making musicals?

Anyway, one of his defences of live theatre was the relationship between a live audience and live actors, spurring on and inspiring each other in the same way, so he argued, that a football crowd can make a team play better. You can never get that sort of relationship with a dead piece of film. How true, Trev, I said, how true. Let's have another bottle.

I'm sitting here now on Monday evening thinking of Trevor, a well-known Ipswich supporter (ha ha, so what does he know about anything?), trying to decide whether I will go to Spurs–Liverpool tonight or watch the match live on Sky.

The arguments in favour are:
- Being there I can help the cause, as Trev said. Yes, my presence will be marginal, and ultimately we're all marginal, as Shakespeare probably said first, except that if all the marginal people combine with one voice we can change the world, or the

score, as he probably also said, because these wise people usually have it both ways. We might then grab one point. Gawd knows, Spurs need all the help they can get at present.

- Being there I will enjoy soaking up the atmosphere, the excitement, seeing my friends, such as R Littlejohn. At every match, even though I go alone, I walk with the crowd, empathise with the crowd, knowing I am part of the world's football family. It's a nice feeling that, hard to describe, and when I do she scoffs not male bonding time again, pass the yuck bag.

- Being there I will see off-the-ball action that the telly doesn't give you: who's truly trying, overall patterns, team behaviour.

- Liverpool are an excellent team. I love watching McManaman. I should see them in the flesh, if I call myself a football fan.

- I have paid £600 for my season ticket. Am I going wilfully to waste it?

Arguments against going are:

- Getting there is a right drag, as is parking, especially on a dark December evening. I'll have to rush my supper and not drink, though I'll have chips afterwards to celebrate a win, or for grabbing a draw. OK, to cheer me up after a hammering. Either way, I'll have chips, that's settled.

- Do I really want to hear R Littlejohn moaning on about Spurs? When I can do that myself, at home.

- You miss so much detail, being there in the flesh. Things like offside, fouls, penalty claims and, most of all, goals, happen in a flash, a mad scramble, a blur, so it's great to have a slo-mo, showing exactly what happened. Plus the expressions. With the telly you get close-ups of every new haircut, tattoo, scratch, love bite, injection mark, though often they only raise more questions, such as what the hell does Asprilla chew? Can't be gum. Is it tobacco? Let me know, if you know.

- Spurs are a dreary team at present. Have been since Klinsmann left. Anderton, the only exciting player, hasn't recovered from his injury and is still lost. Sheringham might leave, and who could blame him? The club itself has lost direction, inspiration, interested only in survival and marketing, especially marketing. Do they really deserve my blindly loyal support?

• I have paid for Sky, but what have I paid? I can't even remember how much it costs for cable, which must prove something, or nothing.

So, friends, what did I do?

Gap of four hours there. Yes, of course I went. But I don't want to talk about it. Let's change the subject. My stamps, for example. When I started collecting, I bought four poor-quality Penny Blacks for £25 each, with no margins, thin and tatty. I felt I needed to have examples of the world's best-known stamps, now I'd become a collector. Around 80 million were produced, so you can get them very cheap, if you happen to be interested in things going cheap. That was ten years ago. My four tatty stamps have just lain there, never looked at, doing nothing. I now know I was stupid to go for cheapness, not quality. If I was selling them I'd be lucky to get £10 each. Now, if I had spent that £100 on just one semi-decent Penny Black, I would have had something to look at and enjoy and today I'd probably get back £250. Are you listening, Alan Sugar? Do you get my drift?

Going for bargains in the £2–£3 million range means you get second division and/or Norwegian players who will never increase in value or be good or interesting to look at. I know, as a tough, no-nonsense biz person, £10–£15 million must seem mad for one player, when you could get four for that price, all with two legs, who would fill a gap, look sensible in the accounts, seem like good business—but will they ever bring present or future joy? Think about it, Alan.

Don't mention the match. I said I'm not talking about it. It wasn't that Liverpool were all that brilliant, though in the end the score could have been 5−0, not 2−0. The first half was drearily even, until the last minute when Spurs went to sleep. The second goal was, well, laughable. All 32,000 of us could actually see the ball jump up like a clockwork toy and bobble over Walker, without the need for any TV close-ups.

The chips, they were good. But I felt very sick afterwards.

DESMOND LYNAM, MRS THATCHER, QUEEN OF THE SOUTH ... FUNNY THING, LOYALTY

13 DECEMBER 1996

I GET ASKED MANY QUESTIONS AS I TRAVEL AROUND THE planet, such as: is Virginia Bottomley really as lovely as she looks? She invited me for tea last week, gave me almost an hour of her lovely time, asking for my comments, any advice, any suggestions, oh, the usual stuff. My seals are lipped on the subject of our intimate conversation, but to answer the question: yes, she is. Even lovelier than she looks.

"Let your hair down, Ginny," I whispered as I left—for it is clear she faces some indecision in that area of her life, too much swimming, I suspect—"and you could be a real stunner, not to say scorcher, no, striker, I mean leader of the Tory attack, that's the word I'm looking for."

The other recurring question is: why do I go to Arsenal? Dr John Davies, no relation, of San José, California, over here in the summer for Euro 96, asked me that very question. And only this morning there was a similar observation in a fax from Maun in Botswana, from Ronald Ridge—yes, a relation, my son in-law. "If you are a Spurs fan, Hunt, as you will keep telling us ever so boringly whether we ask you or not, why do you persist in going to Highbury?"

Let me try to answer. No, don't go away. You could learn something. Loyalty in football, as in life, is a complicated matter, rarely related to logic. I follow Motherwell because my mother came from there. I follow Queen of the South because we lived in Dumfries for three years when I was little. I follow Carlisle United of course, because it became my home town. I follow the career of Will Carling and his successor as England rugby captain, Philip de Glanville, because they both went to Durham. As I did. I'm now looking out for Gabby Yorath, a new face in TV sport, and a very bright blonde — eat your heart out, Ginny — because she, too, went to Durham. I followed Margaret Thatcher because, many years later, my wife had her room at Somerville College, Oxford. I cheer on Damon Hill because his father, Graham, was once very kind to me and gave me a ride in his new super car at Le Mans when I was young and in Le Mans to do a story and had no idea what the heck was going on, and, oh, the people, the noise. I follow Desmond Lynam for his moustache. Right, I hope that's all clear.

The reason I started to follow Spurs, back in 1960, just arrived in north London, was that they were exciting and brilliant and about to do the double. I could have picked Arsenal as my local London team. They were marginally nearer, but so awfully boring. When my dear friend M Bragg came down from Wigton, which we sophisticates from Carlisle look upon as the absolute sticks, he chose Arsenal, presumably because by then they were not quite so awfully boring. And so it has remained. With football following, when you are born with a team, inherit a team or alight on a team, that's it. You never change. Players and managers, and even directors these days, they are all pure mercenaries, fickle and frivolous with their affections, followers of finance, not football. It took me a long time to creep through the turnstiles at Highbury, except, of when Spurs were playing there. I used to use that old joke: "Oh, yes, we are very lucky in north London. We have two excellent teams: Spurs, and Spurs reserves." Boom, boom. I think Bill Shankly first used it, only it was Liverpool and Liverpool reserves.

Then I went once or twice to Arsenal's ordinary games, when friends had a season ticket to spare. God did not strike me down. No cockerel in the sky crowed thrice and disowned me. I had, of course, to hide the fact that I had gone hoping to see Arsenal lose, which, alas, they have not done enough these past few seasons. But what I was mainly going for was a good match, to see some skill and excitement. Very slowly I came to realise that I am primarily a follower of football. Spurs is the message. But football is the medium. Or the other way around. Marshall McLuhan, the author of *The Medium Is*

The Message, told me himself either way was true. Or wrong.

So for the past ten years I have gone to a match every Saturday when I am in London, which means the winter six months of the year, alternating Spurs with Arsenal. My son, and almost all my Spurs friends, think this is diabolical behaviour, that I am doing something evil. Not just supping with the enemy, but contributing to their coffers.

This season, with Spurs playing so badly, I have even wondered why I didn't choose Arsenal in the first place, not that I will, of course — wash your mind out — but it is much easier to get to. We are still in the same house. It's just that the outside world's road systems have changed. I now need an hour to get to White Hart Lane. I can do Highbury in half an hour. On Saturday I was back in the house before the Spurs game was on *Sports Report*.

Yes, I went to the Arsenal – Derby match. Oh, I did enjoy it. As ever, I sat with fingers crossed inside my pocket, waiting for the other side to score, taking care not to stand and cheer should they do so. I don't want to be thumped. You don't go through the usual agonies of despair when you don't really care.

You can also see things objectively. For example, I have noticed something that none of the proper reporters at the match commented on, not being inside the Arsenal crowd. They have turned against David Platt. You can feel it, sense it, sigh it. Poor lad. He's going to have problems ahead.

Two seasons ago the Arsenal crowd hated Martin Keown, moaned and groaned when he was in the team, jeered every clumsy tackle. Now they like him. He has pulled himself around. Those universities where you can do a PhD in football — Liverpool, Leicester and Cambridge — should analyse the reasons.

Derby were the better team, no question, and the Arsenal crowd sensed it. Arsenal were lucky to equalise in the last minute, so they came out relatively happy. Even happier when they heard Liverpool had lost. But not as happy as me. When I heard Spurs had won at Coventry, I gave them a loud clap. In my pocket, of course.

THERE IS LIFE AFTER FOOTBALL,
EVEN IF IT DOES INVOLVE THRASHING
AROUND IN GREY SOUP

17 JANUARY 1997

I GAVE UP PLAYING FOOTBALL WHEN I WAS 50, PARK FOOT-
ball, nothing too strenuous. Dartmouth Park United, we were
called, and we played every Sunday morning on Hampstead Heath.
It was coats on the ground in summer, real goal posts in winter.
More than 20 years I played, and for about ten of them
I realised my ambition, which was to play with my son Jake.
We argued all the time, screamed and shouted. Had to play on
different sides in the end to stop us fighting but, oh, I did enjoy it.

We had to register as a club in order to book pitches, but all we
did was pick two teams from whomever turned up. So one week it
was 13-a-side and the next seven a-side. In my twenties I had played
in proper teams, in proper leagues, but travelling became a drag.
Dartmouth Park United was just a local dads' team, containing
ordinary local dads — mega TV stars, a Labour life peer, a few local
waiters and carpenters. Plus a lot of foreigners, passing through,
who saw this rubbish game and asked to join in.

I was sick on Sundays if we lost, but on Monday life went on.
Real players, when they lose, have a whole week to get through,
with nothing else in their lives, and everyone, everywhere, remind-
ing them they got stuffed last week.

When I gave up I was still fit enough to play, but not fit enough
to recover from playing. I'd often spend the whole week in deep-
heat treatment just to get ready for Sunday. Stupid really, to have
staggered on for so long, especially after two cartilage ops. No
wonder I have arthritis in both knees.

I was sick about giving up and had to arrange my Sunday walk
so I didn't pass our pitch. Even now I avoid a bloke called Ray,
still playing at 60, because I know when we meet he'll say, "Yes, still

playing at 60." And I'll hate him.

The worst thing was wondering what to do next. I did try jogging for a time, until I realised that was really, really stupid. It came to me in a flash one day when I was jogging along the pavement with my hood up and I could hear my bones echoing in my ears. Jogging in a city is the same thing as hitting your legs with lumps of concrete. So I gave up, that very moment.

And became very bad tempered. Now I like to think that I am a very easy-going person, don't have rows or scenes with people, never have had — apart from with my dear wife, but that doesn't count, what else are they for? — but I found myself getting rather ratty. I then realised that for 20 years I'd got rid of any bad temper on the pitch. All that screaming and shouting had exorcised it. What could possibly take its place? I needed something to exercise and exhaust me, something that was also communal and competitive. I'm still looking.

In the meantime, behold, I am a swimmer. Twice a week I go to the baths — Kentish Town in winter and Cockermouth in summer. KT is a health hazard: I never had a verruca until I started going there. Cockermouth is much cleaner and nicer. People talk to each other at Cockermouth, leave their clothes on the benches and don't bother to use the lockers. At Kentish Town the only person I ever talk to is Alastair Campbell, who goes with his kids. Spin doctor and swimmer, but not at the same time.

There's nothing communal or competitive about swimming, though I make up races in my mind against the oldest and most infirm, seeing if I can catch them up, without their knowing. Then I go champion, champion, under my breath, when I beat them to the imaginary tape. I hate walking to Kentish Town and I hate getting undressed and dressed again. Being in the water is fine, but otherwise it's all such a drag. If I was rich — what am I saying? I am — I'd have my own swimming pool. *She* says she'd leave, if I ever did. No space anyway, unless we gave up the garden.

But it keeps me fit, and I like the pleasure of minor exhaustion when I do my final fast length, well sort of fast-ish, and can then look forward to stuffing my face. One of the things about exercise is the compensatory element. I work harder beforehand, get more done, knowing I'm going to go swimming, and feel more justified afterwards in guzzling. If Freud hadn't been so obsessed by sex, he might have worked out a replacement theory for such actions. He himself was, of course, a great walker, doing two hours a day round Vienna at lunchtimes, to get himself ready for the afternoon's sessions on the couch. One reason he put people on a couch was because he couldn't bear to be stared at for eight hours a day. He would, if asked, have said it was all sexual sublimation, both walking and swimming.

You don't get injured swimming, not in the way you do playing football, but swimming in chemicals does affect your eyes and ears. I wear earplugs, but can't get the hang of goggles. At Kentish Town everyone wears them, but not so many do in Cockermouth. I hate them. I just can't see a thing. They cloud up so quickly and I can't see the oldie I'm trying to beat. It's like swimming in grey soup. Perhaps that's why people wear them in Kentish Town baths. To pretend they're not there.

The best swimming is outdoors. What bliss to be alive and in Lakeland and swimming in the lakes. Only a dozen times last summer, compared with every day for three months the year before. Even better when it's the Caribbean. And that's where we are off to, as I write. Already got the cossies packed. You wondered if there was going to be a point to all this. In the old days I played beach football, and usually knackered myself in the first week. Swimming is a fairly decent substitute, for life and for hols. And you don't get kicked.

SHE'S ALLERGIC TO ALBERT FINNEY;
IAN WALKER DRIVES ME MAD.
BUT DON'T ASK ME WHY

7 MARCH 1997

HERE'S A LITTLE QUESTION FOR YOU. TONY BLAIR SUPPORTS Newcastle United. His 13-year-old son Euan supports Liverpool. His 11-year-old son Nicky supports Manchester United. Lots of families are like that, for lots of reasons, most of them lost in time, but in this case they each have a different reason for following a different team. Any guesses?

No, it's not to do with spreading the pre-election net, nothing as cynical as that, goodness no. Think of three genuine reasons. While you're thinking, I'll carry on.

I was reading the theatre reviews — because I read all reviews of books, television, films and plays, saves such a lot of time and money — and I said, hey, this play *Art* is getting some good reviews, are you going to see it?

I go off, on my own, every Saturday afternoon to footer, while she goes off, on her own, to a matinée in the West End. One day I'll try to devise anticipation, stimulation and satisfaction scores, to see who has the most fun with the least aggravation. "No," she said. "I'm not going to see it. I'm allergic to Albert Finney."

Now if we'd gone on *Mr and Mrs* together, an ancient TV prog about husbands and wives, and that had been the trick question, I would have failed. I know she's allergic to Vanessa Redgrave, always has been, and Brian Walden, but taking a skunner to Albert Finney, that's a new one to me. Just shows you. Pays to talk and keep in touch.

This is the chance all *appearers* take, people who prance upon the public or political stage: that, for no logical reason, some punters will take against them. Charles Dance — that's another actor she hates. They're coming back to me.

Yet I can't think of any footballer I really, truly, deeply hate.

Could it be because I'm a nice person without an ounce of hatred, or because it doesn't work that way in sport? Dennis Bergkamp, I don't like his mouth—rather mean, I always think, and I don't like Lee Dixon's head, but in each case it might be because they play for Arsenal. I don't like Nigel Clough's body—not that he's offered it to me—but I wouldn't accept it. "Oi!" I'd say, "Nigel You keep that body to yourself."

David Beckham's eyes, never cared for them, narrow and nasty. John Hartson, pity about that unpleasant complexion. Teddy Sheringham—does he have to have such a dreary haircut? And that Ian Walker he fair drives me mad the way he takes goal kicks. That's about it, really.

On the other hand I have a whole host of people I like, just because they are people I like. Nothing to do with being good or bad footballers. Steve Claridge of Leicester, ooh, Ivy, he's one of my favourites. Love his half-mast socks, his scruffy looks, his lumbering gait. Vinnie Jones, he's got such presence it's hard to take your eyes off him. Ditto Julian Dicks. Also Asprilla. I watch him wondering what he's going to do next. He doesn't know. Nor does his team. In fact, it looks as if he has never met the team before. I like Ian Wright, the way he skips, not walks, springing on his toes. I like Ravanelli for his grey hair and Zola for his sunken cheeks, and Peter Beardsley for looking like the deprived end of the litter.

Good footballers, who cost good money, are not necessarily the ones you like, even if you are glad to have them in your team. Such as Shearer. Oh yes, it's exciting when he scores, and he's feared by all, but he's somehow nondescript, lacking charisma, a footballing functionary. And when he gives a post-match interview, gawd, it's like listening to a speak-your-weight machine.

There are managers I like for equally non-logical, non-football reasons. Joe Kinnear always looks as if he has just come out of the crowd, one of the fans, ie, like a real human being, not someone who is either receiving treatment or has just been dug up and is still half frozen, like, say, well, Trevor Francis.

I used to have Frank Clark, now of Man City, marked down in my mind as a boring manager, just as he was a boring player, until the other day he came out with a throw-away remark, delivering it without a flicker. I had to wind back the video, just to see I hadn't misheard. "I look after the football side and the chairman orders the pies."

Not side-splitting, but for Frank Clark, pretty neat.

I like Martin O'Neill for his intensity and intelligence. Complaining about that dodgy penalty which Chelsea got was understandable, but on that occasion he was all emotion. Standing 50 yards away, he could not have seen the incident properly. That the ref was wrong is irrelevant. Managers can see very little: they can only guess. They can't see because they are in the dug-out at pitch level, and every pitch rises in the middle for drainage reasons. All they can see is half the pitch, the half nearest to them. They have a false or no perspective on the rest. That's why so many managers sit in the stand, making notes, only coming down in the second half, when it's panic stations and all emotion.

But I do like Martin O'Neill all the same, and will follow him, and his career, wherever he goes.

So why does Tony Blair follow Newcastle United? Strange, in a way, as he is Scottish through his parents, by his birth, by his schooling at Fettes. So you might have expected him to follow Rangers. He doesn't see it that way. Durham became his home town, where he lived at a formative time, when his dad got a job as a university lecturer. Newcastle were the big local team, so, like most little boys in that place at that time, he followed them.

Euan follows Liverpool because that's his mother's home town, where her family came from. So why didn't Nicky follow suit? Ah, because by chance in his formative years, they happened to have a nanny who followed Man Utd—and later went on to work for them. Nicky, who liked the nanny very much, followed her team. You see, following football or footballers does make sense. And it also makes non-sense.

MY TEN-POINT MANIFESTO FOR CHANGE.
OTHERWISE KNOWN AS
A LIST OF STUPID SUGGESTIONS

NEXT SEASON, SO WE ARE TOLD, GOALKEEPERS WILL BE penalised for holding the ball for more than five seconds. Or is it taking more than five steps? Something anyway to stop them messing around and deliberately slowing the game down — though I have a memory they tried this in the past, but life went on, referees forgot, and goalkeepers returned to their old habits.

If I were in charge, allowed to make the changes I'd like to see happen, this is what I'd like to see happen, if I were in charge. I think I'm becoming influenced by that boring Ronseal advert, which is shown during ITV and Sky matches. The one where the man repeats everything. Does exactly as it says it will. And drives you potty. Advertisers obviously believe all football fans are do-it-yourself wallies, unaware of the social changes, and that we now prefer Chardonnay and Beaujolais to Ronseal. Taste so much better. Anyway my ten changes:

1 All teams reduced from 11 players to nine players. This is a serious suggestion, arrived at after close observation of a) the speed, strength and endurance of the modern player and b) the fact that in almost every game the midfield is totally congested. Nobody has time or space to do anything, should they get the ball. And notice how often when someone does get the ball, by default or by pressing, that he immediately gives it away, either by default or the other team pressing. I'm mainly talking about British players here. Foreign players don't give the ball away as often. They have the Latin, been better trained, got more skill, nicer hair and smarter shorts.

Because they are twice as quick as they used to be, twice as fit and work twice as hard, it's like having twice as many of them on the pitch. So, cut them down. It would save two elevenths of the wage bill — and all ticket prices could be cut accordingly.

2 Someone, somewhere, to teach Trevor Francis that it's not Noo-castle. Where does he get that from? The Bronx?

3 All teams to put a great deal more thought and effort into their goal celebrations. Earlier in the season there was a flurry of fancy formations, shirt lifting, hand slapping, formal posing. But now they all seem to have forgotten, as the season drags on and they become too weary or goals become too serious for messing around. The other week I caught Valencia versus Seville. I was just passing the telly, on the way to get some work done, and blow me, the telly turned itself on. Honestly.

When this Valencia player scored, he ran to the corner on all fours, then cocked a leg as if peeing against the corner flag. I wouldn't make this mandatory, but it certainly shows a bit of imagination.

4 Half-time to be reduced from 15 to ten minutes, as it was from the beginning of time, till the Premier League arrived. I used to be able to make it back to the car for *Sports Report* at five o'clock, but now that matches finish five minutes later, I always miss James Alexander Gordon reading the results and have to guess from internal evidence, cross references, textual analysis and chance remarks what vital things have happened elsewhere in the football world: ie, how did Carlisle get on.

5 Haringey Council to sort itself out. I have parked in the same spot in Lordship Lane, Tottenham, at the same time, for all Spurs matches for the past 30 years. I can tell to the nearest thousand what the crowd will be by the number of cars already parked when I arrived.

Last Saturday, after the match, I found a parking fine of £40 on my windscreen. Never happened before. If they have changed the rules, why didn't they warn everyone? Rotten buggers.

6 Referees to go back to simple black, not all this fancy dan, silly stripes or spew-like stuff splattered on their shirts. Don't they realise we find it such a mouthful having to shout, "Who's that bastard in the black with the fancy dan, silly stripes, spew-like stuff splattered on his shirt?" What is the point? No team plays in black, so there's never a clash. Can't be marketing, either. Kids don't rush home saying, please please I must have this season's spew-splattered refs' shirt, Mum.

7 An experimental season with no offsides. This is the single most annoying, most irritating rule for players and spectators alike. It's *coitus interruptus* for the attacking team, being halted in full flow, and encourages total negativity in the defending team. But worst of all, it's not an exact science and forces the referee to make an instant decision, based on a blurred vision. There has been talk recently of a battery of cameras and computers to help the ref, but that's been rejected as it would slow everything down. So why not try no offsides? It worked in the playground, didn't it. A new generation of Jimmy Greaves poachers would be bred, but is that necessarily a bad thing? New methods would be devised to counter it, such as a defender staying back, which would spread out the game and stop all this crowding in the middle.

8 Andy Gray fined £10 every time he says, "It's as simple as that."

9 Once the season has begun and the fixture list printed, plans made, tickets bought, Saturdays booked and life organised, Sky to be fined £1 million for every game it wilfully rearranges.

10 Make it a hanging offence for players to shout "Our ball, ref", when they have kicked it into touch, knowing they kicked it into touch, having seen the ref watching them kick it into touch, having been observed by 35,000 people as they kicked it into touch. It's all right for us to shout it, oh yes, even when we know the truth, even when we know the ref knows the truth. That's why we go to matches, as a relief valve, an escape hatch, to shout out stupid things and make stupid observations and stupid suggestions. Such as all the above. Thank you.

1997–98 SEASON

*Haircuts, Sex and
the World Cup*

LIFE WITHOUT FOOTBALL?
BETTER TO RISK UPSETTING THE
GHOST OF WORDSWORTH
8 AUGUST 1997

WHAT A LONG WAIT IT'S BEEN. ALL SUMMER I'VE HAD MY magnifying glass out, searching for snippets, trawling for titbits, peering for paragraphs, even in the smallest of print, in the most obscure of back pages, but, since that tournament in France, what was it called, oh yes, Tournament in France, there's been nothing, *nada, rien*. "Rubbish," she says, "the football season never ends. There's always a stupid match on somewhere." Would that there were, pet.

In July I was reduced to watching cricket and, do you know, it's not totally boring — just 99 per cent boring. I could see for the first time that watching, over by over, can become mesmerising. Just one more over, you tell yourself. OK, after this one, all right, this next one, something must happen, if I'm still awake, still alive. Something did wake me up, in fact. I jumped in the air thinking, hurrah, life has fast-forwarded itself. It was the noise of the lads in the crowd, as bored as me, shouting "Stand up if you hate Man U."

Then I watched bits of the tennis, even though it was being played by blokes I'd never heard of. During the men's final I went out for half-hour walks to the lake, timing it to miss the really pointless sets, ie, most of them, but I was there for the last one. Who won? Can't remember. All I recall is the emptiness of tennis commentaries. Never again will I criticise Ron Atkinson or Bob Wilson. Megabrains, mega-observers, compared with those tennis twits uttering utter banalities.

Golf. How could I have been driven to that? Is there a game less suitable for watching? In the flesh, being there, you can only ever watch one sliver, stuck on the same spot, over and over, like only ever reading the first page of a novel. So what television does is zap you back and forward, watching someone's balls in the air, then someone else's balls not in the air. Nothing is connected, nothing makes sense. What a headache I got. Fun for the camera crews, with their trendy angles, but not for me. Almost as bad as watching *This Life*.

Near the end of July, tiddly back-page paragraphs began growing like tadpoles, spawning columns, ready to leapfrog all over the sports pages, until, oh joy, football pullout sections burst forth, even bigger and better this year, with pundits parading their stuff, predicting winners and losers in the season ahead. I have them all, oh yes, carefully filed. Just so I can say ha ha, you got it all wrong, when I meet them at Highbury or White Hart Lane.

We are in Lakeland till October, willingly, wantingly, but how was I going to survive? Apart from a diet of Carlisle United or crackling *Sports Report*. So last week I drove into Cockermouth, false beard, women's clothes, went into this back-street shop and said: "Psst, how much for a dish?"

No one in our village has one, very low class, how could you, Hunt, don't you know this is the National Park, your Mr Wordsworth wouldn't even allow white-painted cottages, so what would he think of a nasty satellite dish, lowering the tone, etc.

The dish man came the next day, even without my telling him how to find our house, which is hellish to locate. "I know it," he said. "Used to work on the bins."

I do like to see socially mobile dustmen. I suppose it doesn't take a lot of skill to erect a satellite dish, but it's a start, till the evening classes in brain surgery begin at Cockermouth Tech.

It has to face south, apparently, but I chose a careful angle obscured by our yew tree, ten million years old, which means no one can see it. Then I painted it Dulux County Cream, the same colour as our house. The dish, not the yew tree. I'd have the heavies round from Cumbria Wildlife Trust (President, H Davies) if I tried to paint the yew. There was something so satisfying about slapping paint on this brand new black metal dish, though the ex-binman looked horrified. Latest model, he said.

He charged only £150, including all the bits, and I was able to turn on at once and got brilliant reception for Channel 5, non-existent up here so far, dozens of quaint quiz shows from Germany, rude quiz shows from Spain, Sky News and Eurosport. I never expected that. I thought you had to subscribe. You do, of course, for Sky Sports, they're not daft. For £17.99 a month I now get 200 channels, 199 of which I'll never watch.

Today has been the first day of my new life. Lovely weather, of course, it always is, and yes, I have been slumped inside this dark room while she has been out walking on the wonderful fells — don't go on about it. First there was Hibs against Celtic. That Tony Rougier from Trinidad, now of Hibs, he looks awful good, compared with Celtic, after all that money. Craig Brown, the Scotland manager not the journalist, was commentating. I was most impressed, though he did show his schoolteacher pedantry now and again. "Aye, that hit the woodwork — or metalwork, as it now is."

I loved it when Hibs scored and their supporters began jeering Celtic. "You're gonna win fuckall, you're gonna win fuckall. "

First match of the new season, 4th August—and they're already predicting the end. Almost as daft as the pundits.

Then the big one—the Charity Shield, Man Utd versus Chelsea. Just settling down, getting my refreshments lined up, when there was a knock at the door. The Loweswater Thought Police? National Park investigators? The binman cometh for a tip? It was Martin, just passing from Bahrain, where he works for Coca-Cola. He and his family are staying with friends nearby and he thought he might just have noticed something on my roof. After all that paint slapping. "Sshh, sshh," I said. "Quick, come in, you're just in time."

For the next 50 weeks I'll be incommunicado. So if you have anything to say to me, pet, between now and next July, say it now.

HOLD ON TO YOUR TUTS.
THE SEASON IS STILL TOO YOUNG TO
START MOANING ABOUT

NEW LABOUR, NEW LABOURING, AND IT TOOK ONLY 100 days for us to realise it. New season, new seasoning? Yup. After only one week, the signs are there. Some new tastes and new flavours, new sounds and sights are already on the way.

Such as Gary Lineker, who now has grey hair, and Fergie with his new specs. He hasn't quite got used to them yet, hence sending out Beckham with a missing "h". It's not clear if they're for long or short distance, to read the small print in contracts and work out whether this new lad he's signed is on £24,000 a week or is it per minute, or for looking right across the training pitch to see who's there, just in case Cantona has returned.

Once again there has been a flood of foreign imports, which everyone is trying to get their tongues round, and a lot of tut tutting has been going on about the fact that one of our leading clubs is bound to field a totally foreign team at some stage in the season, such as Chelsea with their 13 foreign players or Arsenal with 12. This will be bad for young British players who won't get a kick, poor petals, and for the future of our game, which we gave the world, tut tut.

Hold on to those tuts. They are not quite deserved. If you study the imports carefully, you'll see there has been a slight change this season. Yes, the quantity is there, no question, but there hasn't been a Zola, a Klinsmann, a Ravanelli or Juninho this season, big stars whom we all knew about. Almost 100 new foreign players have arrived in the Premiership but I wouldn't recognise any of them if I met them in my porridge. OK, perhaps Lombardo at Crystal Palace, but that's because he's a baldie head, or Paolo di Canio at Sheffield Wednesday, but that's because he's come from Celtic.

Out of those 100 only about three other names will be known to most fans. Overmars at Arsenal, I had heard of him, but not the six other foreign players Wenger has signed. Also Martin Dahlin at Blackburn and Karlheinz Riedle at Liverpool. But that's about it, leaving 95 players who are unknown, untried, unrecognisable, but now over here. Not much money has actually been spent on them, even the five so-called names. It's presumably part of the attraction, that they come cheap.

The Big Names who have been bought for Big Money are in fact, wait for it, English. Collymore at £7 million, Ferdinand at £6 million and Le Saux at £5 million are the most expensive new signings in the Premiership. Then there's Ince at £4.25 million and Sheringham. at £3.5 million. So no more tuts please about the end of English players as we know them. The good ones are not yet on the dole.

A new season means three new clubs in the Premiership— Bolton Wanderers, Crystal Palace and Barnsley. I predict one of them in three weeks' time will be top of the league. It's one of God's more amusing little tricks. Then they're never heard of again. I have on the wall beside me a framed copy of the first division league table for 24 August 1974, which I kiss every morning on my way to the Amstrad. The leader that day was Carlisle United. Whatever happened to them?

We also have four new grounds to get our eyes round, which is the most I can remember in any season. Derby, Bolton Wanderers, Sunderland and Stoke have all rehoused themselves, so farewell to the Baseball Ground, Burnden Park, Roker Park and the Victoria Ground. I haven't memorised the new names, got all season to do that, apart from Sunderland's Stadium of Light, already known as Stadium of Shite by Newcastle fans, and Bolton's Reebok Stadium, soon to be Reject Stadium, if things don't go so well.

All the pitches I've seen so far are still virgin and green, now that is a surprise. Not just because of the good weather keeping them fresh, but because our commercially mad clubs have so far not sold off the last remains of their souls. In rugby and cricket great swathes of turf are multicoloured, multi-lettered, advertising some potty product or other. How come football hasn't followed suit? It won't last.

Fantasy Football, under various names, various disguises, and I hate them all, has gone absolutely mad. Every broadsheet newspaper has now got some sort of football game and I get caught every time. Oh this is interesting, I think, reading down a list of names of players with values stuck beside them, I didn't know they were for sale. Then I discover it's another bloody newspaper promotional game, covering two whole pages with a load of cobblers and nonsense and bollocks. Why don't they print them as supplements or get idiot readers to write in, instead of cluttering up the sports pages?

New shirts on the refs in Scotland. Have you spotted them? Sort of grey and black with a lot of "V"s. Not as horrible as the English refs last season, but totally unnecessary.

Some new sponsors on players' shirts, but that's not so unusual. Chelsea is now Autoglass and Man Utd seems to have added ViewCam to Sharp. They pay millions, these firms, to have their names on young firm chests, but is it worth it? Both Southampton and Sheffield Wednesday are emblazoned with the name Sanderson, but what or who are they? The trendy wallpaper place or that hardware shop in Wigton where I bought my garden ladder in 1987?

Three letters on the front of the shirt seems to be the flavour this season — JVC at Arsenal, AST at Villa, ORA at Barnsley, CIS at Blackburn, TDK at Palace. Gawd knows what they mean, but it will give me something to ponder, probably rude, when they arrive at White Hart Lane and start running rings round the Spurs defence, as they doubtless will. Oh no, I mustn't start moaning, not now, only a week into the season.

CARLISLE'S PITCH, THE BEST IN THE LEAGUE, LOOKED GREAT, AND NOT A SHRIMP IN SIGHT

22 AUGUST 1997

I LOVE GOING TO THE MATCH, OFTEN MORE THAN BEING there, and most times much more than having been there. Going, I feel part of the brotherhood of football fans, that I am walking shoulder-to shoulder with followers of every match that has ever been and ever will be, amen.

Even more so when it's the first home match of the season, oh the excitement and anticipation, hope and expectation, camaraderie and communitarianism, whatever that is. Not reached Cumbria yet, still stuck on the M6, held up in a contraflow argument near Birmingham.

It's 40 miles to Brunton Park from where we live in Lakeland, but I glide there in my new Jaguar, new to me, but four years old to the maker. Don't think I'll take it to White Hart Lane or Highbury when we return to London. Don't want any of those poor people, what I read about in the southern-based papers, taking out their class resentment by scratching my motor.

I give a lift to Guy, who is 16 and lives on a farm near Caldbeck, and then in Carlisle I join up with my brother Johnny, so we are a gang, we happy three, as we walk down Warwick Road to the match, as if going to the beach. Beach? Carlisle? I was in shorts and sandals, you must remember last Saturday, the heat my dear, the people, and felt overdressed compared with lads bare-chested and lasses with naked midriffs. What a lot of women go to football these days, everywhere, and so many families. And such flaxen-headed little children, Angels not just Anglo-Saxons, proof that Cumberland has been ethnically isolated these last thousand years. Two of my own three children were golden-headed when young. Now look at them.

We went into the new East Stand, very smart — best seats right in the middle, only £11, about a third the price of Spurs with twice the leg room, where the steward in a white shirt, collar and tie called me sir. Very polite. Or had he seen my Jag? I bought a programme, price £1.50 — I like to think this is a column of record — and turned to the team sheet where it said "Carlsile United".

Being a bad speller, I can always spot bad spelling, but you'd think they'd get it right in their own programme, just as you'd think Manchester United's Official Sticker-On of Names on Shirts would know how to spell Beckham.

The pitch looked brilliant, as ever, the best surface in the Football League. They took Cumberland turf to Wembley when it was first laid and out jumped Solway shrimps. I learnt that at school, around the time I thought it was dead funny to go around saying "I've a broad arse". I still think that's funny, but you have to have heard of Carlisle's star of the Forties and Fifties, Ivor Broadis.

Around the pitch they had laid a brand new, bright blue carpet, very smart, very colourful, which will look good on television, should Border TV ever progress to colour.

My brother told me to look out for Matt Jansen, Carlisle's new young star, who reminded him of the young Peter Beardsley when he played for Carlisle, and for Warren Aspinall, who is very good at kicking people. I watched the Watford team warming up and didn't at first spot Jason Lee, as he now plays *sans* pineapple haircut, but I did spot someone who looked the spitting image of Ronnie Rosenthal, so I said to Johnny, look, he's the spitting image of Ronnie Rosenthal, we all love him at Spurs, always gets a huge cheer when he comes on, usually as sub, as he's so useless. And blow me, it was him. Sorry, was he, let's get the grammar right, the verb to be is followed by the subject, I was taught at Carlisle Grammar.

Behind my back, Spurs have let Ronnie go to Watford on a free transfer, which sounds expensive. He was sub again. Poor Ronnie.

You can have a ride in my Jag if you like, Ronnie, but no scratching.

"Taylor is a Turnip," shouted the Carlisle United fans as the game began. Graham is Watford's manager, probably another free transfer, so do we not like him. Nothing in it in the first half, just a lot of huffing and puffing in the tropical heat, then Ronnie came on and, guess what, Watford scored twice. That was it.

Jansen did look good, brilliant jumper for his size, good skill, but he faded. My brother thinks he used to have asthma. Never heard of a pro footballer with asthma, just swimmers and runners, but they must exist. I spent all my teenage life with asthma, playing football till I was red in the face and had to lie down to breathe. There were no inhalers in those days, no wonder drugs, just things to distract you while you were ill, such as having your chest rubbed with Vick's, which was what my grandmother did, then a cold silk scarf which felt really nice but didn't actually stop the asthma.

I also liked the look of Alan Smart, Carlisle's main striker, another addition to my long list of onomatopoeic players. That's not quite the adjective, but players who have names which sound like how they play, such as Roy Keane and George Best. Speedie was on that list, though it was his temper which was speediest. It began with Frank Swift, though he was safe rather than swift. In fact it's not such an apt list, now I think about it, but it's something to do on the way home when you've been stuffed and there's no Premier League results to listen to.

It was sad going home, trailing those 40 miles when you've been beaten, even in my lovely car. Young Guy said he'd been told a scout was at the match to watch Jansen. From Barrow or Accrington Stanley? No, from Newcastle, so he'd heard. Chose the wrong match. So did we. But it's going to the match, I always say, which is the best fun, not what happens afterwards. A bit like living. I find that's always more fun than dying.

THE WORSE OUR FOOTBALL PLAYERS ARE, THE MORE WE SEEM TO LOVE THE GAME

29 AUGUST 1997

THERE'S SOMETHING I DON'T UNDERSTAND ABOUT FOOTBALL. There's something I don't understand about life, such as why it is that photocopiers are still so bloody expensive. In the past 20 years fridges, televisions, washing machines, camcorders and fax machines have all plummeted in price, yet photocopiers still cost a fortune. It's a mystery.

I also don't understand why there are no waterproof shorts. I was caught in a shower in Cockermouth, wearing the shorts and sandals I've worn every day since May and intend to keep wearing till October, so I went into a shop, examined their waterproof jackets, coats, leggings, and asked for a pair of waterproof shorts. "You what?" said the girl.

I came out convinced I'm on a winner. When I'm back in London, I'll start manufacturing.

The football mystery is a bit more complicated. You know how well football is doing, massive following, ever so fashionable, men and women and families of all classes flocking, acres of it in papers of all brow sizes, millions of hours on TV, record transfers and wages, yes, yes, I know you know all that; though I was surprised to read that Manchester United's total income of £55 million this year will make it the world's highest-earning football club. Can this be so, can this be true? Also interested to learn which British club has sold the highest number of season tickets this year. Guess. Go on. No, not Man U. It's Celtic. They have 40,000 season-ticket holders. Amazing.

And that is where the mystery begins. Celtic, let's face it pal, are a rubbish team. Man Utd are failures. Come on, admit it. When it really matters, when it really counts, namely in Europe, they are useless. Ditto Liverpool, Newcastle and Arsenal, three of our so-called best clubs. Rangers have won nine league titles in a row, or is it 19, or 99, who cares. It's all cobblers. Whenever it comes to playing outside these shores, all British clubs are craparoo. England itself has not won a pot for more than 30 years.

And yet look at the success of the game here at home, its passionate appeal, its intellectual following, its enormous popularity, its ability to attract and pay top wages for the world's best players. Despite the fact that the basic product, compared with the product produced elsewhere, is so poor. If we were talking economics, it wouldn't make sense. Yes, economics doesn't make sense either, but economists think it does. Common sense would suggest it can't go on, all this success, all this conning of the population, when what's being sold is of such inferior quality.

I'm not trying to work out why we do so badly in Europe. That's another subject. The question is simply: why does this appear not to matter? Why is our football doing so well, being enjoyed by so many, when it's not really very good and any half-decent foreign team can come over here and stuff us, no problem? That to me, friends, is a mystery.

All right then, having started this, I'll try some explanations. Perhaps it's because we're so insular. We're not just an island race, but a blinkered population, tied blindly to our local or chosen favourites and don't realise foreigners play it better. Or we do know, but don't actually believe it. We might admit, down the pub, that Barcelona are better than Blackburn, both Milans are better than Man U, Real Madrid better than Newcastle, and OK they get huge crowds, so I'm told, and they have incredible stadia, twice the size and magnificence of Old Trafford, yeah, you have a point there. Then we sup up — and forget it. We are, you see, in denial.

Or is it all to do with being caught up in a feeding frenzy? Football is fashionable, this year's taste thrill, everyone must have a bite, a desire which will soon fade and be forgotten, like Hula-Hoops, Rubik Cubes and Mr Blobby.

Or could it simply be the money? By a sequence of events not directly related to football, billions are pouring in because Rupert Murdoch, who wouldn't recognise a corner flag if he met it up his bum, is set on world media domination.

Well, that's three attempts to explain the mystery. A fourth could be a footballing one: that our football is not worse but different, faster and more furious, full of blood and guts, far better to watch than those sterile if skilful European games.

That doesn't really wash, not if you saw Barcelona against Real Madrid last weekend. I found it on Eurosport, twiddling the knobs, trawling the ether for anyone kicking a football. I got a German match first, which was jolly interesting. In German, as in almost every other language, they use many English words for football terms, as we invented the game, but I hadn't realised they also use associated phrases such as "match winner" "golden goal" and "hat trick". I keep telling my wife, awfully educational having satellite TV.

The Barcelona–Real Madrid match was brilliant to watch. Gawd, the blood and guts, the speed and excitement, the crowds and the passion. It'll make this weekend's Arsenal–Spurs game seem like Noddy's tea party. I also noticed they had an electric car, like a milk float, which came on to the pitch to carry off the injured. Good idea, huh? Wish I'd thought of it. More useful than water-proof shorts.

Anyway, after watching TV last week, I have come up with the best explanation for my football mystery. It came to me during the Chelsea–Barnsley match when the supporters of poor old Barnsley, 5–0 down, started singing, "We're going to win 6–5, we're going to win 6–5…"

The next day, when Sheffield Wednesday were being thumped 7–2 by Blackbum, some of their fans were dancing a celebratory conga round their seats.

That's it, I thought. That's why we love our own football, enjoy it so much, despite all its faults, all its failures. While loving it, we are mocking it. It's a vital element in our postmodernist, quasi-ironic attitude to football which few foreigners could possibly comprehend.

THE RECENT LACK OF FOOTIE
GAVE ME TIME TO SCRUTINISE THE
PREMIERSHIP WINE LIST

12 SEPTEMBER 1997

I KEPT THINKING ABOUT FOOTBALL DURING THE FUNERAL, which I know I should not have done. "As a mark of respect" I should have been thinking of higher things. I used quotes there because that phrase is now part of our legend, part of our everyday chat, ever since I saw it on a public lavatory in Workington announcing it would be closed for the funeral. I say it all the time. As a mark of respect, I am now going to bed. As a mark of respect, I am now having this glass of wine.

The first comparison was in the camera work. Goodness, aren't they clever these days? All that arty stuff from the ceiling of Westminster Abbey, zooming in and out, making kaleidoscopic patterns, but of course we have that in football with those arty shots from the airship high above the ground, giving us a plan view. I spotted a camera crane leaning and twisting out of the trees in the Mall, looking towards Buckingham Palace, just like they have in European football. Didn't spot a dolly anywhere, a camera on wheels on a track, but they probably did have them somewhere, as they often do in football behind the goals. I couldn't work out all the camera angles on the M1, how they got totally empty shots of the hearse, yet there must have been a camera ahead on a car or motorbike. I can't always work it out in football either, but it does give you something to do, when the action is boring or the service slow.

The funeral has a narrative, as in football, which means it was impossible to come in halfway and work out what was going on. You had to know what had happened before, who had been spotted, who had said what, otherwise you wouldn't understand the clapping, or the silences, or what Earl Spencer really meant by his elliptical references. Just like in football. If you don't watch from the start, you don't know why they are booing, why someone is angry, why someone is limping, why they are laughing or what the crowd means when it chants those elliptical refrains.

Then the playbacks, replays, slow motion repeats which we got for the rest of the day, just like every post-match analysis, looking for meanings we missed, players we didn't notice, actions that didn't seem important at the time. I shouted at David Dimbleby when there were members of the Royal Family he didn't identify, things he didn't explain, or famous faces in the crowd he missed, just as I do when Motty fails to explain, or talks bollocks, or tells us facts he has preplanned and is determined to unload.

Then there was Elton John, the well known football fan, famous for his Watford connections. Even my wife knows that. She also knows he wears a wig, is gay, was a friend of Princess Diana, in fact she knows all the minor stuff about him but — and this was the most amazing part of the whole funeral — she didn't know he sang. When he came to the piano, she had no idea what he was going to do next.

How can you go through life, pet, and not know that? Tell me some of his songs then. I did, and she hadn't heard of any of them. I think she half thought he might be a comic, like the other Elton. Or perhaps even a historian, like the other other Elton. He used to look like a comic in his silly-glasses period, rather than a singer. Of course he did sing, and very well. And that was also like football. We have good singing at almost every game.

. . .

Now, at last, after all these interruptions, we are getting back to football again, with a lot of exciting stuff in Europe coming up. This probably explains why everywhere I go, people are asking me the same question: tell us, Hunt, what is the best thing to drink while watching football?

Well, friends, this all depends on the occasion and the mood, but I find it is best to combine the character of the drink with the character of the team you are about to enjoy. I am grateful to the Waitrose wine catalogue, just received, for all the sparkling adjectives.

For watching Manchester United, try a deep, rich red, with a gutsy, robust bouquet, such as Chateau Alex claret, *grand cru* of course.

Chelsea needs something with a classy finish, hinting of southern hills and Mediterranean herbs, but with an ambiguous aftertaste, so go for a chianti.

Arsenal suggests acidity up front, but with an ageing, oak-like quality, dependable on most occasions. Not quite up to the quality of a premier Chablis, but I think you'll find a medium Muscadet quite acceptable.

Spurs calls for a cheap Chardonnay, an anonymous blend of bargain wines from many parts, some a bit indigestible. It should go down well with most things, and also might go down, full stop.

Newcastle needs a balanced wine, with a hint of sediment, still trying to settle, lacks a clear-cut nose and not quite as full bodied as it should be. A Shiraz perhaps.

Blackburn has a crisp, quaffing style, to be enjoyed now, but will fade if kept so perfect with Beaujolais Nouveau.

Rangers has a plump, full-bodied middle, which would indicate a Côte de Gascogne.

Liverpool should require a rich Fleurie, something with great power and depth on the palate and an elegant structure but this is not vintage Liverpool. Best to stick to a basic burgundy.

Leicester is a young team, vibrant and unfussy, so something fresh and amusing from the New World, such as an Australian Cabernet.

Aston Villa can't score so a blanc de blancs is called for. Leeds United can still leave a nasty aftertaste, but is trying to be workmanlike. Stick to cooking sherry or Barr's Irn Bru.

Wimbledon is heading back for its roots, so get out the lager. Man City still lacks maturity. A case of alcopops.

Carlisle United, well the way things are going, it looks as if we'll be back to drinking sheep's piss. Cheers.

I'VE DONE IT IN TURKEY AND EVEN IN MOSCOW, BUT I'D FAR RATHER DO IT AT HOME

19 SEPTEMBER 1997

I GOT OUT OF THE SUBMARINE, HAVING SPENT AN HOUR AT a depth of 80 feet learning some jolly interesting things, and went into the hotel bar to watch England against Moldova. As one does. So where was I? Answers in your mind, please. Then I'll tell you.

I don't like watching football matches away from the comfort and kindness, calm and silence, not to mention the fridge and wine bottle of my own armchair, but over the decades, for various reasons, like all football fans I've found myself stuck elsewhere when something really, really vital was going on.

There was that hotel in Gozo, Malta, where I watched Manchester United win the European Cup in 1968. Lousy black and white TV, awful reception, but goodness, such excitement. We were living in Gozo at the time, what a mistake that was, and I'd searched everywhere on the island before finding a place with a TV. I'd expected to be on my own, an expat, miles from home, and was looking forward to settling down in an empty room, but the whole male population was already there, hanging on to every wall, cheering every move. I should have realised earlier in the week because in every car, every bus, the driver had a little plastic medallion of Bobby Charlton hanging from his driving mirror, beside the Blessed Virgin and other assorted Religious Superstars.

One May I went on a spur-of-the-moment holiday to Turkey with my two daughters. Nice place, nice hotel, till I woke up on the Saturday and realised it was Cup Final Day. What a mistake, going away at that time. But the Turks are football mad, so I knew it would be on somewhere. Are we not told that our own dear Cup Final is watched by trillions, both here and on Mars? The TV lounge was chocker, all cheering and screaming. I felt quite proud that our game should be so popular, till it turned out they were watching some local Turkish match. The English Cup Final came next — and as soon as it started the whole room emptied. People left, looking at me pityingly. Not bad judges. It was a boring match. Manchester United again, as far as I remember.

As for watching in the flesh in foreign parts, now where have I been? Oh yes, the Lenin Stadium in Moscow. This was in 1986 when we were guests of the Russian Writers' Union. They'd asked in advance what me and the wife wanted to see while we were in Russia, and I said, straight out, no ballet and no tractor farms, thank you. I can get all that in Kentish Town. What I would like is a bit of your footer, please.

We were taken in a huge black car to watch Torpedo versus Spartak. Rather eerie. It was full of military, making sure there was no rowdy behaviour. No one cheered or clapped, even for a good move; but there was noise for any mistake, or for too many back passes, or when play was boring, in which case they all whistled.

In Douala, in Cameroon, it was totally different. When a mistake was made, by either side, the whole crowd erupted in laughter — clutching themselves, pointing fingers, rolling around. We could learn something from that. It must be a far more effective humiliation to be laughed at than called a wanker.

While in the Seychelles I was watching a match when I heard a player shouting "Manongl" I thought, that's interesting, could it be an Indian dialect version of some old French colonial phrase, so I asked an Indian gentleman beside me to translate. The answer was "man on". As shouted in every UK public park.

So anyway, where was the submarine? No, not at the seaside but on Lake Windermere. I was in Southern Lakeland last week for a couple of days with my dear wife and sister, staying in this hotel called Lakeside. On the pier, right outside the hotel, I noticed a sign offering a dive in a submarine, only £39.50 for an hour. Cheaper than an hour in a hot-air balloon, which I've also done recently —

well, I don't get a lot of thrills at my age.

Can't say I'll go in a submarine again, as it was about as exciting as sitting in a car wash, but it was an experience. Quite scary when water started coming in, but the pilot said don't worry, it's only condensation. Did you know submarines have a pilot, not a captain? I also learnt that the biggest mountain range in the world is not the Himalayas but is underwater, in the Pacific. He also told us if that female body found recently in Coniston Water had been dropped just 20 yards further on, where there's a valley some 100 feet deeper, it would never have been found by a diver.

I then dashed straight into the hotel bar where I knew there was Sky TV. I sat on my own, got the drinks lined up, my feet on a comfy stool, thinking this is the life. For the first 25 minutes it was brilliant. Gazza was up for it. Wright looked bright. Then suddenly I was surrounded and overwhelmed by a surging sea of humanity.

I'd forgotten there was a conference on in the hotel. They'd been out on the lake for an evening sail, supper and a jazz band on a steamer, and had now arrived back, tanked up, ready to carry on drinking in the bar. Half were American, with no interest in football. The rest weren't interested either. Most of them stood with their backs to the TV, obscuring my view. In seconds I couldn't hear a bloody thing and was choking with the cigar and cigarette smoke. God, was I spitting. I wasn't even able to fight my way to the bar for another drink.

If only we'd stayed at home in Loweswater, I'd have seen the game in comfort and silence. So how was it for you? Did they really play well against Moldova? No, don't tell me. I've still got a headache. It was either the submarine or the cigar smoke.

WHATEVER HAPPENED TO THE RAPE OF THE LOCK? ENG LIT, INNIT?

26 SEPTEMBER 1997

FOR THE PAST TWO SATURDAYS, 'FOOTBALL FOCUS' ON BBC1 has been trying to decide which goalkeeper has the longest throw. Could it be Walker of Spurs because he can throw to Edinburgh? Or Big Ogi at Coventry, who throws to Dublin? The winner was Seaman of Arsenal. When he throws to Wright, he throws Overmars. Ha ha. Straight from a Christmas cracker, or possibly the top of the page in the *Dandy* or *Beano*.

Is this a sign of clumbing down in football? *FF* does consider itself a serious prog, dissecting matches, allowing its intellectual heavyweights, in other words Jimmy Hill, to get steamed up about affairs of the day such as bungs in football. God that was boring, as if any fan didn't think it happened, as if any fan cared. On reflection, it's impossible to dumb down *FF*.

But something new has happened this season. In all the broadsheet papers, there is not just extra space for sport, which is good, or entire sections, which is even better, but whole pages devoted to what are more or less jokes, dopey lists, odd facts, fascinating surveys, silly connections, daft bits of word play, all to do with football. Every posh paper now does it. Hurrah for that. Better than being put to sleep by Brian Glanville and his thoughts on *catenaccio*.

At one time only the tabloids did silly football stories. I remember once travelling to a match with a *Daily Mirror* photographer, in the days when I did match reports, and he was carrying with him a pair of toy guns and a holster. His job was to grab the star centre forward after the match and get him to wear them for a photo — shooting for England. The tabloids have always specialised in corny puns.

I have this image of these brilliant, young, first-class brains who in ye olden times would have been trying for All Souls or the

Foreign Office but their fantasy now is work experience on *When Saturday Comes*. After several years of slog they get a paid job at last, if only just, on the sports pages of the *Independent* or the *Guardian*, where they spend their days compiling lists of footballers with funny haircuts, foreign parts or fairy names.

I made that last one up. I haven't seen such a list, but when I couldn't sleep last night I was thinking of Valery and Dahlin who plays for Blackburn, Lilley of Leeds, Trollope of Derby, Vieira of Arsenal, Gayle of Wimbledon, and thinking I could probably find a whole team with effeminate-sounding names. Or a whole team full of verbs, such as Given and Rush.

When I did sleep, into my head came a Middlesbrough cross-word in which the answers were Merson and Emerson. Then an Italian one which revolved around Winter of Inter. I woke up before I found the questions.

So is the arrival of a joke page in the so called serious press a surer sign of dumbing down? Nope. You can't trivialise what is essentially a trivial game. It's just that when you have more fans, from a wider selection of brains and brows and classes, you need more people and more space to cater for them. The broadsheets can't afford ghosted columns by star players or managers, or pay for scandals and confessions, so they have to use their imagination. In Italy and Spain they have even more space devoted to football, but they take it much more seriously, going for endless if piddling facts and exhausting if pointless analysis. Here, we go for fun facts.

When I did a book called *The Glory Game* in, goodness, was it 25 years ago, about a year in the life of Spurs, I bunged in 40 pages of appendices, using up all the bits and pieces I hadn't been able to work in, little surveys I'd done for my amusement, such as the players' motor cars, houses, newspapers, holidays, future hopes, political feelings.

For 25 years this has been about the most popular part of the book, judging from the letters. Readers remember Perryman saying "Aren't all players Labour?" when they weren't then and aren't now.

If we have heroes, we usually want to know more about them, eager for any morsels of information. When the Romans marched through Britain, there were people hanging around the routes, hoping for a gape at the centurions, fainting at the very sight.

In the 18th and 19th century, when romantic poets were big, people went mad for locks of their hair. In Austin, Texas, where they have the world's best collection of Eng Lit manuscripts, they also have collections of hair from Keats, Shelley, Byron.

Wordsworth's gardener at Rydal Mount also used to cut his hair and he made an extra bob or two selling cuttings to tourists. Strange that collecting hair died out while autographs are still big business. Both are liable to fraud, but with a dodgy bit of supposedly famous hair a DNA test could now prove ownership.

I see that Sky has spent a fortune on a new football soap, *Dream Team*, which starts next month and will have Big Ron Atkinson playing the part of Big Ron Atkinson.

There's also a new football magazine just out for those of a more literary taste, called *Perfect Pitch* and published by Headline. They know that most football fans like something to watch or read, laugh about or wonder about, in between the matches.

Footballers are today's Big Heroes, so we are eager for any bits and pieces, odds and ends, stuff and nonsense. Samples of footballers' hair are hard to come by, now that there are so many shaven bonces, and not all of them can do joined-up writing, or are in any fit state after the match to even try, but football trivia, dreamt up by clever people with vacant minds, well, it's all around, innit.

A SMALL GAME FOR SPURS, A BIG DAY FOR CARLISLE. AND BOTH OF ME WERE THERE

MOST OF US HAVE TWO TEAMS, BECAUSE MOST OF US ARE two people. We have the team we were born with, which came with our father's milk, which we would inevitably follow because of family or geographical reasons. In other words, the team picked us. Then there is the team we acquired later in life, which appealed to us at a certain time, at a certain stage, often because, go on admit it, they were successful and famous and exciting. In other words, we picked that team.

The former we support through thick and thin, effing and blinding, cursing and moaning, but we will not waver because we are supporters, our team needs our support. With the latter we are celebrators, joining the party after it started, gatecrashing other people's triumphs, missing out on the decades of struggles, but wanting to be there sharing the success.

The latter is supposed to attract a nasty lesser breed, the sort who follow Manchester United yet have never been to Manchester in their lives and have absolutely no connection. They are despised by those who call themselves True Fans. But True Fans, come on, should be tolerant. If we believe the gospel of football, we should welcome converts at whatever stage they arrive, from whatever direction. From my observations, many of those who start from false or fashionable reasons, stay with their team, pick up the history, buy the season ticket, buy the attitudes and encourage their horrible offspring to overdose on the club's horrible merchandise.

I used to be able to tell the exact age of kids who didn't support their local team. The older ones followed Liverpool, till along came Man Utd, soaking up the easily influenced, the weak-willed, the slavish.

I chose Spurs as my London team in 1960 because they were

more exciting, more fashionable. If I'd arrived in the Thirties or the Eighties I would probably have chosen Arsenal. Gawd, how life would have been different. The wallpaper in my son's bedroom would not have been white and blue, nor his socks, shorts, shirts, scarves and duvet. Yes, OK, don't say it. It was I who bought him all that horrible junk.

Of course I still follow Carlisle United, and have gone through almost 40 years with two vastly different teams, from two vastly different lives. I think, friends, we should all have a Carlisle in our baggage. Are we not all big and small, optimistic and pessimistic, inferior and superior, failed and successful?

So guess what happened last week. Carlisle played Spurs. I never thought they'd meet again in my life. The last time was on 24 August 1974, when for a brief moment Carlisle were in the top division and I was there—to watch them beat Spurs 1–0 and go top of the league. Part of the folk memory for all Carlisle fans, but completely forgotten by Spurs fans; except they might remember what happened the week after: Bill Nicholson, their most successful manager, resigned.

Who was I going to support? Same as last time: Carlisle. Spurs are a Big Club, despite the crap way they are playing at present, and will have many Big Games to come, we hope, while Carlisle will always be a Small Club, depending on the luck of a cup draw, this time the Coca-Cola, for the occasional excitement.

"Up Street", as we say in Carlisle, it didn't seem like a Big Day, but then it was a wet midweek evening and everything in Carlisle, as in most small towns, closes down at five o'clock. The city centre is now pedestrianised and is so much more attractive, even more historic, than it was when I lived there; but it means the silence and emptiness is more grave-like. But we do have a Pierre Victoire, and by banging on the door at six o'clock, my brother, my dear wife and I were allowed in for an early supper.

I thought she might come with me to the game, as she is Carlisle born, a true local, while I only arrived there aged four from Scotland. Her surname is pure Border and appears in Walter Scott's *Marmion*: "The Forsters, the Fenwicks, they rode and they ran." Not a great line but it is a mensh. I went through the whole poem last week and do you know, there is not a reference anywhere to Melvyn Bragg. Huh. Call himself a local.

She couldn't of course come, not after what she said at the High School meeting in the 1950s. Carlisle had drawn Arsenal in the cup, another ancient folk memory, and all local schools were given a half day off, as it was a mid week game, gawd knows why. Was there no flood-lighting in those days? Anyway, she stood up in the school council and said the school should not close, she would lead a protest. At the time she was hoping to be Joan of Arc when she grew up. I bet the teachers panicked. You don't realise when young that teachers are just as keen to skive off as pupils.

There was a big crowd last week, 13,571, yet there were some empty seats. Perhaps the pulling power of Spurs is not what it was. For most of the first half, Carlisle were the better team and Spurs soon had Gary Mabbutt warming up. He was just below me, doing those self-conscious stretching exercises that all subs do, trying to look fit and focused to impress the manager. But then he stopped and I thought, oh no, has he pulled something? He was warming up his hands if not his legs by signing autographs — for Carlisle fans. Well, I suppose we don't get many ex-England players at Brunton Park.

Then Spurs got a penalty for no apparent reason. They didn't appeal for it and seemed as amazed as everyone else. Carlisle fans shouted "Ginola you poof", just for someone to boo, and cheered "Sumo, Surno" when fatty Warren Aspinall got the ball, even though he fell over it and gave away the second goal. So that was it. A Small Occasion in football, but A Very Big Day for all followers of THFC and CUFC: ie, *moi*.

TONY BLAIR IS ABSOLUTELY RIGHT.
IT REALLY IS A GAME OF TWO HALVES

24 OCTOBER 1997

JUST GOT IN FROM MY FIRST GAME OF THE SEASON AT
Spurs. Yes, a bit late, but we've been living in Lakeland till now. I
was back in time to have made the midweek defeat by Derby, but
we had something else on that evening. Now what was it? Where
did we go? I know I was furious, having agreed to go to this do,
before I'd realised Spurs were at home. I hate paying £600 for a
season ticket and not using it. Double worse hatred is paying £30
a month for Sky, which was showing the game live, and not being
able to see it, either.

I'll look in my diary and see what passing, piddling event made
me miss the football. Oh, Downing Street. Almost forgot. Down
Whitehall, on the right, big gates, you can't miss it.

I said to Tone, Tone I said, did you not check the fixture list when
you sent out the invites for your reception? Ah, he said, we didn't
know that Spurs would be drawn at home in the Coca-Cola Cup
that night, did we?

I didn't of course say that, but I did ask him if he'd seen the
England–Italy match. Hellish tense, he said, especially the last ten
minutes. Bonding, I think it's called.

At the reception, I met a few people who'd been to receptions
under previous prime ministers. Under John Major, I was told, you
always met a lot of cricketers. I looked around for any footballers, as
Tony does follow Newcastle United, in theory, but the only sports-
man I saw was Greg Rusedski.

The last proper conversation I had with a prime minister about
football was with Harold Wilson. I'd gone to see him about something or other, and we got talking about football. I remember him
showing off by reciting the players in the Preston North End–
Huddersfield cup final of 1938. Later he sent me a letter adding that

Preston won 'with a penalty in the last minute of extra time'. That sentence was typewritten, but he put an asterisk beside it and at the bottom of the letter, in his own fair hand, he wrote: 'After hitting the crossbar'.

What a clever clogs. What a know-all. But what a good letter. I have it as a star exhibit in my rather wonderful collection of letters and autographs of prime ministers, which goes back to Walpole.

The traffic was awful getting to Spurs, and parking hell, for a Sunday afternoon. Why do I bother? Why do I drag all this way, just to suffer? Watching on telly, and the match was live, you suffer for only 90 minutes. Going there in the flesh, or what's left of it, you lose almost four hours of your life.

There was one bit of good news. The awful middle-class family who sat behind me all last season, with their awful, noisy, affected children, were not there. God, they drove me mad. The new North Stand is still not completed, but behind the goals they have installed a TV camera on a dolly to get close-ups of all the excitement. If there is any. Unlikely. The way Spurs have been playing.

The programme cost £2 compared with £1.80 last season. Appalling, especially as it's full of pages of adverts listing the firms which have executive boxes. That also drives me mad. What a waste of space. I'd have thought they would want to keep their names quiet, spending their shareholders' money on treats for themselves at a club which is playing crap football.

So I had a headache before the game had even begun. Made worse by the Sheffield Wednesday supporters' band playing just below me, the one which now follows the England team. "You only know one song," sang the Spurs fans.

Very observant. Made a change from singing anti-Gerry Francis songs, which they've apparently been singing all season so far.

Then Spurs scored. Not just once, but three times, and it wasn't even half-time. Some mistake, surely. The first was jammy, slipping under Pressman's body, but the third, by Ginola, was brilliant. I was up and cheering and in my mind I could see Ginola as a born-again Hoddle — same hair, same shirt outside his shorts, same arrogance, spraying passes all over the park.

Yes, the good times are coming back. Come on you lilywhites. Who cares about £2 for a programme? That one tune band is quite amusing, actually, especially the half-naked fat bloke trying to conduct it. And I rather miss those over-excited middle-class kids.

Three more wins, and we could be up at the top of the league. Could be in Europe next season. We have been unfair to Gerry Francis. He couldn't help all those injuries. Ginola really is a brilliant buy, just look at those silky skills, his touch, his vision and terrific hair. And we have got Sol Campbell, the best young defender in England, Europe, the universe. He didn't desert the sinking ship like Sheringham. And young Walker, is he not the country's best young goalkeeper? Come on you Spurs.

Then came the second half. Don't talk about it. They just buggered around, back to their old stupid habits. Fox really is useless, and he's fat. The defence is a joke, even with Campbell. And how Walker got into the England team, I don't know. Why does he take for ever with every goal kick? Ginola, what a lazy sod. He never tracked back once. And he should get his hair washed. All Francis has done these past three years is buy has-beens, never-wases or Third Division players. Gerry, Gerry, Gerry — Out, Out, Out.

Sheffield Wednesday got two goals back and looked set to equalise, if not win, but Spurs somehow lasted out and sneaked a dodgy, lucky, unlikely, undeserved victory.

So we all came out smiling, or with what passes for smiles on faces that have seen such suffering, seen such agony, all in the space of one game. I think Tony is right about football. Following it is hellish.

FOOTBALLERS USED TO BE TOPS
AT SELF-DESTRUCTION.
SADLY, SENSE NOW PREVAILS

31 OCTOBER 1997

WHY DOES THE WORLD LOVE A BAD LAD? ESPECIALLY A BAD lad with skill and talent, flair and originality, who then throws it all away and self-destructs?

Two questions there, I think, trying to creep out. First, why does the person himself — and it usually is a him — do it, wilfully ruining his own life? That can be complicated, depends on many matters. Just been to see the Oscar Wilde film and that doesn't really make it very clear. So my answer to that question has to be very simple: I dunno.

As for the second question, why do we love him, the self-destroyer, I can make a better stab at answering. He is doing it for us, doing all the things we would often like to do but would never ever do because we're too scared, too conformist, too pathetic, too boring, so we just watch, fascinated, going tut tut, but enjoying every minute of the rise and the terrible fall.

What a joy George Best was, doing all those stupid things during the week, drink and sex and girls, disappearing or passing out, ignoring the coaches and the trainers, driving them to distraction, then turning up on Saturday, usually late, and playing a blinder.

Stan Bowles, I loved him as well. So silly, spending all his money on horses so he ended up with practically nothing. But what a player. Rodney Marsh, he was a good-time guy as well, and that Frank Worthington, putting all his energies into his clothes and his hairstyle rather than his work rate.

Jimmy Johnson, wasn't it great that time when he was supposed to be in training for Scotland's World Cup but decided to go rowing on his own into the Atlantic, half smashed by the sound of it. Jim Baxter, he was another one who dissipated his natural skills. Is it something in the Celtic character? Not really. Londoners have done their bit to keep our tongues clucking. Charlie George, he was a right goer in his day, though not as wild as Paul Merson and Tony Adams. Their drugs and drinks antics kept us all agog. Something rather dreary about them, now they've gone straight.

And as for Robin Friday, he was probably the wildest, most self-destructive of them all. Robin Friday? You haven't heard of him? Where have you been? Living in Reading in the 1970s, that's where you haven't been.

I did know his name, but didn't know anything about him until I read a book by Paul McGuigan and Paolo Hewitt called *The Greatest Footballer You Never Saw*.

Oh no, this isn't a disguised book review is it? I hate that, feel really conned when I get into a column and find it's about a book. I also hate columns where they mention their children and don't name them or give them twee names, or columns which are really a rehash of some trivial human-interest story or stupid survey which they've been given by the features editor and told to put a spin on. Is it a column like that? Certainly not. This is a theme column, sparked off by a topical angle. Now back to Robin Friday.

He was a total piss artist, womaniser, druggie, gambler. He had a criminal record, was married three times, was always in fights, abused himself in every way, didn't give a bugger for any sort of authority, but had amazing natural flair for football.

He wouldn't train or follow tactics, wear shin pads, but when he was out there he thrilled the crowd, either with skill or his daft-ness. He once grabbed Bobby Moore by the balls, long before Vinne Jones ever thought of such amusements, and gave the V-sign to referees. After scoring a goal he took off a policeman's helmet and kissed him.

Afterwards he'd go to pubs and dance, on tables, or go night-clubbing in an old raincoat, bollock-naked underneth except for his boots. Everybody, apparently, loved him, rarely had a bad word against him. He lived life, to the fool. He really enjoyed himself That's the romantic view. In reality he was a nutter, the ultimate nightmare for any manager, wife or friend.

He played for Reading between 1973–76, then had a short spell with Cardiff. Then he disappeared. He died in 1990 aged 38, from alcohol and drug abuse. So it goes.

Will we ever see his like again? Well Gazza has tried over these past few years to amuse, annoy, upset and outrage the nation, but now he seems to be settling down. On Sky TV last Sunday, asked about whether he was leaving Rangers, he spoke for at least 30 seconds without putting out his tongue, making a stupid face, swearing, farting, belching or pouring beer over the interviewer's head. He'll be in William Hague's shadow cabinet next.

The best way today for a young person to self-destruct in style is to be a pop star. Followed by artist, actor and, at a pinch, novelist. The modern young footballer has little chance. He's on a diet from birth, so avoids most of those nasty foods and drinks. His body is monitored every second, so any dodgy drug will quickly show up. His bank balance is monitored by a team of accountants and advisers who will make sure he capitalises on his skills and keeps the millions rolling in till he retires at 36, which is when he can abuse himself and his money.

I blame the Italians. Coming over here with their sensible lifestyles, showing our native-born idiots and halfwits that three girls before a match, a spliff at half-time and 15 pints of lager-top afterwards are not quite the best way to impress coaches or influence Glenn.

The stakes are so high in football these days that self-abusers and self-destroyers really haven't much of a chance. But we live in hope.

THE NEW BREED OF FAN HAS PAID FOR RESULTS, AND WANTS ITS MONEY'S WORTH — NOW

12 DECEMBER 1997

I HAVE JUST COME IN FROM WATCHING SPURS — AND IT was really interesting. Not exciting. Interesting. In fact I don't think I can remember a more interesting Saturday afternoon in 30 years. Considering we got stuffed 6–1 by Chelsea.

My seat is in the West Stand, right in the middle of row 18, which is a drag if you want to go to the lav or get a drink, as you have to clamber over everyone. But it does mean you don't get disturbed when other people leave.

There are always half a dozen or so who depart four or five minutes before the end, to catch transport, avoid the crowds, but today I watched fascinated as all around me rows began emptying, hordes of people standing up, all furious, some even frothing. They were season-ticket holders, like me, who had paid around £600 for the privilege, yet there was still 20 minutes to go. They were deliberately missing 20 per cent of the game. Amazing.

"Having spent all that money," I said to the bloke on my right as he left, "aren't you going to wait to the end?"

"Fuck off," he said. As if I'd personally been responsible for his leaving.

"Lucky old Christian Gross," I said with a smile to the bloke on my left as he, too, got up. "It can only get better from now."

"Like fuck it will," he said.

So I sat there, almost on my own, in a half-empty stand. Those who'd paid most left first. Wasn't that interesting? Yet it was Gross' first home match as manager, the start of his brave new disciplined regime. Why, he even has the lads staying in a hotel the night before home matches, first time that's happened. There was an eerie silence which meant I could hear every word floating over from the

Chelsea supporters, down to my right. Nothing amusing or subtle. Perhaps they, too, were stunned by how the game had turned and could think of nothing wittier than: "Going down, you are shit, you are scum."

In the first half it had been pretty even. Zola and Di Matteo were doing little, most of it badly, and the Spurs crowd had shouted "Inger-land" every time either made a mistake. Which I smiled at, being easily amused.

When the final whistle blew it was so easy leaving, none of that pushing and shoving. I caught up with this flash family I hate, who sit behind me, with two noisy boys who never stop shouting inane abuse, even when things are going well. I did enjoy seeing their contorted faces.

"That Gross is useless," said a refined looking man as I walked down the concrete steps. "He's changed nothing." "Well, some local hotel must be pleased by his arrival," I said. "Let's see, 18 in the first team squad, plus manager, coaches, staff, that's probably 25 extra people they had last night ... "

"Do you want fucking kicked?" said the refined man.

I then caught up with two girls, arms round each other, as I walked through the car park, zigzagging between the Mercedes and the BMWs. What wonderful business Spurs and Arsenal players have brought to the luxury car market of north London. How they must be grateful for all these young millionaires.

"What a bloody shame," said one of the girls.

"It's the players I feel sorry for," I said. "They have nothing else in their lives, poor things, whereas we can go home and soon get over it, but they have to live ..."

"You taking the piss?" said one of the girls. I then noticed they were with two enormous blokes, so I hurried on.

In the High Road I met a friend who lectures at LSE. "We're ahead of the pack," I said. "It's like we had the industrial revolution first, right, so now as a secondclass nation, with no industries, no nothing, Britain is in advance of everyone else. Same with soccer. We are in the cycle ahead of Man Utd…"

"What the hell are you on?" lie said.

"Fisherman's Friends," I said. "Would you like one?"

In the queue at the chip shop there was an old man behind me, looking very mournful, waiting for his savolard. Or savollo. After all these years in London I still don't know what those sausage things are, or how to spell them.

"Cheer up," I said. "Man Utd couldn't exist without us."

He stared at me as if I was an alien, or an Arsenal fan.

"I mean, if you have winners, you've got to have losers," I said. "If you have a top of the league, there must be a bottom. If three come up, three have to go down. So we all have a part to play…"

I though he was going to choke on his savoy thing, or ram it up my bum, so I ran to my car. I have this weekly competition with myself to get to the car before the strains of *Sports Report* have ended.

I switched on and found myself smiling when the results came through: one-nil to the Arsenal, of course. I smiled most of the way home. It's a little trick the Maharishi taught me, all those years ago. I can't reveal my mantra, but it's a form of levitating, rising above oneself.

There is, you see, a new breed in football: wealthier, better-educated, more fashionable people, but alas, some of them are nastier, meaner, greedier than the ones before. They are not interested in years of blind, abject loyalty. They have paid good money, big money, and they want satisfaction, right now, at once, this minute, or boy will they make someone suffer. The clubs are also greedy and mean, and equally shortsighted. In a way, they deserve each other.

So, friends, that's why this season could turn out to be awfully interesting. For supporters of Spurs, Everton, Man City, oh, quite a few really. Anywhere that the worms might turn.

THIS YEAR'S WORLD CUP LOOKS GOOD
FOR PHILATELISTS AND GERMANS ALIKE

9 JANUARY 1998

WHAT I'M LOOKING FORWARD TO IN 1998 IS, OF COURSE, the World Cup, especially the really exciting, really stunning World Cup stamps which I'm sure France and lots of other countries will be producing.

On the walls of our bathroom are hung my framed football stamps. Among them is a 1966 first-day cover signed by the whole England team, including A Ramsey, rather a coup, as no one ever thought he could do joined-up writing.

My best exhibit is probably a history of the World Cup in stamps. Which I created. Quite amusing, quite unusual, a talkingpoint, as they say on Friday evenings on Sky TV when it's been a really boring Second Division match and there's nothing to talk about but they hope you won't switch off because at half-time they'll be analysing the talking points, such as that disputed corner flag, that controversial scarf the chairman was wearing and whether the striker's haircut was offside or not.

For about ten years I was mad keen on stamps, for reasons we won't go into, then I gave up, for reasons I can't remember. One of my many madnesses was thematic collecting, which means collections on a theme. In the US they call it topical collecting, because you collect on a topic. Don't say you don't learn things. I got rid of my Wembley Exhibition stamps, my Columbus stamps, my railway stamps and all my other thematic stuff, but I kept all my football stamps.

I have my World Cup collection ever so nicely framed, with two or three carefully chosen and well mounted stamps to represent each of the 15 World Cups from 1930 in Uruguay to 1994 in the US. I did little labels in my best handwriting but, alas, the steam has faded most of them. They give the venue, the final two teams and the score. People washing themselves in our bathroom don't come out all that clean, because there's very little room for washing, but awfully knowledgeable.

My favourite football stamps, as you've asked, are the set France produced in 1938, the last time it held the World Cup. They show a bloke heading the ball and a goalkeeper diving. They are not quite in sync, but very artistic. I also like England's 1966 World Cup set, which is very balletic. The 4d one has two players high kicking, which is now against the law, and reveals acres of their bare thighs. I suppose that's why David Hockney had them pinned up on his bathroom wall. Or was it a photo of Denis Law? I went to interview Hockney in 1966, when he'd just won his Gold Medal at the Royal College of Art. I wasn't quite aware at the time of the nature of his interest in footballers' naked legs, having lived such a sheltered life.

Depending on the quality of this year's stamps, I might add further information, such as the top scorers in the World Cups so far. Do you know who's leading? Just Fontaine of France, who scored 13 in 1958. Then comes Sandor Kocsis of Hungary, with 11 in 1954, and Gerd Muller of Germany, who got ten in 1970. You thought Gary Lineker had scored most. He is well down the list, with six in 1986.

As for the World Cup winners, well, you know that. Brazil leads with four wins, followed by Italy and Germany with three each, Uruguay and Argentina with two each and England with one. That makes 15, unless I've missed one out. It's the steam fading the handwriting. Not my fault.

But we all know that what you learn from statistics is what you learn from history. Bugger all.

Not that this is going to stop us looking into the future and predicting, based on what has happened in the past. After all, what else have we got to go on.

Right, look at that list of winning countries again. Notice something? Only teams from Europe or South America have ever won.

I predict that will be the same again this year. It is too soon for a country from Africa or Asia to win, or one from Concacaf, wherever that is.

I also predict that whoever wins this year has already won. That's because the top teams are still the top teams — except for Uruguay, the only ex-winner not in this year's World Cup. It's a long time anyway since they had their wins — in 1930 and 1950.

I am therefore predicting that France, the home nation, won't win, nor will Spain, Romania, Denmark or Colombia, all of them well-fancied countries, none of which has ever won.

The winners have been evenly split between South America and Europe — with eight wins for a South American country and seven for a European. Almost always a European team has won in Europe and a South American team in South America. The only exception was Brazil's victory in Sweden in 1958.

OK, Brazil also won in 1994 in the US, which is technically outside their own continent, if you call South America a continent, but they were at home if you count the Americas as one continent. Columbus did, but then Columbus didn't know where he was. (He did, actually, in the sense that he could find his way home exactly, wherever he roamed, which was amazing, but he didn't know what was round the next bay.)

Now that football stars are all mercenaries, used to working in foreign lands, wherever the money takes them, acclimatisation should not be such a handicap as in the past. But I still think home continent counts.

I am therefore going to tip Germany to win. Beating Brazil in the final. The other semi-finalists will be England and Spain. Thank you. Now chew this after you have burnt it, then swallow. On 12 July I don't want proof of my daftness.

FACE TO FACE WITH A CROATIAN
AMBASSADOR FOR FOOTBALL

16 JANUARY 1998

I DON'T JUST SIT AROUND AND WATCH FOOTBALL. TELE-vision only fills up five nights a week, plus Sunday afternoons. Or go to see Spurs and Arsenal, which normally means every Saturday. Plus all the reading of the back pages, mustn't forget that. OK then, I do mostly sit around and observe football. But now and again I get out and meet a living, breathing footballer. In the flesh.

Which was why I was at Derby County's training ground, watching them go through another morning's training. Derby are among the most foreign of British clubs, even more than West Ham or Chelsea, with 12 of their squad from foreign parts.

Their captain, Igor Stimac, having trained, was finishing his pasta and salad. He stood out as a mature figure among the rather gawky youth players he happened to be sitting with, a prefect among schoolboys, but he is 30-years-old and six foot two. He can speak four languages, unlike most British players, unlike most British people. He's also seen things they will never experience, such as living and playing football in a war zone, with bombs flying around, people being shot. Igor is Croatian, formerly of Hadjuk Split.

"Pass the fucking juice, then," he said to one of the young players beside him. I'd somehow not expected him to swear, as if his experiences of life might put him above swearing, which was silly. A football club is an industrial setting. He has picked up the English used around him.

We looked for a quiet corner to chat; but there were phones and noise, so I said, "... er, what about going to your house?"

One's chances of getting into the home of a well-known player in London or Manchester are zilch. Even getting ten mins after training without having to pay some agent is unlikely.

"No problem," he said, going off to change his training gear.

While I waited I talked to Jim Smith, Derby's manager, widely known as the Bald Eagle. I asked what it was like, having all these foreigners. The coaches love it, he said, it brings variety and atmosphere. They settle down quickly.

In London or Manchester a new player can have six months in a boring hotel feeling lost and fed up, but at Derby most move into a new house locally, thanks to a club director who has a building firm. "I should have been an estate agent," said Jim.

Igor's house was a show house, on a model estate, with every mod con. But when you are from war-torn Split, anything with four walls and a roof would have been amazing. In Split, Igor had an apartment, but a lot of the time there was no water and no electricity. Beside him on his new estate live another Croatian, two Costa Ricans, two Italians, a Dane, a Dutchman, an Estonian and an Irishman—all of them Derby players. They provide support for each other in a foreign land, especially the wives, who, for all the big money at their disposal, live isolated lives, liable to move clubs, towns, countries at any moment. In their own homes they speak their respective languages, but with each other they speak English.

Igor and his wife, Suzana, have two children, Luka 7 and Mia 2½, who speak fluent English. Igor had never been to England till he joined Derby—but Suzana had. She was Miss Yugoslavia when she was 17 and came to London for a beauty contest. She has not had the advantage of going out to work and training every day like Igor, so she's had to pick up a lot of her English from watching daytime television. Her swearing is thus a bit limited.

Igor also speaks Italian, picked up on holidays, and Spanish, after playing in Cadiz. Very handy at the club. He's the only one who can speak to the Costa Ricans and Italians in their languages.

They love everything about England, apart from the traffic and weather. "In Croatia," said Igor, "we have 300 days of sun a year. Here it's only about three days." I took this as a wild exaggeration, till I looked at the map and saw where Croatia is on the Adriatic.

Yes, that's been one of the things they've found — our ignorance of Croatia and what really went on in the war. Many of the younger players at Hadjuk Split abandoned football to fight for their people. The internationals such as Igor felt it was their duty to keep playing and represent their new country abroad.

"One of the nicest things that happened since I've been here was during Euro 96. The club shop decided to buy 500 Croatian shirts to sell to Derby fans. They didn't know if anyone would buy them — but all 500 were sold in a few weeks."

Since coming to Derby, Igor has bought two night-clubs in Croatia, which his brothers look after. "One is in Split and the other on an island called Brac. This is where the young and rich go, the jet set of Croatia."

Croatia has a jet set? "Oh, yes! My club can hold 4,000 people. When I've saved some more money, I'm going to buy a hotel in Split."

Nice to think that some of the trillions floating around football today are ending up with people who have had a hard time and not simply boosting Sky TV's profits.

As for the football here, he finds the skills and technique as good as anywhere in Europe, but he still hasn't got used to the drinking. He managed two hours at the team's Christmas party, while others poured down the pints. "In Europe, a young player on a night out will have a glass of wine then think it is time to look for a nice meal, or a nice shag. Here all they think of is the next drink, and the next pub…"

Yes, it must be a culture shock for foreign footballers coming to Britain, but their arrival is beginning to change our ways. And not just the training methods. Alex Ferguson says that at Man Utd he now has seven players in his first-team squad who are teetotal. The next generation might not drink beer at all. But will any of them be able to speak four languages and have survived a war?

HOMERS, HAIRCUTS AND HUGE SALARIES.
YES, IT'S GOOD TO BE BACK

6 FEBRUARY 1998

Where have you been for the past three weeks, Hunt?

The West Indies: Barbados, St Lucia, Bequia, Tobago, Grenada.

Following the cricket?

Gerroff. Don't follow those fairies. I was mainly following the footer on the back pages of five-day-old newspapers. Last year when I was away, there was this amazing news that Kevin Keegan had packed it in. Couldn't believe it.

This year I spent every day trawling waste-bins for news of Kenny Dalglish throwing in the sporran, Christian Gross chucking in the cold sausage or Jürgen Klinsmann taking his educated right foot back to Germany.

What is an educated rightfoot?

One that passed the 11-Plus. It often used to happen that one foot failed and went to the sec mod and felt for ever a second class foot. Now with comprehensive education, all footballers can kick each other with either foot.

What is a cultured left back?

One that doesn't spit or pick his nose.

When the commentator says, "There were no Newcastle shirts in the Villa half," what does that mean ?

Precisely what it says. Bodies are now so expensive, costing up to £15 million, plus huge amounts spent on hairstyles and ear-rings, so bad weather can cause havoc. To reduce the risk of injuries or looking unkempt, Noocastle often send out a team consisting only of shirts.

Why did you say 'Noocastle'?

I thought I was Trevor Francis in disguise.

Why does Barry Venison now always appear in disguise?

As a player he had long, bleached, 1970s-style hair, which didn't get him very far. No, hold on, he did play for Galatasaray for one season. Now as a television commentator he's acquired short dark hair and hintellectual specs and no longer looks like a girl.

When a manager calls a ref a 'homer', is that because he thinks he looks like a girl?

I thought that when I first heard the expression in the Spurs dressing-room in the 1970s. Bill Nicholson would pick up the programme, turn to his assistant and say, "Bloody hell, a homer."

How does he know? I thought. And has he got photos? It refers, in fact, to a referee who is suspected of being easily influenced by a home crowd.

You mean bribes?

No, crowd emotion and constant abuse. For example, whenever a home player is touched, even with a zephyr, the home crowd go mad, scream at the ref, criticise his eyesight, then when one of their heroes takes out a Kalashnikov and shoots dead the opposition's star striker, they say he's just pretending to be injured.

A Zephyr? Wasn't that a sort of Ford car?

Yup. Klinsmann now drives one, recycled, showing he is anti-materialist and environmentally sound.

Why has Klinsmann stopped smiling?

Same reason as Dwight Yorke. Playing in a rubbish team soon wipes the smile off anyone's face. Plus playing with Collymore.

What is his problem?

I blame his mother. No top player is called Stanley, not since Stanley Bowles first turned out for Carlisle United. In fact, no one is christened Stanley today. Frank Dobson's National Health bill has banned it for ever.

Has the Barnsley crowd been banned from singing, "It's just like watching Brazil"? Haven't heard it recently.

No, it's because they now realise Alan Brazil was a very poor role model. Baldy bloke, played for Ipswich. Now commentates for Sky's boring Friday evening games, where his speciality is:

"Goodness me!" or alternatively: "The boy done well."

Tell me, who are the boys who really done well?

There are currently 14 players earning more than £1 million a year. In order they are: Alan Shearer on £3.5 million, followed by Ryan Giggs, Paul Ince, Les Ferdinand, Teddy Sheringharn, David Beckham, the aforementioned Collymore, John Barnes, Robbie Fowler, Ian Wright, Paul Gascoigne, Paul Merson, Andy Cole, Graeme Le Saux. All millionaires.

You're making it up.

Not me. It's been made up — sorry, carefully estimated — by BBC Radio 5 Live *Sports Yearbook 1998*. The money also includes sponsorship deals.

Are you sponsored, Hunt?

Yes. I get a free Cumberland sausage every time I mention Carlisle United.

Did they also pay for your West Indies trip?

Watch it. That was work for a book. Someone had to do it.

So what's it like being back?

Cold. I got back just in time to watch Chelsea on the telly, and goodness, what changes while I've been away. Zola has had his hair cut using the same knife and fork as Le Saux. Mark Hughes has gone grey.

Then I went to see Arsenal against Southampton and they've changed the typeface on the electronic scoreboard and I couldn't read the names. Only afterwards did I realise Le Tissier had played. He was a total non-participant. Never have I seen any player do so little for so long, as Churchill almost said.

Who?

Fred Churchill. Played for Carlisle reserves in the Fifties. Right, that's two sausages. Oh, it's great to be back.

THEORIES ABOUT SOUTHERN SOFTIES ARE COBBLERS; LIKE MOST THEORIES, ACTUALLY

13 FEBRUARY 1998

I'VE JUST COME BACK FROM WATCHING ARSENAL AGAINST Chelsea, oh no, what an intro, as if anyone outside London would be interested, as if only the metropolis mattered, as if London were the centre of the known universe, as if nothing and nobody existed outside the M25. Good job I said it. Get the retaliation in first, as Nobby Stiles used to say.

I like to think, friends, that I am rarely guilty of any superior southern attitudes. The media as a whole might be London centred, because that's where it mainly comes from and thinks the Sun shines out of its Arsenal; but not our Hunt, not with his roots.

What really gets up the bum, up the nose of those north of Watford is that while Londoners go on as if London is the Top Dog, the Bee's Bollocks, everyone else knows that London football is crap.

Oh yes. Bring out your facts. Make sure you have a big enough trolley. Since 1892 a London team has won the league title (First Division and then Premier) only 13 times. Pretty useless when you realise London has always been up to ten times the size of most other cities. Liverpool has about a 20th the population of London — yet it has won twice as many league titles. I mean Liverpool as a city, counting both teams. Liverpool FC have won 18 league titles and Everton nine. London has around a dozen professional teams, depending on where you draw the boundary. Yet only Arsenal with ten, Spurs with two and Chelsea with one, have managed the league title. Pathetic. Should be ashamed of themselves. All that money, all that catchment area, all that glamour.

In bars and prisons, clubs and senior common rooms, they have oft discussed this interesting anomaly. The usual theories go as follows:

Southerners are softies.

This belief is fondly held up north, making them feel tough and gritty, by heck.

London has too many distractions.

Chaps get led astray, you see, with all the bright lights, hair salons and assorted temptations.

I think both these theories are cobblers. In fact I think most theories are cobblers. Good fun, amusing, passingly interesting, keeps people in employment and provides PhDs, but total rubbish, like all theories assembled with hindsight to explain the inexplicable past. What happens is that you come across some facts, whether it's more women than men in the population, which is true, or more heart attacks in Motherwell than Madrid, which I've just made up, but why? I mean, why should there always be a reason? In assembling any statistics you're bound to have differences. So some clever clogs scurries off to think up explanations. Why can't figures just lie there, doing no harm? I personally believe southern players are no softer than northern players. They have just as much mental and physical muscle, an equal determination to succeed. Look at the stars of England's 1966 World Cup team: Moore, Hurst and Peters. All from London. In recent years most of England's managers have been Londoners, such as Alf Ramsey (born Dagenham), Ron Greenwood (born Alperton), Glenn Hoddle (from ... er, near Heathrow Airport I think, out that way anyway, look I haven't got time to check every boring manager's place of birth). And of course Terry Venables, who as we all know was born in a West End nightclub and weaned on champagne.

As for the other theory, about London being a distracting place to live, I think it works the other way. It is a plus for famous players to be living in London. They have more chance of living a normal life, able to move around, be anonymous. A football star in a northern or Midlands city has no escape from the pressures and the fans.

Historically football began in the industrial north and Midlands and it was always strongest there, so in the early decades the north did much better. That has probably affected the figures. It took 40 years, until 1931, for even one London club, Arsenal, to win the title.

Today's match was pretty boring, so if you believe southerners can't play, it would prove your prejudice. But of course the new element in football is not north and south, but foreigners. This is why the north-south divide, in either the geographical sense or the make-up of the team, will become increasingly irrelevant.

Today at Highbury I did notice that the softies, ie, those not prepared to put themselves about, unwilling to get stuck in, were not the southern Brits but the foreigners — such as Anelka and Overmars of Arsenal, who were either ineffectual or anonymous, and di Matteo and Zola of Chelsea. Zola was only a sub, but did nothing when he came on.

So what does that prove? Not a lot. Though you could argue that London clubs attract mercenaries, passing through our lives, here for the money and the bright lights, and not awfully keen on getting their hair messed up.

Manchester United, so we tell ourselves through narrowed lips, sighing heavily, nodding sadly, are currently our best team. Few would argue with that. But are they northern, or what?

If you take away the Irish, Welsh and overseas players in their regular first team you are left with four locals: Butt, born in Manchester, Scholes in Salford and the Neville brothers from Bury. All good players. But there are also three definite southerners: Beckham from Leytonstone, Pallister born in Ramsgate, and Sheringham from London. Cole was born in Nottingham but was an Arsenal apprentice. So he's not northern.

Black players were at one time classified as having no bottle. They wouldn't make it. They couldn't stand the winters. When that was quickly disproved, it was said you would never get a black goalkeeper. They didn't have the temperament. Now that's seen to be rubbish as well.

So let's agree it doesn't matter where you come from. It's what you do with what you arrived with that matters.

FRANCE 1, SPAIN 2.
ITALY 3, ENGLAND 0.
UNTIL NOW, THAT IS

27 FEBRUARY 1998

ABOUT TWO YEARS AGO I GOT A CALL FROM A BLOKE WHO asked if I'd like to write some football stuff for a brand new sports daily that was about to come out. I said yes, and hung up.

Those calls have been coming since I was in short trousers kicking a ball made out of old pink 'uns across the sands at Rothesay, or was it that beach in Brazil? Anyway, it's one of our oldest football fantasies. No, nothing to do with those dopey games in the *Independent* and elsewhere. The dream is that someone, one day, will begin a national newspaper devoted entirely to sports.

Why hasn't Britain got one, we who created almost every sport? Yet other countries have. It's one of the mysteries of the modern world, along with why Joe Royle would want to go to Man City and why Bates really wanted shot of Gullit.

There was then silence for two years. I'd even forgotten that this bloke, Bob Harris, had ever rung me. I did meet him, about 20 years ago. He used to cover football for Thomson Newspapers, then I think he went to the *Sunday Mirror*. I had noticed recently that he was in the money. Well, he must be, having 'helped' Kevin Keegan with his latest book. He's also ghosted for Bobby Robson. Big money in football ghosting these days. Fergie has supposedly got a one million advance for his new book. Hugh McIlvanney, who is said to be holding his pen, will do well.

Then blow me, Bob rang today to say all systems are go. A new national sports newspaper, *Sport First*, will hit the streets, or at least the chip shop queues, on 15 March.

That's a Sunday. Well spotted. They're not producing a daily, not just yet, says Bob. That will come later. The person putting up most of the money is some publisher-printer called Keith Young. He does lots of magazines, from some parliamentary magazine I'd never heard of to the *Church Times*.

It's been a hard two years, says Bob. Once the national dailies got wind, they started increasing their sports coverage, "even the *Financial Times*." There are rumours that at least one of the two racing papers, *Racing Post* and *Sporting Life*, will soon branch out and cover all sports.

But so far we haven't got one national sports newspaper, yet France has the excellent *L'Equipe*. Italy has three: *Gazzetta dello Sport, Corriere della Sport-Stadio* and *Tuto*. Spain has *Marca* and *AS*. Poland has one, so does Hungary. Even Russia, where everything is falling to pieces, including its football, has got a daily sports paper.

I asked my son, who is awfully clever and has lived in both Spain and Italy, why do they have such papers and we don't? Was it, I suggested, to do with Spain and Italy's long-established middle-class following for sport, with high-quality football reporting and analysis, whereas in Britain, until recent times, football was followed by the working man and read by the working man, with very little money? Bollocks, he replied. So rude, this younger generation.

Italy and Spain, he says, didn't have national newspapers the way we have, yet traditionally they have national clubs—in the sense that Juventus is followed all over Italy, and Real Madrid all over Spain. Local papers naturally preferred to cover their local clubs, so to follow the big clubs, far away, you had to buy the national sports papers. That's his theory.

"And I'll tell you something else," said Bob Harris. "No English-speaking country in the whole world has a national sports paper. Not in the US, Canada, South Africa, Australia or New Zealand."

What about *Sports Illustrated*? "Ah, that's a magazine. I said national newspaper. It's a brilliant mag, but it's still a mag, and subject to magazine deadlines."

The new paper, to be edited by David Emery, will have 48 pages and be bang up to the minute, so Bob says. They've spent £1 million so far in development.

They will have a hard struggle competing with the present sports sections of the national papers, especially on Sundays and Mondays, when they are now so enormous, with large staffs and massive budgets. But naturally I wished them well. Readers need options. Hacks need many outlets. "Yes, but will you write for us?" asked Bob.

Well I've so much on, two books on the stocks, bit of this, bit of that, plus my Spurs and Arsenal season tickets to service.

"Then how about doing match reports?"

Nah, you have to be a young hack to enjoy that. You get a rotten seat for a start, well you do at Spurs, mine is so much better. Most of the pleasure is taken out of watching football when you have to think about what you are going to write. When there's a goal, or a controversial incident—a 'talking point' as they say on Sky—there's a mad panic in the press box to work out what the hell happened. With all the television close-ups, you can easily be made to look a right prat.

Then there's the hell of getting your copy across. I hated having to shout down phones that didn't work. Presumably it's now all laptops and modems. Even so, I bet they go wrong and you find yourself still in an empty stadium, hours after it's over, or hanging around car parks to get quotes from some bastard.

One of the pleasures in watching football is having unconsidered opinions, ones you don't have to substantiate. "Loada tossers. That centre forward is on the juice again. My tortoise could have saved that goal."

After you've said that, or listened to all that, you can go home and forget it. Well, till you watch it again on telly.

The only attraction would be not having to pay for my copy of *Sport First* on 15 March. I'd insist on a free copy, delivered to my door. I collect first editions. I have number one of the *Daily Mail*, *Daily Mirror*, *Picture Post*, *Private Eye*. (Guess the most valuable?

The *Eye* has it by a mile. Reason — so few were printed.)

If I want to be sure of number one, perhaps I'd better write something for them. Just in case there is no number two.

.

PREMIER LEAGUE SEASON TICKET?
THAT'LL DO NICELY, SIR

6 MARCH 1998

I WAS COMING HOME FROM SPURS LAST SUNDAY EVENING — yes, you can have matches any day, anywhere, any time—and I decided to have a car wash. The last one was in October in the Lake District and my old Jaguar is getting a bit cakki, or maybe cacky. I'm not sure how you spell that, or how the word came into my head. Hasn't passed this way, through my little mind, for 40 years.

I was in the garage forecourt, trying to work out how the car wash operated, when this police car came whizzing up behind me. A cop flung open the door and rushed over to me. Naturally I wound the window down, getting ready to help the agitated officer. Perhaps he didn't know how to operate the car wash either.

"Do you know what you just did?"

"No idea. What?"

"You hit that roundabout as you went round."

I looked back into the road, Tottenham Lane, and yes, I had come round a roundabout, one of those stupid flat ones, made out of bugger-all. I wasn't aware of hitting anything, or of there being anything to hit. So I looked puzzled.

"You been drinking, Sir?" he asked, suspiciously.

"Certainly not, officer," I said. "I've been to Spurs."

Not quite a logical answer. But I never drink at football matches, with all those common people, all that smoke, and those nasty plastic glasses, ugh.

"Not even a glass of beer?" he sneered, shoving his head into my car, as if to get a whiff of my breath. Or did he think I was John Prescott? Tubby bloke, double-breasted suits, got a lovely wife, lovely motor, you must have seen him on the television.

"Is this your car, Sir?" he asked.

"Of course it is," I said.

"Got any identification?"

Bloody cheek. As if I'd stolen it. I don't exactly go to football in my best gear—well, I haven't got any—but I wasn't totally dressed like a tramp. These cords, let me see, must be only 17-years-old.

I opened the glove compartment for my service book, but it wasn't there. Anyway it still has on it the name of the bloke I bought the car from. I felt in my pocket for my Visa card, which normally I carry, but I'd left it in my other coat. Yup, two-coat Hunt. Then in the other pocket I found my Spurs season ticket. I handed it over to him.

He opened it—and his mood immediately changed. All smiles, all deferential. Sir this, Sir that.

"You've got a very nice car there, Sir, and a very nice season ticket, Sir. Mind how you go."

And off I went, *sans* car wash. That can wait till the summer.

So what is the moral of this exciting story? Yes, put my name at once on my car's service book. I know that. No, the point is my season ticket does happen to be top of the range, with the price printed in it: £561. It indicated that I was a man of substance, a person of consequence.

At one time an Old Etonian tie might have done the trick, or a CD [Corps Diplomatique] plate, or a House of Lords parking pass. But we now know most of those indicated con-man or someone who didn't have a bean. But a paid-up follower of football today is someone not short of a bob or two, a person of some wealth. How could you follow football otherwise?

The latest report from the Norman Conquest Centre for Football Research at Chester University, published last week, says the average Premier League fan spends £1,300 a year supporting his team. That's his season ticket, getting to and from matches, and includes an average of £689 a year on buying rubbish from the club shop.

Then of course there's the cost of having Sky TV, which every true follower must acquire. That's almost another £400 a year. And if you want some decent, good quality reading on football you will have to subscribe to *Four Four Two*, which costs £2.60 an issue, or *Perfect Pitch* not as frequent, but that costs £7.99.

Next year season tickets will cost even more, especially at Chelsea. Their obvious aim is that only millionaires, or similar, can watch their games.

I do feel sorry for those poor people, living on the breadline, who are reduced to a diet of *Sun* back pages and the scraps that terrestrial television sometimes throws their way. How can they survive? How can they hold their heads up in the pub, argue the toss about England's World Cup chances, when they have never seen a live match in their life, and probably never will, unless they win the Lottery? What does that do to their self-esteem, their self-worth, their position in society? That Harriet Harman should be working on schemes to help them, not faffing about with single mothers and pensioners. Oi, get your priorities right, Harman.

I must make sure I carry my Spurs season ticket all the time from now. Be handy at the bank, if I forget my cheque book or bank card. "Certainly Sir, that will do nicely, just take away as much money as you want."

It'll probably get me tick in pubs and restaurants and entry everywhere when it says house full. "This way Sir, as you are a season-ticket holder..."

I forgot to tell the copper that actually I have *two* season tickets. Well the one for Arsenal is shared, but he couldn't have known that. And I have *two* subscriptions to Sky — in London and in Lakeland. Does that make me doubly wealthy, in the top ranking of football's ruling classes?

It's not just today's players, all of them millionaires in the making, or the Premier League clubs, all of whom now have incomes about the same as Botswana, but the fans in the stands, the paid-up followers, who are now members of the moneyed élite.

Think about it this way, pal. We are all hurtling through the same world on the same train, heading in the same direction. It's just that some of us are travelling first class.

FOOTBALL IS NEVER BORING, RUUD.
YOU JUST NEED TO KNOW
WHAT TO LOOK AT

20 MARCH 1998

SOME TIME BEFORE HE LEFT FOR WHEREVER HE HAS LEFT for, Ruud Gullit—remember him?—said that he wasn't obsessed with football. He could take it or leave it. As an example, he said that if he was watching a match on telly and it was boring, then he had no compunction at all about turning over and watching a film.

Wash your mouth out, Ruud, I thought. And wash your mind out, or you could be out of a job soon. Successful football managers are obsessives. They may not like it. It may not be good for them. Or their families. Or even their players. But that is the nature of their beastliness.

Then I thought, am I obsessed? I would never turn off a boring match to watch a film, but then I've never watched a film on telly, so his whole analogy was wasted on me. Just as I have never read Brian Sewell in the *Evening Standard* I see his page and I think, goody, I don't have to read that, just as I used to be pleased to see an article by Bernard Levin. All newspapers, all media, have bits that are ignored by many people. They play a part, have a function, by being totally boring.

Football must come into that category for many people, but not for me. I will read anything, watch anything footballish. My eyes home in on the City pages when there is the merest mention of Man Utd shares, or Spurs, or even Caspian. Not sure what Caspian owns, but it is footer-based. I think.

I maintain that there is no such thing as bad weather, only bad clothing. That's what I used to tell my children for years on Lakeland holidays, and they would say, "Oh shut up, Hunt, don't be so stupid."

By the same milk token, I maintain that there is no such thing as a boring football match. Just that some are more exciting than others. So here are nine things to look out for when the game itself is not quite as exciting as it might be.

Nets: I am doing my own survey of goal nets around the world. Thanks to television close-ups, which get sharper all the time, and cameras on dollies you can see details never seen before. Not just how goalposts are hung, and their respective supports, which vary enormously, but I've spotted two types of mesh. One has square holes, very popular in the English Premier League; but in Scotland and parts of Europe they favour six-sided meshes, sort of diamond-shaped. Do look out for them.

Architecture: This is a rich and marvellous subject, now that we have so many wonderful new grounds. I half close my eyes and think, does that skyline mean it's the McAlpine Stadium at Huddersfield or the Reebok at Bolton?

Haircuts: They always set my mind off wandering where it will go. At present I am wondering why Di Matteo waited till now to go slaphead, when he has been surrounded for two seasons by baldies. Because Vialli became manager — so he's doing a bit of creeping?

Even more intriguing is Sheridan of Barnsley, with his ancient 1930s sweptback middle-parting. He must get the piss taken out of him in the dressing room, yet he has persevered. Good lad.

Shirt sponsors: We know the famous ones sported by the famous clubs, but some are names I've never heard of, I'm always yelling at the commentator to tell me. Aberdeen shirts say "Living Design". What the hell does that mean? Atlético Madrid shirts say "Marbella". Is that a place or a cheese? Most interesting of all are Barcelona. They have no sponsor's name on their shirts. That is a real statement — of club pride and power, willing and able to turn away free money. I wonder if that makes them unique among the world's top clubs.

Ground advertisements: I am often on the edge of my seat trying to spot them whenever a game is boring, sorry, not awfully exciting. When I see the ad for Jiffy Condoms at West Ham I think, what on earth would the founding fathers of 1900 think if they came back today? Then I think of the Spurs and Arsenal directors who until the 1970s allowed no ads around the ground, considering them vulgar.

The ads for Vin de Bordeaux and for *The Times*, which you now see everywhere, indicate how fans have changed in socio-economic terms in the past ten years. Then I think, hold on. Fans may have changed in their social habits, but in the case of *The Times*, it's the newspaper that has changed, going downmarket.

Moving adverts: The ones that change as you watch them. Very exciting in a dull match, but bloody distracting if the game is good. How are they done? Is it timed automatically or does someone operate them when play is on that side of the pitch?

Players' bonding rituals: I have a list of these new habits, which I intend to send to Desmond Morris. Celtic get into a huddle before every match, arms linked, heads down, cuddling together. Big Jessies, they would have been called at one time. I watched the African Nations Cup and was delighted to see the Egyptians actually kissing each other on the cheeks when they came on the pitch as subs or got taken off. Very touching.

Faces in the crowd: I look out for women, randomly sampling to see if one out of ten fans is now female, as I read somewhere. I think it's cobblers. More like one in 50.

Managers' mannerisms: I keep close tabs on Fergie's specs and his chewing gum, on those who always stand in the dugout, such as Dalglish, or start off sitting in the stand like George Graham, or those who make notes and those who don't, and then I think about what it might show about them.

You see, friends, all human life is there, at every football match. Plus a whole host of social, cultural, artistic, economic and commercial signs and symbols. A healthy boy or girl can never be bored. So

Ruud, don't turn over. Just open your eyes wider, and your mind. Thank you.

WE FANS HAVE TO GET IN TRAINING NOW IF WE'RE TO SURVIVE THE WORLD CUP

10 APRIL 1998

IT'S BEEN A LONG, HARD SEASON. AT THIS STAGE IT'S NOT surprising that tiredness sets in, wear and tear affects body and spirit. It's easy to understand why freshness, sharpness and concentration start to fade. There are so many matches, one after the other. So you have to make allowances when standards slip, or even worse, out of the blue, there is a sudden desire to fall fast asleep. To be expected, really.

What, football players failing asleep, when they're being paid all that money? Course not, stupid. I'm talking about fans. And about time, too. No one seems to worry about us getting jaded and knackered, suffering from too many matches, hoping we might be substituted and given a short rest. No chance. We have to keep at it, till the last whistle of recorded time, or extra play, even penalties. Take today, for example. A real beezer of football watching. Eight hours before the mast, or at least before the remote control.

First, I watched *Match of the Day*, recorded last night. I knew that Sunday was going to be a mega day, so I went to bed early, as managers always suggest, wanting to be fresh. Then I did a quick 20 lengths at Kentish Town pool to get myself ready.

I don't think I can remember such a day. Three live games on television, all of them staggered, at 12, three and five o'clock, two on Sky and one on ITV. Presumably so that millions of idiots, sorry fans like me, could catch all three.

It began with Arsenal *v* Wolves. Premier against First Division, names-on-backs *v* no-names-on-backs. Why is it only in the Premiership they have names on their backs? We know them all, the cut of their jib, their side profiles, their haircuts, even when they go down in a heap. After all, we've watched them for 10,000 hours already this season.

There was great excitement in the crowd. I thought Bob Wilson summed it up very well. "Fantastic support here from the supporters."

Yes, nicely put Bob. Very succinct. Who would have guessed supporters were there to, well, support?

I noticed that Adams and Overmars hadn't shaved. Not surprising, as it was such an early start. They did well to turn up in time, and in the right strips, considering they'd probably just got home after their Saturday night out. Big Ron, my favourite Big of all the Bigs in football, was helping to commentate. "Am I imagining it, or are there four Vieiras out there?"

Perhaps he'd been out late as well.

When Arsenal went ahead, I didn't really want Wolves to draw level, otherwise there might be extra-time. First time I've ever thought that. I always look forward to extra time, and penalties if possible, as it means extra value for your television licence or your Sky payments. It's like living to 100 and hammering the pension fund. It creates a warm glow, knowing you have won and the system has lost You've had something for nothing. And then you die, happy.

Next came Sheffield United *v* Newcastle. "Winning would mean immortality," Sheffield's acting manager, Steve Thompson, said. A most interesting thought. If that really did happen, he'd hammer his pension fund for ever.

In the studio Nigel Spackman, who used to be the Sheffield manager, was asked for his prediction. "I'm not sitting on the fence — I think it will be a draw."

That's the sort of homespun, *faux-naïf* philosophy that gets you a fellowship at All Souls. Also in the studio was John Beresford, used to be full-back at Newcastle, a tough, no-nonsense, hardworking bloke. Today he was dressed like a pimp in a touring version of *Guys and Dolls*, wearing an electric blue suit with matching shirt and tie. They have no thought for the poor viewers, these footballers hoping for a media career. Don't they realise what it does to our eyes when they dress as if they're inspecting a tart's boudoir?

Several times the camera zoomed in on an elderly Newcastle supporter who looked as if he'd been watching football continuously for eight million hours. But I did eventually get the point. It was an artistic reference. What's the name of that Lowry painting of the football match?

There was then a close-up of two Newcastle players, Albert and Speed. No, not the old time music hall act, do concentrate, but two of their modern stars. Each was looking incredibly brown. They'd either been under the sun lamp or in the West Indies for the weekend. I screamed at both of them. Oh yeah, don't worry about us, stuck here in front of the telly, never missing a match. OK for some. Poncing off to top up your bleeding tan.

"There's a lot of tired people out there," Andy Gray said. Very true, though I think he was referring to the players.

Finally came the Scottish Cup semi-final between Rangers and Celtic. Like the first two, the pace was frantic, the commitment total. After 15 minutes I felt as exhausted as Goram looked. Is he really an old-aged pensioner? And does he get those elastic stockings for free on the NHS?

I'd always thought Walter Smith, the Rangers manager, was awful dapper in his suit. I'd decided he was the only three-piece-suited manager in the UK, if not the universe. But today I realised I was wrong. It's a cardie. Yes, a blue woollen cardigan, knitted by his mum, perhaps. How touching.

I noticed that Wim Jansen, Celtic's manager, was giving directions by whistling with his fingers in his mouth. Could he be the only manager in the world who does that? Or was he whistling for his dog? Or his lost youth? Or was I falling asleep? No, no, I did manage to keep awake, right to the end. In fact I enjoyed all three matches. They were played at such speed, without one nasty or vicious foul. Hurrah for British football. And British television.

Now I really must get some sleep, as I am in training. What for, you ask? Oh, come on. Today was just a trial run. We fans have got to be on top form for the big stuff to come. For 10 June to 11 July. If I can't keep awake during eight hours of football, what chance do I have of surviving four solid weeks of the World Cup?

FOOTBALL MIGHT NOT BE BETTER THAN SEX, BUT AT LEAST IT LASTS A LOT LONGER

17 APRIL 1998

BETTER THAN SEX? IS FOOTBALL BETTER THAN SEX? IT ALL depends, squire, on what you mean by sex, what you mean by football — are we talking playing or watching? — and what you mean by better. That was my initial response when an old friend happened to bring the Subject up.

I do have old friends, which always surprises my children. They think blokes don't care, don't keep in touch, aren't interested in bonding. (Unless they're talking about the other sort of Bonds. Remember John Bond? Used to be manager of Norwich, with the bouffant hair, wonder what happened to him, and his son Kevin Bond, played for Man City, didn't he, then he went off to America.)

Their dear mama, even at her age, can be on the phone for hours to her female friends, bonding and empathising away till her ears are red, I am fuming and the bills are enormous.

"Whatjawant?" is usually my reaction if someone rings me. I reckon I can deal with most calls from most so-called friends in two minutes. No wonder you don't have real friends, they say, the way you treat the ones you do have. But I can think of three friends, straight off, whom I meet regularly. Once a year, anyway. OK, sometimes the gap is two, even three years. But I've known each of them for 30 years.

And it was one of them I was having lunch with when he started talking about sex and football. I said that footballers always maintain that scoring a goal is orgasmic, even the ones who can't spell it. It is the ultimate thrill. So nothing new in that observation, squire. (His name isn't squire, though I did once have a friend called Squire Barraclough. Wonder what happened to him? And does he know what John Bond is doing?)

My friend explained he was talking about watching football, not playing it. These days he finds himself watching five nights a week. That did surprise me. When I first knew him 30 years ago he had absolutely no interest in football. I remember trying to get him to go to one of the 1966 World Cup matches with me, in Sunderland, I think, Russia versus Hungary, I think, and he said No Way. Course he didn't, not in 1966. "Get stuffed." That's what he said. He did go to some potty public school, then Oxford.

"Ah, but in 1966 I was sleeping with my wife five nights a week," he replied. "That's why I didn't want to go."

"And the rest," I said,

He thought hard, then soft, his lips slowly opening, a thin smile creeping among the wrinkles at the remembrance of times past. That particular wife is long gone, but he's had a second wife for 25 years, and they're awfully happy. And yet, and yet, when it comes to options for evening entertainment, he finds himself preferring the footer, if footer there is on.

If real football is indeed sexual, and orgasms, or similar, really do happen when playing, then is watching football sexual sublimation? Are we, friends, subconsciously taking part in a sexual act while watching, let's say, Man Utd *v* Liverpool on a Sunday afternoon, or even Carlisle United against Burnley on a Friday evening? We ordered a second bottle while we pondered.

There must be PhD students already at work on such connections. Alas, I missed a seminal event on 23 March, as advertised in the *New Statesman* on 13 March (page 42, look it up if you don't believe me). This was a public discussion in London E2, tickets £1.99, entitled "The Ingerland factor: football, new lads and lasses". The blurb said it was about the "World Cup, psychoanalysis and gender relations". Oh help.

I might, however, be able to attend a forthcoming debate called 'Freud meets Football' which I see from the *Ham and High* newspaper is to be held at the Freud Museum in Hampstead on 21 May.

If you make it, do have a look at Freud's couch. I visited the house last year, expecting it to be black leather and brutal, stark and austere; the couch, I mean, not the house. It's covered with gaily coloured cushions, Persian rugs and stuff. More like a Turkish brothel than a medical consulting room.

We all know about Freud's obsession with sex, so Freudians are bound to see sexual undertones in football, but will they prove that football fans find it better than sex?

Look, I said. You're 63, much older than me, but still able to totter around, marvellous really, in fact let's totter on to our third bottle. What I would agree with is that while football is not necessarily better than sex, it's longer than sex.

He took a while to take that in; well, he is 63. I didn't mean the sexual act lasts longer than a football match, for clearly it doesn't. Oh come on. Stop boasting. A match lasts 90 minutes. Forget extra time and penalties or we'll never get through this bottle. Which normal bloke can manage nine minutes, never mind 90? And that's including foreplay.

What I'm saying is that an interest in football is there for life. It never goes stale. My father-in-law recently died aged 96. Right to the end, when he had no interest in the world at large, I would ring him on Saturday evening after *Sports Report* to discuss Carlisle United's result, and he would come to life. Wainwright, the great walker, was a great football fan. He was a founder member of the Blackburn Rovers supporters' club in 1939 and his passion continued till he died in 1991, aged 84.

When I get depressed, which doesn't happen often, well never really, I think of all the matches I've got to come. Then I think I shouldn't be watching so many matches now, when I'm hale and hearty. I should be saving them up for the winters ahead. Then I have a final think and realise, hey, there will be even more matches to come, the way things are going with all this bloody pay-per-view stuff and this digital nonsense. The future is bright. The future is football.

CAN YOU NAME THE ONE PREMIERSHIP CLUB WITHOUT A SHIRT SPONSOR?

24 APRIL 1998

THE LAST STRAW WAS JENNI MURRAY. I WAS LYING IN BED, half dozing off, waiting for the *World Tonight* on Radio 4, hoping it was going to be Isabel Hilton, who has such a lovely voice, when on comes Jenni Murray, who has quite a lovely voice, but lovely in a traditional BBC southern counties way. She had popped up to do a trail for the next day's *Woman's Hour*.

Nothing unusual about that — except that, bloody hell, it was being done to the background of football chanting, using lots of football clichés and phrases. Can't remember precisely what *Woman's Hour* items she was on about, but they had bugger all to do with football. Gawd save us, woman, I shouted. Give us a bleeding break. I can't take it any more.

That day I'd picked up the evening paper and there was an advert for a pop concert given by Madness. The illustration was not a photo of Madness, as one might expect, or even some musical symbol. It showed Stuart Pearce in his England shirt, screaming his head off. How the hell did they drag him in? What's he got to do with a pop group? Then I thought, oh aye. His nickname is Psycho. The group is called Madness. Hah bloody hah.

Then I noticed a British Telecom advert for something called BT Internet. The illustration for this is a goalkeeper making a save, his face not visible, so they don't have to pay him. But what was the connection between a goalkeeper and BT? Oh no. "Internet" equals "into net". Joke, huh?

It will all get very much worse between now and the World Cup. Football is fashionable. Football is everywhere. Football sells. Those three examples were unofficial, in the sense that they connected themselves with football without huge fat fees being exchanged, though perhaps they'll send Psycho free tickets for the Madness concert.

Just think what is yet to come from the companies that have paid massive amounts to be officially connected in some way with the FA, or our leading clubs, or our leading players. Between now and July they'll be milking their investment till we all end up screaming for mercy.

I expect there'll be acres of jaw-aching stuff from Green Flag — 'Exclusive Sponsor of the England Football Team'. And from Carlsberg — 'Official Supporter, England Team'. And from Snickers — 'Official Snack Food of World Cup '98'. From William Hill — 'Official Bookmakers at Wembley Stadium'. From Citizen Watches — 'Official Timer of the FA Cup'. And not forgetting Walkers Crisps — 'Official Partners' of the FA.

These are just some of the firms that took page ads in the programme for the recent England–Chile game at Wembley. Gawd knows what it all means, what deals those weasel words represent. There must be some difference between a partner, a supporter and a sponsor, but I bet they all paid many millions. As I'm sure Budweiser, McDonald's, Wilkinson Sword and all the others did as well.

I quite like some of the football-related commercials, such as the Nike one featuring Ronaldo playing footer in the airport and that fat bloke and the football chanting in the Coca-Cola ad, but I hate the One-to-One ads. Ugh.

Then there's all the advertising during the games themselves. Even the trainer runs on the pitch with logos on the side of his bag and you get close-ups of the injured player recovering on Lucozade. I wonder what they pay to have their bottles shoved sideways down the gobs of sweaty footballers? It can't be an accident. I feel sorry for milk. Milk used to be big in football. What did they do wrong? What price would they not pay? Lucozade used to be a boring drink for elderly invalids; now you get all these hunks swigging it. Must be worth it, whatever it costs.

I'm surprised referees haven't started selling space on their shirts. They don't get paid much. The players are absolutely covered, and they get well paid. Correction. Not every team has a shirt sponsor. Can you name one Premiership team without a shirt sponsor? You've got two seconds.

A few weeks ago I mentioned in passing that Barcelona were the only world-class club without a shirt sponsor. Next day I got a letter from Jim Fitzpatrick, MP for Poplar and Canning Town. Yes, I was surprised. Alastair Campbell I expect. Make a nasty comment about Burnley, and he comes round and duffs you up. Mr Fitzpatrick pointed out that West Ham play in virgin shirts. No, not Virgin, that used to be Crystal Palace. Virgin meaning their shirts are naked and unadorned.

My first reaction was, huh, hasn't he got better things to do than writing to me on piddling points when he could be putting his piddling points in the House of Commons? Then I thought, he's wrong. Last I looked, West Ham had Dagenham Motors on their front. But that was a year ago. I looked again — and he's right. So I wrote a grovelling letter, saying how clever of him to notice, how good of him to write, and other insincere cobblers.

All the same, I could hardly believe it. Barcelona don't have a shirt sponsor as they see their shirt as a symbol of their Catalan heritage and don't want it adulterated. They're also pretty well off. But West Ham, they need all the pennies they can get. Must be some explanation. So I wrote to Peter Storrie, West Ham's chief executive. He's just replied, saying that being sponsorless is purely temporary. "We have had a contract signed for some while but it has not yet been completed due to technical problems on their side."

Who is their new sponsor? He doesn't reveal. Perhaps the problems are to do with putting something unusual on the shirt front, such as a female face, say, and promoting a product aimed at women. That's why I suspect their new shirt sponsor could be Jenni Murray and *Woman's Hour*. Look out in the next two weeks in case her phizog is covering the hairy chest of John Hartson and the rest of the lads. I won't actually be here to see it. I'm off to see my daughter in Botswana. Cheers.

YOU CAN SEE WHO'S GOING TO
WIN WORLD CUP 1998 JUST BY
LOOKING AT THE PHOTOS

5 JUNE 1998

I WAS SITTING WITH A NICE PILE OF CUT-OUT-AND-KEEP World Cup guides, free supplements, special surveys, World Cup history in 152 parts, CD-Rom of the World Cup stadiums, your baby's guide to the World Cup superstars, World Cup full-colour charts for the blind, special World Cup condoms in five different tastes, your petrol station guide to World Cup night driving, *People's Friend* knit-your-own World Cup tea cosy, *Marie Claire* blow-up-and-suck-your-own inflatable David Beckham, souvenir World Cup alphabet for the hard of understanding, unique World Cup abacus for the hard of counting, eat Snickers and be World Cup sick for free, drink Coke and feel World Cup drunk, eat one more World Cup analysis and overdose.

Oh yes, I have them all. In fact I can hardly get into my office for them. I will keep and treasure them for ever, especially those which feature Paul Gascoigne as one of the stars to watch in World Cup '98. They'll be collector's items like a misprinted penny black or a Jeffrey Archer novel not signed by Jeffrey Archer.

My wife came into my room just as I was re-reading my favourite one: *The Fifa World Cup Book*, published by Carlton, price £6.99. Lovely glossy paper, yummy colour pix. On page 44 it acclaims Gazza as one of England's five World Cup '98 'star performers'. (The others being Seaman, Ince, Shearer, Beckham and Southgate. Southgate? Yup. That's what it says. It is an 'officially licensed World Cup product'. Do they know something no one else knows?)

She picked it up and straight away, without any prompting, flicked through the colour photies of each World Cup squad and gave me a run-down of the *real* chances of the 32 teams, based purely on their visual appearances.

As you know, nature has ordained that when any team is being photographed they line up in their kit in two rows, one row crouching, next row standing. Optional extras for the back row include arms crossed, arms behind back, arms hanging loose like a gorilla, or arms around each other, as if cuddling. For the front row, you can either crouch, as if on a potty, rest on one knee, or half crouch, as if farting.

Either way, it provides an excellent close-up inspection of every individual face, every posture; hence she was able to give me her totally inconsidered opinion on who's going to win the World Cup just by looking at the photos

"Iran? Dear God, that's not Iran is it? They don't look manic enough to be Iran. Ooh, look at those nasty strips. Who are they anyway? Oh yeah, Saudi Arabia. Why has someone poured paint all over them? Those Danes look nice, except for the one's who look horrible. Paraguay don't look like Paraguay, I mean they don't look South American, do they? No, seriously [flicking back through book], all the other South American teams look South American. Hunt, why does the Croatian team look so working class? Tell me, I want to know.

"Are those the Scots? They look surprisingly couth, for Scots. Is that the USA team? What a rabble. They look like tourists. What have the Colombians done to their hair? Cameroon must have a chance. Very tasteful shirts. Those South Africans look happy, especially number 6. Something funny about the French. Not at all chic. Hey, I didn't know Austria was in the World Cup. You've never mentioned them. No chance. Just look at them.

"I'm not impressed by England. They look so untidy, except for Ince. He's the only one who looks together. There's only one lot I fancy — Italy. No seriously, just look at them. Yes, one or two are a bit desperate, but you have to admit they're the most attractive looking team, very handsome, I think they'll do best …"

So that's her politically incorrect and footballingly wonky

survey. It was interesting how she picked on Iran, expecting them to look manic, but then we are all pretty prejudiced when it comes to Iran, understanding little about what's been going on, either in their football or in their politics. It so happened that I found myself talking to Afshin Mobasser, a producer with the BBC's Persian World Service, for a Radio 4 World Cup prog, *The Ultimate Goal* (tonight, Friday 5 June, at 11.30, hurry, hurry). It's about the cultural and social effects of the World Cup rather than the footie itself.

Naturally, we talked about those 5,000 young women who turned up in the national stadium in Tehran, to welcome back the lads, disobeying their religious and political leaders. Women in Iran are not allowed in mixed crowds, nor should they watch men playing any sport. There was even a move to make all footballers play in tracksuits, so that women watching on television would not see any bare knees. This was so ridiculed it never made it into law. Now the laws generally relating to women are being relaxed, all because of football.

I had never realised how passionate Iran has always been about football. It was only after the 1979 revolution that the new leaders tried to curb its importance, jealous of its influence. It hasn't quite worked, judging by those 120,000 crowds in Tehran, the biggest for any World Cup qualifying game.

I had also not realised that the Iranians are not anti-western. Just their government is, so Afshin said. Ordinary Iranians love football and love foreigners, even Americans. This was backed up by Guy Oliver, the producer of *Futbol Mundial* for Sky, who has recently been to Iran. He was scared stiff before he went, believing all the stuff we have been led to believe, but found he was welcomed everywhere when he said he was covering football.

The 21 June game between the USA and Iran will not be political dynamite. Just normal football passion. Are you listening, pet? So no more silly remarks about manic Iranians. But the rest of your comments will probably be proved spot-on. Italy to win.

THE FOOTIE'S FINE SO FAR, BUT THE REAL EXCITEMENT IS ALL IN THE HAIRSTYLES

THIS IS MY WORLD CUP ROUTINE, AS YOU'VE ASKED. GET UP, get working, work really hard, work like buggery, then take my seat at 1.30 and watch really hard, watch like buggery for the next ten hours. Yes, it's hard, but then I have been in training.

And I deserve it, look what I've done in the morning, doubling normal production. Do wage-slaves in their offices do that? I think not. They spend the mornings scheming to skive off in the afternoon.

We've been in Lakeland for five weeks, and the weather has been mainly rotten, which is a relief. I've missed nothing, huddled in front of the telly. It's in a little room at the back of the house, book-lined, with my collection of Lakeland books. I have this big comfy chair, with wide wooden arms, perfect for a line-up of drinks, goodies, fruit, enough to get me through three games. Beside me is a small table made of bamboo, with my red clipboard, WC charts and notes I have made on every game so far. I give marks out of ten for excitement, deportment, hairstyles.

Damn, this cheapo Amstrad doesn't do drawings, but you can imagine it, you're clever. No other furniture, except a stool for my tootsies. A small WC leads off the room. Lavatory, not World Cup, do concentrate. It also has a shower. If overcome by utter exhaustion, or endless extra-time when we get to the second round, I could just live in here till 12 July and never go to bed.

From time to time, my dear wife pops in, smiling, bringing another cappuccino and some delicious gingerbread made by our neighbour, widow of the vicar of Loweswater. She is world class at gingerbread, would get in anyone's team. All winter she stashed it away in her freezer, knowing I'd need massive supplies.

Smiling? Did you say smiling? Why aye, man. My wife is happy that I am happy. Ignore those silly articles in the popular press about wives/partners being pissed off. My random sample of one partner/ wife in one household proves conclusively the opposite.

She reads every report, every interview, follows every game, which is jolly handy because when I do manage to snatch half an hour between games, and join her for a walk down to the lake or round the fields, we can discuss the football.

No, she never actually watches any matches. She sits in the conservatory, reading, trying to match my rate of three matches in ten hours with three novels in ten hours. Who has the better fun, huh? Next day, she can't remember the title or author and I can't remember the score. But ah ha, I have my notes.

As I sit in my little room, I do give occasional shouts, being unable to control myself. "QUICK SCOTLAND'S GOT A PENALTY!" Or "HURRY UP THIS NIGERIAN BLOKE'S GOT GREEN HAIR!" She rushes in, gets her specs on, but usually too late. The ball is in the net; or he's changed his hairstyle.

"Tell me, why is it you are obsessed by hair?" she asks sweetly, still smiling. "Because you are losing yours."

Shut the door behind you, woman.

"And I was just wondering," she continues, "if football is an addiction, will the World Cup act as addiction therapy, so that afterwards, no one will watch football ever again? Hmm. What do you think, Hunt?"

The football, well it's been terrific, so far. Only two boring matches, Paraguay – Bulgaria and Saudi Arabia – Denmark. All the rest have been fascinating, positive and attacking, played in excellent spirits. There has been no thuggery, no nastiness, not even pettiness. Players have got back at free kicks and hardly bothered to protest at throw-ins. It's almost as if they like each other, a World Cup camaraderie, not bearing grudges against other countries the way they do against each other at home. Once we get to the knock-out stages, this could all change. They'll revert to cheating and kicking lumps out of each other.

French television coverage has been poor. Not enough different angles. And I could do with more close-ups of the crowds enjoying themselves. But no more Mexican waves, thank you.

The most tiring, toughest, most stressful games to watch so far have involved Scotland or England. Whether they play well or not is almost irrelevant. Sitting here, all tense in my little room, I try to think of all the other billions around the globe in their little spaces, with their little emergency supplies of gingerbread, being unable to get any pleasure either. Watching your own team is too nerve wrecking, too worrying, like watching your own children.

Watching other teams you can see things clearly, dispassionately, such as: have you noticed how players try to copy the style of the dominant or star player? Not just football style. I mean things like boots. If the star has white boots, or blue or red or yellow, then others will copy. Or hair. Look at Brazil. Ronaldo has a skinhead, so the rest are now following. Hadji of Morocco is growing a pony tail, so three others in the team are doing the same. That Japanese, the one who looks like Paul Scholes crossed with Gazza, the one with the red hair, he's got two others copying him, but so far they've only got round to using bottles of henna.

Have you noticed that, pet? Yes, yes. I promised not to mention hair again, but it's really interesting, players spend so much time on their hair, why do you think Beckham is now a blond, and the fans as well, there's this Jap fan I spotted in the crowd, even he's been at his hair. I wonder if that barber in Cockermouth can fit me in between matches.

FOOTBALL IS A SUBSTITUTE FOR WAR —
SAME SPIES, DIRTY TRICKS
AND DISINFORMATION

3 JULY 1998

SO MANY NEW PEOPLE HAVE COME IN TO FOOTBALL THANKS to the World Cup, folks who have never seen a match before, who sit down and say, heh, it's quite interesting really, now, what colour is England? Ten minutes later they are experts.

Ten minutes after that they come out with what they think is an original observation, an observation which has been observed since 1872 when the world's first ever international match took place between England and Scotland. "Heh, it'sjust like war."

This week, especially, they have been observing it, with England against Argentina. We've also had other deadly enemies fighting it out with balls not bullets, such as the USA and Iran.

But how true is it? Is Football a Substitute for War? A Mere Shadow? Vaguely similar? Or is there bugger all connection?

It so happens I was there, during the last time we had a world war. I've also followed every World Cup since 1950, when England first entered. Yes, bit of an expert, go on, ask me anything.

I saw front-line service in the 1940's from my infant and primary schools in Carlisle and Dumfries, and from what I remember it was jolly good fun. You got to wear gas masks. Play in air raid shelters. Now and again Yankee soldiers in jeeps threw chewing gum at you as they drove through. You had to give them a "V" sign, which I found awful hard, but my mummy arranged my fingers for me.

There were some hardships. *The Dandy* and *Beano* were both titchy, only four pages each, what a swizz, and I didn't see my first banana till I was ten when I said what's this mum, a phallic symbol? Only joking. I was 11 before I knew that.

The hardships I have endured during this present World Cup have been far, far worse. After that stuffing by Romania I came out in a rash. Honestly. All up my legs. I think it's tension, doctor, and fury at England's crap performance.

But enough about me. Let's look at the global picture. Eleven similarities between war and the World Cup.

1 **Size.** The WC wins hands down. In the last war it was just us against the Nazzies; no, someone else came in later, yes those Yanks, wondered what they were doing, and oh yeh, the Japs, I can remember cartoons about Japs. And the Eyties. OK, let's say ten countries took part. Nothing really, compared with 172 countries for this year's World Cup.

2 **Numbers.** Front-line troops might be small, but the back-up WC armies are enormous. Over 37 billion have been watching this year's World Cup, from every country. By comparison, WW2 was a little local difficulty.

3 **Cost.** Again the WC wins. Sponsorship alone cost £2 billion — most of that on Ronaldo. The bill is not yet in for the Romanian team dying their hair blond, but it won't be cheap.

4 **Casualties.** The war wins here. But don't forget, there could be bloodshed when the lads who've been stuffed get home. Remember what happened last time in Colombia. And there's a few French cops with sore heads and shopkeepers with broken windows.

5 **Uniform.** Mandatory for both war and footer. Not just in the trenches but all camp followers must sport appropriate colours, even Prince Harry. Did you see his scarf? Dinky, wasn't it, though he only put it on when we woz winning. Note also the return of face paint — a throwback to tribal war.

6 **Patriotism.** The WC and WW2 authorities are very big on this, hence the national anthems, badge clutching, shirt kissing. You could argue that WC football is purer than war. No mercenaries are allowed. OK, that Lopez bloke from Brazil changed his nationality to Japanese to get in the team, and the Jamaicans did much the same. Then so did Lord Haw Haw.

7 **Espionage.** Very much so, as Glenn always says. In war and footer, every army employs spies, dirty tricks, disinformation. Glenn has been particularly good at this, as has been mentioned in most dispatches. Truth is, naturally, the first casualty of both war and football. Do you really believe he was always going to play Beckham and Owen? Pull the other. It is also not well known that Brian Moore is a double agent. No real patriot could be so over the top and blindly patriotic.

8 **Propaganda.** In the war, the national press kept our spirits up, telling us a load of old lies about how well our lads were doing, or were about to do, getting us all excited and elated. This role in football is now taken by the BBC and ITV.

9 **God.** One of the confusing things about both war and football. He plays for both sides. Whether Muslim, Catholic, Protestant, the lads know he's on their side, hence all the crossing. Not the ball. Themselves. And for sure, God does like a winner. He is willing to lend a helping hand when necessary. Ask Maradona.

10 **Memoirs.** The WC can't possibly compete with WW2. I remember as late as the 1960s when I joined *The Sunday Times* spitting blood when yet another boring episode of Monty's memoirs were being run, instead of them using my brilliant stuff. Motty's memoirs will certainly not run as long.

11 **Titles.** After it's all over, every winning general gets a gong. In war they always do. Earldoms and peerages were showered everywhere, once we'd won. But what about football? Alf Ramsey did get a knighthood, but had to wait a year. Bobby Charlton didn't get his till 28 years later. Geoff Hurst has had to wait until this year for his title — 32 years after the war, sorry the World Cup, was won. Bleedin' shame. Don't expect Nobby Styles to turn into Sir Norbert until 2016. As for Glenn Hoddle, after England's defiant showing against Argentina, his dukedom will have to wait a while yet. Perhaps an OBE, for bringing to an end the nation's stress and anxiety levels. Seven out of the eight remaining nations have got the worst of theirs to come.

1998–99 SEASON

George Graham, Hoddle, Henry,
Beckham and C.U.F.C.

NEW THIS SEASON: A PLAYER WITH A TASH; TWO PLATINUM BLONDES; ADS FOR SOLICITORS

4 SEPTEMBER 1998

FOUR WEEKS OF THE SEASON GONE SO FAR, AND WHAT HAVE we learnt about life and death and the meaning of Dalglish? That football is like politics, John Major took over from Thatcher because they wanted an opposite. An end to arrogance, bossy boots, ranting and ravings and radical change, so they brought in nice, unthreatening, John, who would comfort not confront, take soundings rather than sounding off. Daglish got the boot at Newcastle because he was seen as negative, charmless, chippy. Gullit has been brought in because he is seen as positive, charming, sexy. So it goes. And when Gullit gets the bullet, they'll be desperately seeking some dour mean bastard. Once again.

I hate the arrival of that word in football. You know the one I mean. No need to spell it out. They were even holding it up in the crowd for Ruud's first match, welcoming the arrival of sexy football.

What is going on? It's supposed to be a man's game, innit? Tough, nasty, none of that emotional, slippery, slithery, sticky nonsense. Coaches traditionally tried to stamp out such elements, balling out those deemed fairies, nancies, girl's blouses, who ponced about, played like tarts. Those are the words you heard on all training grounds. Football was meant to be effective, not attractive. I blame those Italians, bringing in short shorts, exposing thighs. Should never have been allowed.

As for fans, we certainly don't want sexy football either. If we were interested in that sort of thing, we would stay at home on Saturday afternoons and watch Anthea Turner videos, the one with the snake.

What's also new about this season is walking. Prime walker is Gazza. It's a good new trick. Needs little energy, being hugely overweight hardly matters, and should prolong his career by, oh, days if not weeks.

What's old this season so far is Shearer. We all gave him the benefit of the doubt last year, because of his injuries, but I sense his head hanging, his spirit sagging, his brows furrowing, his limbs getting heavier. He should have moved to Europe two seasons ago, which would have jerked some new life into him. He's lucky with Ruud coming to inject some new energy into his life without him having to get off his bum and go somewhere, but this could be his last season at the top of his career. The future could be downhill, or walkabouts with Gazza at 'Boro.

Owen was predicted to mark time or fade or become petty this season, but so far his curve is upwards and onwards, amazing really. If Shearer and Owen both play for England against Sweden this weekend, who would you put money on to score? I fear, however, for two of this season's big signings—Dwight Yorke and Kevin Davies. They look burdened, frightened rather than stimulated by their good fortune.

The big money, as ever, seems to get spent on strikers. Stam at Manchester United is an exception, and could well be a waste of money, but generally, when a manager wants to improve his team, he lashes out on a new striker, thinking this will be seen as exciting, not to say sexy. This is very often a mistake. If only managers had experience of life, not just football, they would realise that the strength of any team, any unit, is the strength of the weakest link. So if you have money to spend, and want to improve, you should always be sifting out and replacing the weakest element, not trying to duplicate the stronger bits. This is what is continually happening at Chelsea.

On the hair front, lots of excitements this season, some of them a fall-out from the World Cup. Oh, come on. You must remember it. Back in the summer, three matches a day on the telly, you can't have forgotten it already. No whole team has copied the Romanians and gone all bleached, but some individuals are trying very hard. Tony Adams of Arsenal has had a light blond rinse but Lee Sharpe of Leeds and Michael Gray of Sunderland have gone the whole bottle and are now platinum blondes. Cadamarteri of Everton has taken off his locks, which makes him very hard to recognise, and Chris Armstrong of Spurs is no longer shaven headed, but rather tufty on top. Even more surprising, he appears to have a tash. Now that really is *new* this season. All right, then. Tell me another Premier player with a tash. In the 1970s, you couldn't get moving for them, cluttering up every penalty area.

West Ham have got Dr Martens on their shirts, so a warm welcome to him, but the most interesting thing I've spotted so far on the advertising fronts was at Bradford. Can't remember what match I was watching, or why, as Sky has a match almost every day of the week, but on the advertising hoardings around the ground I noticed not one but two firms of solicitors boasting their wares. Lager adverts at football grounds one can understand, or for *The Times*, as it's now a tabloid, or even condom ads, as football is now so sexy, but solicitors? Probably aimed at crooks in the crowd, the sort you get in directors' boxes.

'Well documented.' That's a popular phrase among football

commentators this season, and one to watch. You say it after you have said something banal and obvious which doesn't need saying but, by saying it, you distance yourself from the banality you have just said. Such as: "Staunton has a good left foot, as has been well documented." Several pundits use it, though not Alan Brazil. He is still too busy saying, "Goodness me".

I thought those stupid bits of Elastoplast on the hooter were definitely last season's fashion and would be gone for ever when Robbie Fowler got injured, but then I counted three in last week's Sunderland team. It seems to have spread like a rash in the dressing room, especially among the really ugly. I know, I'll put a bit of plaster on me nose and no one will see how ugly I am and when Ruud gets round to chucking everyone out at Newcastle, I might get into his sexy new team.

HERE'S THE REAL STORY: CHRISTIAN GROSS IS BEHIND MURDOCH'S MAN U BID

I CAN REVEAL THAT THE PERSON BEHIND THE MANCHESTER United takeover bid is — England manager Glenn Hoddle. He was desperate for a football shock-horror story, the bigger, the better, to take attention away from him, at this moment in time, very much so. Selling his book to *The Sun*, and all the associated nonsense, then getting stuffed by the Swedes, were two cock-ups about to bring him down. So he rang Rupert, suggested this Man Utd takeover story, which suited Rupert as he is in secret talks, I can reveal, to take over Carlisle United.

Don't scoff. I have it on the best authority. My own. Glenn is still in his job. Every paper is filled with Man U. We have all forgotten about Sweden. Ergo, it must be true. Or as true as anything ever is in football.

What you have to remember about football, friends, is that only those 90 minutes on the pitch are real. All the rest is fiction.

Take Glenn himself, master of the art of fibs and fantasies. He regularly lies about injuries, to fool the opposition, so he maintains, but really to hide his own indecision. Faith healing is, of course, pure fantasy. Saying he had to write his book to put the record straight, that's another fantasy. Saying he had no control over *The Sun* buying his book or how they serialised it, well, that's more fantasy. I'd call it bollocks.

Two years ago, I did a book about Lottery winners which by chance appealed at the time to several newspapers. We got a handsome bid from the *Sunday Times* and an even handsomer bid from the *Daily Mail*. We didn't let anyone else see the manuscript, or make a bid, as we feared spoilers — that failed bidders would cobble up their own spoiling version and publish earlier. We chose *The Sunday Times* bid in the end, though smaller, in the belief that it would help the book more, that *ST* readers were book buyers. They guaranteed a good display and agreed I could read all the edited copy and the headlines. These conditions were easy to impose. Glenn could easily have done the same. He was in the driving seat. He could have dictated exactly how his book was presented — and still made himself a packet. (With hindsight, I wish I'd gone for the bigger packet. The *Sunday Times* serial didn't help sales of the book at all. Alas.)

In Tony Adams's new book, some other liberties with the truth appear to have been taken, according to Niall Quinn, writing in last week's *Guardian*. In the book, Adams describes how he and Quinn went on a two-day drunken bender at Windsor races just 48 hours before Arsenal's big match at Liverpool at the end of the 1989 season, the game that won them the league. Not quite true, says Quinn. Their drunken trip to Windsor in fact took place 18 days before that vital match. "That was just not sexy enough for the publisher," so Quinn presumes. Or maybe Adams has forgotten the dates entirely.

Footballers say they hate the tabloids, rubbish their views and coverage, ridicule their scandals and supposed transfer talks, but are more than willing to take their money, then try to disown responsibility, when it suits them.

Chairmen will swear loyalty to managers, say their jobs are guaranteed, when we all know they are lying. Managers will say their star player is not for sale, is going nowhere, no chance. Footballers will say they were not offside when millions of us clearly saw they were. They will deny penalties when there was no doubt at all. "Our ball!" they always cry, from the moment they wake up in the morning, but I can excuse them that, poor things. They know not what they are saying. It's conditioning, innit?

Bryan Robson says that Paul Merson and Gazza are bosom pals, best of muckers, so all this talk about Merson wanting to get away from Gazza's bad influence is rubbish, anyway Gazza is not a bad influence, he is as pure as the driven slush, a model player and human being etc, as are all Boro's players.

The Premier League tells itself it is the best league in the world, which most of us like to believe, as it sounds nice, feels nice, but one moment's thought and we know it is self-delusion. Have we got Ronaldo playing here, or Denilson? Did Kluivert rush to join us, or Zidane? Yes, but we do have loads of famous Italian stars. Funny how not one of them got into last weekend's Italian team.

The football authorities say that they will not let Murdoch get away with this, whatever it is, and will have a full investigation, oh yes. Downing Street says that Murdoch will be treated like any other multi-millionaire global magnate, the sort whom craven Labour leaders scurry half-way across the world to keep in with. No favours will be given. Certainly not.

You have to laugh. After all, lies are funny, if you are merely a humble spectator at the football feasts, content to turn up and meekly pay your Danegeld to Sky, buy the shirts, mortgage your house for a season ticket.

That one about Glenn Hoddle being behind the Man Utd bid was very funny. Didn't you think so? But of course it was a lie. Come over here. Keep your voice down. I have it on even more excellent authority that the *real* person behind the Man U drama is—Christian Gross. Oh come on. Manager of Spurs, just half an hour ago. You can't have forgotten him, even though this has been a monster week for Football Stories. But of course you have forgotten him. And that was precisely Christian's object. He engineered all this so he could creep home to his snow cabin in Switzerland with no fuss, in quietness and tranquillity. Rest in peace.

YOU CAN'T WATCH FOOTBALL
WITH NOISY PEOPLE

18 SEPTEMBER 1998

LAST WEEK, I TOOK MY WIFE AND SISTER FOR A CITY
break, three days in an exciting, exotic location, no, not Paris or
Barcelona or Venice, but Glasgow. And it was brilliant, really exciting and fascinating. So was the hotel we picked, the Malmaison,
which I'd never heard of before but is now my second favourite
hotel on the planet, after Cobblers Cove in Barbados, for its individual style, food and staff.

I was a bit worried at first when its awfully artistic brochure
arrived, thin on facts but fulsome with fantasy fotos, telling me bugger all about what l really wanted to know. So I rang to ask, er, I was
just wondering, if by chance, I know it's a bit common, not to say
vulgar, but have you got Sky TV, anywhere in the hotel?

I'd realised just as I was about to make a booking that while I
was there it was going to be Chelsea–Arsenal. One has to get one's
priorities right. No problem, I was told. Each bedroom has it. Can't
get more artistic than that. After an awfully artistic meal in the
hotel, my wife and sister went off to the pictures to see *The Horse
Whisperer*, said to be a chick film, ie, said to appeal to soppy people,
such as women. I settled down in my room, like a man, nice glass of
wine handy, lying on my bed naked, except for my boxer shorts.
Didn't want to muck up the artistic bed clothes, did I?

I switched on five minutes before kick-off but couldn't find Sky
Sports 1. Must be my fault, not understanding this awfully artistic
TV set with its fancy menu and fancy instructions. All I could get
on the screen was "NO SIGNAL". What was going on? Had
Chelsea or Arsenal been taken over by Carlton or some other TV lot
and were refusing to appear on Sky, just to sicken Murdoch? Or
was it my Stupidity, unable to work the TV?

I rang reception. An awfully nice girl said she would come up in five minutes. She didn't appear, so I rang again. She said she was sorry, she was alone on reception, but would get some bloke to investigate, if she could find him. The match was by now well started. I could have missed two goals.

The bloke eventually rang with a complicated story about problems on the roof, workmen had been doing something, it wasn't my stupidity, a cable had somehow been disconnected. But he was sorry, it wouldn't be mended till tomorrow.

"Oh God," I shouted. "What the fuck am I going to do? I have organised my whole evening, my whole life, round this."

He suggested I go out into Sauchiehall Street, three blocks away, and find a pub showing the match. So I dashed out of the bedroom, then dashed back in again. Wandering half naked down Sauchiehall Street would probably get me arrested. I threw on my trousers, shirt and sandals and dashed out again. Then back, to get some money.

I ran like hell, panting hard, screaming and swearing. Yes, just a football match. Yes, there will be others. Yes, I have been less worked up for much more awful things going wrong in my life. Yes, as bad as a drug addict, half crazy for a fix, liable to do something really stupid. I know all that. Just shurrup. I have lost bloody half an hour of the match so far.

The first pub didn't do Sky. The second was so full I couldn't get in the door. At the third, which was called the State, an apt description for what I was in at that moment, I managed to squeeze in and even got a stool at the bar.

I don't know if you watch football in a pub. I never do, and hope never to again. The screen was huge, about 12 feet long, so that was good, suspended from the ceiling, which wasn't good, because in minutes I had a crick in my neck. But the picture quality was amazing. So much detail, every expression and movement absolutely clear, and terrific sound, every thump and collision magnified like thunder. Which it had to be, for the noise in the pub was horrendous. How can folks eat, drink, talk in such conditions, let alone watch football? At home I don't let people breathe in the same room.

In front of me were four young women in their twenties, thin and slight, knocking back pints and smoking for Scotland, screaming and shouting, laughing and yelling —*with their backs to the screen*! Around me I could see a few other groups, equally uninterested in the football. How could they bear to be in this hell-hole when they were not following the football? Most people were watching, or trying to, and there were loud jeers or cheers when news flashes came in from other matches, such as Man U being one down to Charlton. Followed by groans when they came back.

I can see there is a certain camaraderie in watching football in such groups. Everything is magnified, not just the sound and vision but the audience, with people standing up and shouting, getting very excited, but dear God, I don't think my ears, eyes, throat, mind and body have ever been so assaulted all at the same time, though where do I go, what do I do?

And it all turned out pointless. The most boring goalless draw I've seen for years. I'd have been better staying in listening to West Ham 3 Wimbledon 4 on the radio, which sounded really good. If I could have got the radio to work.

I was slumped on my bed, shattered and exhausted, when *les gels* got back. Good film then, my pet? "Even worse than the book," said my wife contemptuously. "Which I would have said was impossible. So how was it for you?"

Don't ask, I said.

"This room smells a bit funny," she sniffed. "Sort of smoke and beer. What on earth have you been doing?"

I said don't ask. I'm not going to think about it. Ever again.

A BUNION ON THE FOOT SPOILS
BLACKBURN ON THE BOX
25 SEPTEMBER 1998

THROUGHOUT THE WORLD CUP I WAITED FOR THE CALL. IN fear and trepidation. Not from Glenn, as he must know I can't play for England, despite my residential qualifications and despite having played for two English clubs, Wardington FC in the Banbury District League, oh they were good, and Dartmouth Park United in the Hampstead Heath Sunday Morning Old Blokes' League, they were not quite so good. I'd have to turn out for Scotland, if that sort of call ever came, as I was born in Scotland of Scottish parents and consider myself Scottish, go on, ask me anything about Oor Wullie.

The call I was dreading was from the West Cumberland Hospital to come in and have my operation. I went on the NHS waiting list last September and they said the wait would be about a year. If I'd gone private, I could have had it in three weeks, possibly three minutes, thank you, that will be £1,500, sorry to have kept you waiting three minutes.

When our dear Labour Party got in, they promised to bring NHS waiting lists down, which of course I totally believed. Then it struck me that if waiting lists did come down from 12 months to say nine or ten months, then my *call* might come in June or July — right in the middle of the World Cup. Oh no. I couldn't go in then, not with 60 live matches to watch. So I crossed my fingers, and my legs, and hoped Labour wouldn't keep their promises. Which they didn't. The call came last week, after waiting exactly one year.

That was literary licence, about crossing my legs. Did you ever see my poorly foot? But you don't want to hear about it, do you? I always skip when I come to people's operations. So boring. OK, I'll tell you. Sort of bunion thing on my big toe, inherited, because my mother had the same bump, so do two of my children. They fuck you up, your mum and dad, but who fucked them up? Their mum and dad. Are you listening, Larkin? Anyway it got bigger and bigger so I couldn't wear shoes, which was a relief, never liked shoes, but I do love the modern Velcro sandals, though they brought on an allergy in my wife. VNA, it's called. Velcro Noise Allergy. Very nasty. Every time I fiddled with the Velcro bit, to make a sandal bigger or smaller, which on a long walk I might do every ten yards, she screamed, "Stop making that bloody noise!"

Then on top of the bunion thing I got a ganglion. Can't spell it, but very ugly, all had to come off, but no problem, quick slash with a pair of shears, crutches for a few days and you'll be walking again in six weeks.

So last week I went into the West Cumberland in Whitehaven and found myself in a ward filled with blokes with tattoos and beer bellies who'd injured themselves playing football. We were on first-name terms with our nurse, that's the style these days. She was doing everything. Bringing huge blokes back from the theatre and helping them on to their beds, fixing tip drips, answering the phone, making toast.

I'd gone in the night before my op, as I had to have an injection, which meant in the evening I was able to walk around, so I walked to the day room, leaving all the post-op blokes cursing their bad luck, strapped to their beds during a monster week for Euro football.

In the day room was an old woman who appeared to be asleep on a chair and a younger woman in a bed with bottles and stuff strapped to her body. Gawd knows how she'd got herself and her bed pushed into the day room. At the back of the room were some hospital staff, eating their sandwiches and chatting. The telly was on, blaring away. No one seemed to be watching it.

Er, do you mind if I change to BBC1? "What's on, love?" asked the old woman. Blackburn Rovers *v* Olympique Lyonnais. "Don't mind me," she said. "Nor me," said the younger woman. "I've only come in here for a …" And she gave me the sign of a fag.

For 20 years I have watched football on the telly in peace and isolation in my own home, now for the second week running, by a horrendous series of coincidences, I got stuck in a crowded room, with other human beings, doing human being things like talking and eating and smoking.

At least the woman didn't smoke, not while I was there, but she and the other woman talked non-stop, mainly about you-know-who.

"It's the woman I blame. They went after him, didn't they. They asked for it. Of course he's going to lie about it. All men do."

Meanwhile I was trying to get to grips with Sutton and Davies as Blackburn's new striking partnership. It's that Roy Hodgson I blame, paid far too much for Davies. How can they talk about him as the next England manager when he can't even manage Blackburn? Lucky Glenn, proving an unconvincing England manager so far, but having no credible rival, apart from Alex Ferguson. That would be interesting, wouldn't it? If I was Fergie, at his age, I'd take it.

It was a really boring match. Not even shouting at Motty for being a total dickhead made it more interesting, though it did alarm the two women. The younger one nearly came unplugged from her drips, but I did apologise, made it clear I was not shouting at her, only the telly.

I'm back home now, thanks for asking. The op was fine, well done West Cumberland, hurrah for the NHS, but I'm fed up resting my leg and trying to be sensible, neither of which I'm good at. I don't think I'll beturning out for Wardington FC again, but l can't wait to give those Velcro sandals a run-out. Sufferers from VNA, you have been warned.

GORGEOUS GEORGE GETS READY
TO TAKE HIS REVENGE

I AM CONTINUALLY BEING ASKED, AS I GO AROUND THE planet, what I think of George Graham. All the sheep around here, locals such as Herdwicks, foreigners such as Swaledales, know well that I be a Tottenham supporter. Naturally, they are interested to hear my reaction.

Not that I'm walking yet, not with my poorly foot, still waiting for the stitches to come out, but even hobbling to the front door I get the same reaction. This very day, Peter the Postman was standing there, smirking. "What about George, then?" George may not, of course, have gone to Spurs. But as of now, at this moment in time, Spurs is where G Graham appears to be bound. So, tell us Hunt, what do you think?

Let me take you back, friends, almost 30 years. To a lovely spring morning when our first-born, Caitlin, was aged about four. There was a sudden commotion outside our house, an air of great excitement, so out I rushed, followed by Caitlin. I propped her up on the front gate to see what was going on. Our north London street was then fairly mixed: old working classes, foreign persons in flats, a handful of young thrusting couples on the way up, such as our good selves. We thought we were but passing through this rather run-down street, on the wrong side of the Heath, waiting till we could afford Something Nice in Happy Hampstead.

It was a wedding. The bridal car was setting off from number 15, next but one to us, and there was Marie, daughter of our Turkish or Greek Cypriot neighbours, I never did know where her parents came from as they moved not long after. But she was stunning, the talk of the neighbourhood, still a teenager, but already with a modelling job. Her bridegroom was a handsome young Arsenal player, Gorgeous George, so he was known.

I held Caitlin up high, hoping for some pennies. In my mind, looking back, pennies were thrown, and in my mind, Gorgeous George was sitting in the wedding car and I gave him a little pretend hiss, being a Spurs fan. But could this be true, or is my mind playing tricks? George was also known as a canny Scot, so would he throw money away? And would the bridegroom set off from the family home with the bride? But I can clearly remember Marie's face and smile, giving a big wave to little Caitlin as she set off happily into her future. Thirty years later, we are still in the same street, while George is the one with the posh place in Hampstead. Caitlin is a journalist and novelist, married and living in Botswana. Marie, dunno what she's doing, but not with George.

Graham is one of modern football's many surprises. Who expected the slow, lazy player, known as the Stroller, to turn into a hard-nosed manager? Only those clever enough to predict that the soppy, Nancy boy, fancy dan, Spurs midfielder known as Glenda would also metamorphose into a successful manager.

It was also surprising that George took bungs, allegedly. Didn't seem to fit in with his brutal honesty towards his players. But then what does anyone know about human nature who only watches on the pitch, or on the box, or in the papers, or even in marriage to them.

His personal morals won't worry most supporters any more than political supporters worry about the morals of their leader. George, like Clinton, is allowed almost any personal sins, as long as professionally he appears to be winning.

It doesn't worry me, either, that he managed Arsenal. Loyalty in football exists only among supporters. To managers and players, it is an alien concept, mumbled about and invoked when it suits them, but they all know it is a total nonsense. Was Arsenal loyal to Rioch, Newcastle to Dalglish, Spurs to Gross?

As for players, they play primarily for themselves, which is how it must be, how it should be. From playground football, to five-a-side training, to a Wembley final, real players don't want to get beaten, whichever team they happen to be in. And if the teams are changed around, by chance or the whims of the transfer market, they will still be keen to win. Or should be.

George has always been brilliant at defence, and Spurs have been crap at defence since oh, god, since Caitlin was a baby at the gate, but I do fear, if George takes over, we could be in for some years of boring football. If it means we don't often get beaten, few will complain. I like the fact that he makes notes. That always seems so sensible for a manager. In every match, there are 100 minor points worth noting, techniques that need improving, habits to be eliminated, all easily forgotten when apparently major points, like dodgy goals, unfair penalties, come along to cloud the mind.

I also like it that he sits up in the stand for the first half. Again, so sensible. I have sat with managers on a touchline or the dugout and you can see bugger all, understand bugger all. And the players can't even hear you screaming.

Why is he going? This has puzzled many commentators. Leeds is just as big a club, they say. The money can't be a major factor. So is it just his posh London house?

I think his main motivation is revenge. He was furious at his treatment at Arsenal, let down by people he thought would always support him, some of whom he thinks were just as guilty, just as dodgy. Now is his chance to get his own back. By putting new life and muscle into Arsenal's old enemy, he might give them a good kicking, hurting where it hurts the most.

HOW I BECAME A FIRST-TIME VOTER
FOR MAN OF THE MATCH

9 OCTOBER 1998

I'VE JUST DONE SOMETHING I HAVE NEVER DONE IN MY life, in my football life, in 140 years of football life. Sometimes I do feel as if I've been stuck here since the very beginning, since the year dot. Who was she, by the way, to have a year named after her?

I was watching Liverpool–Chelsea when this irresistible urge came over me. No, not to have another glass of wine, as I'd had a bottle at Sunday lunchtime, well I am recuperating from my foot operation. Also celebrating Spurs being higher in the league than Arsenal. They were, for almost 24 hours.

So I was pretty relaxed, not caring who won, with around 70 minutes of the match over, when on to the screen flashed the telephone number for Man of the Match. Usually I scream when they start this stupidity. How can you vote for anyone when there's still 20 minutes to go? Who would be idiotic enough to ring up, at their own expense, when there's nothing in it for them? You'd have to be a barm pot, a total plonker, or pissed in the pub even to think of ringing them.

So I did. I wanted to see how it works. All these years I've suspected it was a ruse by BT and Sky, to encourage halfwits to ring up and be forced to hang on for hours, listening to some crap jingle, till they give up.

It was 1–0 to Chelsea, a first-half goal by Casiraghi. He'd played well, I thought. Vialli had jumped in the air when he'd scored, gesturing in triumph, rather unseemly for a manager, but it did give me a good chance to examine Vialli's tie. He's taken to wearing a sort of old school striped tie, but he can't tie it properly, so he looks like Just William.

Liverpool had been pretty useless. Owen hadn't had a chance, nor Fowler. Ince had been prowling around, upsetting only himself.

Redknapp looks lovely, with a nice light tan at present, where has he been, but I'm still not convinced by him. I fear he could be the Ray Wilkins *de nos jours*, as they say in Italy. Watching on telly, as opposed to being there, you only see players when they're on the ball, which mainly means midfielders. If strikers aren't striking, you can almost forget they exist. Defenders tend to be seen in long shot, so you're unaware of their best work which is often off the ball, cutting out, closing down, things the television eye doesn't see.

That's been my real, GCSE-level reason for ridiculing television's Man of the Match. What do we know, who only know what we are given to know? Any road up, Casiraghi, I'll vote for him. First goal for Chelsea. Bound to get a sympathy vote. Then came the first problem. Where the hell's the bloody telephone in this bloody house?

I'm still in Lakeland where the little telly is in our little library, lined with my Lakeland books, plus one little chair. My dear wife never watches telly up here, not like London, where she watches *EastEnders* and *Casualty* and other soppy stuff. Strange that she eschews such frivolities up here. Eschews. Can't believe I've written that, must be the first time in ten million words, though most of them were the same words. It's a sign. Me and Casiraghi, both getting a first on the same day. I've just got to ring and vote for him.

I ran into the living room but couldn't see the phone. I followed the lead and my wife was at the end of it, on the couch, talking rubbish to her chum friend Valerie Grove, rubbishing various literary folks.

Give me the phone woman, this is urgent.

I had to grab it from her in the end, then lead the lead back to the door of the TV room. That was as far as it would stretch. Through the doorway, I could see Casiraghi coming off. Oh no. Well, I'm still going to vote for him. I dialled 0660 1122 33, as instructed. Got through right away. A voice said welcome to Sky Man of the Match, if you want to name your man, speak after the tone. It then said if you want a chance to win a replica shirt of the Man of the Match, hold on.

Hold on. Do I want to walk round Loweswater with a Chelsea shirt saying Casiraghi and frighten all the Herdwicks? Of course I do. I was then asked to name the ground where the match was taking place. I also had to give my phone number and town. Now that was hard. There's not a town for over 30 miles unless you count Cockermouth. So I said, Cockermouth, spelling it out slowly. People never get it right, or think you are being really, really juvenile.

While I was calling, Liverpool had started storming back. Redknapp, who had done bugger all, scored a brilliant goal from a freekick. Just as I thought. Everything can change in minutes.

It ended 1 – 1, but I had to hang on, to see who had been voted Man of the Match. I always switch off the minute the whistle blows after any live match. Who wants those boring pundits, all those statistics. I like foreplay before play, not after. Casiraghi had got 17 per cent of the votes, Redknapp 25 per cent and Ferrer 51 per cent. Who? Oh yeah, Chelsea's Spanish full back, with the deprived-looking face and the sad haircut. He did bugger all, as far as I could see. In fact, in the *Independent*'s report next day he didn't even get a mention.

Just rung Sky Sports and spoke to Chris Haynes who said oh yes, Man of the Match is very popular, very viewer friendly. For a big match, they can get up to 35,000 calls. It's computer driven and the winner is picked at random, from those who voted for the winning player. That day it was Robert Hunt of Falmouth who got the replica shirt. Lucky.

So, I'm persuaded it's not a fiddle, but I still think it's a nonsense. It means, though, I need never do it again. I can now go on to the next thing I have never done before.

"THE REFEREE'S A VIRGIN."
OH YES, SPURS FANS ARE DEAD WITTY

30 OCTOBER 1998

GEORGE GRAHAM'S FIRST HOME MATCH WAS ALSO MY FIRST home match. Of the season so far. I hadn't been to White Hart Lane since May, at least I think I went in May, I can't remember that far back, though it will be in my diary, in which I record all scores and all sores, such as my sore knee, sore wrist, sore toe. Correction. My toe has now recovered, after the operation. I learnt three things recovering from the operation. The best homeopathic medicine is sunshine. The best painkiller is wine. The best recuperative treatment is work.

The first surprise at White Hart Lane was the price of tea. It's gone up from 60p to £1. Diabolical. Bigger cups, which I don't want, as my seat is in the centre of a row and I try to go to the toilet as little as possible. I complained to the child on the counter and he said, yeah, diabolical. At Arsenal, where he also works, it's still 60p. I suppose Spurs need every penny to pay George his £1 million a year.

Then I went into the Spurs souvenir shop, as I do at the beginning of every season to check out the latest rubbish, sorry, treasures. My way was barred. They wouldn't let me in. It happens at the beginning of every season. And I always forget. You're not allowed into the souvenir shop holding a cup of tea. Dunno why. Unless they fear fans will throw the contents over the new away kit. Personally I think it's rather fetching. You've probably seen it, a sort of senatorial purple, a snip at £70 for shirt, shorts and sox.

I asked the security man at the door to keep an eye on my cup. "Don't drink it," I said. "I've spat in it." I say that every year and he never smiles.

Couldn't see any women's knickers with a cockerel on the front, they were very big last year, but they have a nice line in Spurs romper suits for babies. I noticed a Spurs bib, two for £5. Also meant for babies, but I bet quite a few lagered up lads will get them in their Christmas stockings from their lagered up lasses.

I bought ten match programmes for £1, good bargain, eh, except that they are all last season's. I buy them every year, unable to resist a bargain, even though I know they won't contain a Spurs–Man Utd prog or a Spurs–Arsenal prog. They always sell out. Instead you get Spurs–Barnsley or Spurs–Wimbledon which nobody ever wants. I take them with me when I go abroad and give them to poor persons. I find they are more acceptable these days than beads.

Inside my bargain pack was one for 24 November 1997, at home to Palace. On the cover was a smiling shot of Christian Gross having his hand shaken by a smiley Alan Sugar. I studied it carefully, because the programme for the match I was about to watch, against Newcastle, had Sugar in exactly the same pose—but shaking hands with George Graham. I wonder if it was computer-generated. Good way of saving money on new photos every time a new manager arrives.

Full house, great atmosphere, as you would expect for George, our saviour. Down below, I could see Ruud, Newcastle's saviour. As was. Doesn't time go quickly in football? Seems only yesterday there were headlines everywhere about Ruud's sexy football. No one says it now. You have to feel sorry for managers, the glow so quickly dims, the smiles so quietly fade, expectations simply vanish, and then, poor petals, they are revealed as mere humans, or less, left with only their measly million pounds a year to make themselves smile.

Beside me were the father and his son who have driven me mad the last three seasons. He is thin and weedy, so is his son, aged ten. They keep up a non-stop barrage of complaints, working themselves into a lather.

"Edinburgh, what are you doing?" screams the dad, clutching his head.

"What are you doing; Edinburgh?" shouts the son, even louder, burying his head in his hands for greater effect.

"Armstrong, you're an old woman!" yells the son, shaking his fist.

"You're an old woman, Armstrong!" shouts the dad, shaking both fists.

I fear one or both will have a heart attack. Every gesture is so violent, every expression so explosive. Then what would I do, stuck in the middle of the row with ambulance men clambering over me to get them out while I'm trying to watch the game?

In front of me last season was a large man who looks and sounds as if he's got a stall somewhere, or access to the back of a lorry. He's still there, with three boys. They are at fee-paying schools, judging by their accents and manner. They talk all the time, which is really annoying, showing off their football knowledge, or rabbiting on about Fantasy Football. Now and again they stand up and shout, especially if it's a dodgy decision. They still shout the same thing. "The referee's a virgin!"

There used to be a nice quiet bloke in a Barbour who sat near me, with his daughter, aged about 13. No sign of them. Perhaps given up their season tickets. I liked them both. Very agreeable. In fact they agreed with everything I yelled, stood up when I stood up, laughed at my dead witty remarks.

On the giant screen, before the match, they showed some clips from old matches. That was new, and a good idea. I gave a little cheer when I spotted Ralph Coates's wispy hair.

Oh yes, the match. It was nice to see John Scales get a game. I'd forgotten he existed. He did well. Newcastle were decidedly unsexy. Shearer, old son, I'd move on if I were you. Before you get nasty worry lines and drooping shoulders. Spurs won 2−0, so it was a good match to begin my winter.

Next week it's Arsenal. Could be exciting. Got a lot to check out. Such as the tea. Can it really still be only 60p?

WHO NEEDS A FOOTBALL AGENT ANYWAY?
OK, I ADMIT IT, I DO
18 DECEMBER 1998

I HAD LUNCH LAST WEEK WITH TWO AGENTS WHO BETWEEN them look after Alan Shearer, Michael Owen, David Beckham, Dwight Yorke, David Platt, Dion Dublin, Gary Lineker, Graeme le Saux, Gary McAllister, Emile Heskey, oh the star names go on and on.

I can't name one of the star agents, as he does not like any personal publicity, so we'll call him Mr S. The other is Jonathan Holmes, whom I have known for years. They have recently come together, in that their respective firms are now part of a much bigger organisation, the Marquee Group, which is ultimately American owned.

I haven't got an agent at present, for reasons too boring to go into. I have thought up and negotiated my last five books on my own, and found that it has saved me time and made no difference to the money. So who needs an agent?

They both looked at me pityingly. Everyone needs an agent, they said, especially when they are beginning. It's true I had one when I started out, but he retired through ill-health, selling his firm to another agency, then in due course this agent left that firm and I thought bugger it, I'll do it on my own.

Publishing and football are two very different industries, but Jürgen Klinsmann, when he was at Spurs, managed without an agent, and he didn't do too badly. Most unusual, they said. Though Klinsmann did have an adviser. There are at present 91 official football agents in Britain, looking after approximately 90 per cent of our players. They know it makes sense. Footballers need help and advice.

But why not just pay for advice, if and when you need it? I was always impressed that Gazza uses Mel Stein, who is a lawyer, rather than an agent, paying him per hour, per job.

Again, they looked saddened by my naïvety. "A lawyer will still present you with a big bill, irrespective of whether you have made any money. Anyway, lawyers are not commercial people. And with one or two exceptions, they are not as close to the game as football agents."

They have both made most of their income over the years from the commercial side of a footballer's life, not his actual footballing life, handling things like advertising, sponsorship and personal appearances. One of them has never taken anything from a footballer's wage, or from his transfer fees. They pride themselves on this, pointing out that, unlike some agents, there is nothing in it for them to stir up trouble at a club or encourage a player to move. But naturally, they are there to listen to a player's moans about his club, his problems, his career, and give advice.

"When I take on a young player, I draw up a ten-year career plan," said Mr S. "I chart the likely stages, his likely income.

Both of them came into football sideways, when by chance they gave help and financial advice to two young players at the beginning of their careers, long before they were known. Mr S's first footballer was David Platt, back in his days at Crewe. As Platty progressed, got to bigger clubs and then into the England team, he recommended Mr S to other players.

In the case of Jonathan Holmes, he met and looked after Gary Lineker while he was still in his early days at Leicester. As Lineker progressed as a player, so did Jonathan as an agent, taking on rugby players and cricketers as well as footballers, all from his Nottingham base. At one stage, he was the agent for all three of England's sporting captains—Lineker, Atherton and Carling.

He has done a great deal to ease Lineker from football into the media, thinking up ideas for TV programmes. They both see themselves, if required, as being a footballer's agent for life, helping them into their next career, whatever it might be, even if it's just sitting at home and counting their millions.

Our top agents, of course, have done pretty well for themselves, capitalising on their years of hard work behind the scenes. "And we do work hard," said Mr S. "I work every evening and weekends and am always available, without any extra charge. Unlike a lawyer."

Yes, you've made your point. Both of them realise how lucky they were, chancing on young players who turned out not just to be star players, but sensible, intelligent, un-daft people. Platty, for example, even wrote his own autobiography, something almost unheard of in football.

Where is Platty, by the way? Not heard of him recently. Waiting to go into management, said Mr S, sipping his glass of water. He then had to go off for an urgent appointment at a London club.

Jonathan and I ordered another bottle of wine while we tried to think of other players in living memory who have also written their own books without help. We only got to three—Lee Chapman, Garry Nelson and Eamon Dunphy.

What football really needs, I said, is someone who knows about football and can write about football. Now that you're branching out, Jonathan, extending the empire, becoming a transatlantic media mogul, I happen to know about this very good hack who hasn't got an agent at present who could just be the soft of person you might like to represent.

Jonathan got up, suddenly remembering he had an urgent meeting as well. But he did pay the bill.

WHAT EVERY CLUB NEEDS IS A
RUN-OF-THE-MILL MILLIONAIRE

8 JANUARY 1999

I HAVE MADE THE SAME SILLY MISTAKE, AS I DO EVERY NEW year, which explains why I am sitting here screaming at my 1999 diary. I bought the same one as last year, sort of long and thin, fits snugly in my inside pocket. It has a plastic cover, which means I can slip into the end folder my basic address book and save myself the trouble of writing out the same old basic addresses every year.

But what I had forgotten is that whoever makes these diaries, Art No 3090 it says at the end, whatever that means, has decided Sunday is a non-day. Sunday doesn't matter. Who needs to bother with Sundays? So they only give a third of the space for Sundays.

I can see the problem. There are seven days in a week so if you give two pages to each week, as this diary does, it is hard to spread them out evenly. If only there were ten days a week, it would be so much easier to divide them. And if each month had the same number of days, that would also help. And as for 365 days in a year, now that's really loopy. Who thought up all this nonsense?

Given this mess, why pick on Sundays? It means I have to draw a line through the bottom part of Saturday, to give Sunday a bit more bulk, a bit more space. That then buggers up the whole weekend, making it look very cramped, not to say scruffy. Looking back at my 1998 diary, I see I drew a line at the bottom of every Saturday. And not very neatly.

There are two reasons why the diary maker is so out of touch, so behind the times in victimising Sundays. Millions of us now work from home, making our own routines and rituals, so Saturdays and Sundays are just as likely to be working days as any other day. We therefore need equal space to write down details of our exciting lives. Got up, got out of bed, dragged a comb through my head. I made that up. No one uses a comb these days.

Second, football fans needs lashings of space for both Saturdays and Sundays. Millions of us go to a match on a Saturday, in the flesh, or similar, then watch a match on a Sunday on Sky Sport. If not two matches. Perhaps even three. How are we going to record all the vital details for posterity if the diary makers don't give us enough space, huh?

I like to write in the score every Saturday. Pointless, I know. All scores get recorded, then these days analysed for ever and ever. There is no need for me to put it in my diary as it if were a personal or exclusive piece of information. But putting it in my diary means I was there. That's how I know, when I look back, when I'm really, really old, I also add a few pithy observations, as I did last Saturday. "Spurs 5, Watford 2. Sinton a plonker, Ian Walker hopeless again." That sort of pith. Well worth recording.

When I watch a match on TV, I add the letters "TV", to show that I wasn't actually there, in the flesh. Last weekend I wrote: "Rushden 0, Leeds 0. I want to be Max Griggs when I grow up."

In years to come, or even months to come, I won't know what the hell Rushden was or who was Max Griggs. But I can see him now, in his little pully, being interviewed after the game, a run-of-the-mill millionaire, un-pushy, un-flash, just someone who happens to have done jolly well in life, building up the Doc Martens empire. What fun to have put his spare change into buying his local little non-league club and creating that absolutely brilliant stadium. And how satisfying to see the stadium full and his little club so successful.

When I get depressed, and I do, friends, about the future of football, with the haves galloping away leaving the have-nots miles behind, I will think about Max Griggs.

The new money flooding into football, from Murdoch or from Sky, is going all one way — to those who already have it. The result is that the average Premiership player can now demand a million a year. Steve McManaman, so it has been reported, will get over £5 million a year if he goes to Chelsea or abroad next season. The report said £110,000 a week, which I read as a misprint, how could it be that much, some mistake surely, but if it's not quite right now, it will be, any moment.

How can this mad spiral be stopped? It can't, as long as we daft fans are prepared to pay more and more for season tickets, which we are, judging by the waiting lists, and TV companies are prepared to pay more and more for every new contract to show matches, knowing we daft fans will want to watch. So, it's all our fault.

In theory, then, it is in our hands, to stop this madness — by not going, not watching. But that won't happen. Our football authorities could sort it out, but that won't happen either, as they can't sort themselves out. Which leaves the govemment. They could create Offoot — the Office of Football, with legal powers to limit excess and try to create fairness in football. If there are bodies to regulate the National Lottery, gas and electricity, to stop overpricing and abuse of monopolies, why not in football? Fat chance.

Max Griggs, in his own little way, is trying to reverse the trend for only the big clubs to get bigger and richer. And he's done it sensibly, in that a lot of the money invested has gone into developing a site of some 70 acres, with leisure facilities, not just a football club, available to the whole community. The money hasn't just gone into the players' pockets.

So well done, Rushden. Wherever it is. I still can't find it on the map. And I'd never heard of Max Griggs until last weekend. But now he's sure of immortality. He is in my diary, oh yes, for ever. Just a shame I didn't have more space to write about him.

A VISIT TO THIERRY HENRY'S
FAMILY HOME

5 FEBRUARY 1999

WHY ARE THERE NO BLUE PLAQUES FOR FOOTBALLERS? Those things on the front of a house, telling you that Stanley Matthews once lived here, or Bobby Charlton, or Pele. If the National Trust can buy Paul McCartney's old house in Liverpool and open it for the world to come and gape, I don't see why it can't be done for famous footballers. These days, they are just as likely to have a world following.

I've agreed to give a National Trust lecture next month, I do like to help, and I'd planned to suggest to their big bosses that there's a little house in Hayes they might consider buying, the home where the infant Glenn first hoddled. They could organise tours, give the world a chance to see the ball of wool his mother used to roll up for him as his first football. Or the wall on the outside privy where he played head tennis. Or the back kitchen door where that first scout from Tottenham skulked, his pocket full of tenners. Or the mirror Glenn first stood in front of, pulling up his shorts, really, really tight, to show off his lovely creamy thighs. Or the bathroom where he had his first truly meaningful one-to-one spiritual experience.

Alas, I now don't think the Hoddle home is going to get a blue plaque. Which is a shame. I'd go, like a shot, as I love looking round the home of anyone famous.

Over the years, I've looked at scores of literary homes, from Wordsworth's Dove Cottage to Robert Louis Stevenson's Valima on Samoa, and masses of homes where artists once lived, from Beatrix Potter's Hill Top to Charles Rennie Mackintosh's Glasgow home, OK that was a repro, but I've never managed to get inside the birthplace of even one famous footballer.

Which explains why ten days ago I forced my wife to go with me to Desirade. That's a little island, about five miles off the coast of

Guadeloupe, which is in the French West Indies, yes, thousands of miles away, but we did happen to be on Guadeloupe at the time, which was handy.

One of the interesting things about France's World Cup winning team was the lack of Frenchmen, true Frenchmen, with blue eyes, wearing berets and a string of onions round their necks. I didn't notice many of them. What we all noticed was the large number of North Africans, such as Zidane, or black Africans, such as Desailly, or West Indians, such as Thierry Henry and Lilian Thuram. The latter two both originated from Guadeloupe, one of two French departments in the West Indies, the other being Martinique. Guadeloupe itself only has a population of 300,000, so it's done well to produce two World Cup stars. Bernard Lambourde of Chelsea is also from Guadeloupe — yet the island hasn't even got a professional football I league.

It was when I was told that Thierry Henry's family was from Desirade, an island so small and isolated I couldn't find it on the map, I said come on, lass, let's go and have a butcher's. Plus someone in the hotel we were staying at mentioned there was a special offer on boat trips to Desirade — only 100 francs round trip as opposed to the normal 150 francs.

I soon discovered why. We were hardly at sea when the young Frenchwoman beside me started throwing up. The waves were enormous and the little boat was taking a pounding. The island has a population of just 1,600 and is only eight miles long, which I know because we walked it, from end to end, in 24 hours. (Our walking rate is three miles an hour.) It is in a time warp, and appeared totally asleep, not to say dead, so it was hard to find anyone to ask the way to the house where the Henry family lived. Or even anyone who had heard of him. That's because I kept on stopping people from French France, middle-class tourists from Paris. The other interesting thing about French football, despite their famous win, is that they are still hardly a football-mad nation, not compared with Italy. "I only follow rugby," said one man. "I only follow games played by French people," said another.

But in a bar at the far end of the island I did meet a local who told me that Henry's family home was in Grande Anse, the little harbour where the boat came in, so we walked back there. No we didn't. Hold on. We got a taxi. It was midday by then and I was knackered, what with the sun and the ti punches. That's what they call the favourite rum punch drink in Guadeloupe. Can you guess why?

Back in Grande Anse, I did eventually have the Henry home pointed out to me, or what purported to be his family's home, it looked like most of the other shacks, but his parents have long since gone. Where to? I asked. Monaco, I was told. They went with him when he went to play in Monte Carlo. Isn't that nice? I like it when lads who do well look after their old folks. Juninho did the same when he came to Middlesbrough, bringing his mum and dad, sisters and aunties and second cousins with him from Brazil.

Leaving Desirade must have been a lot easier. OK for a day trip, and we did enjoy it, but there are clearly a lot more mod cons and facilities in Monte Carlo than in Grande Anse. Or in Turin. Henry has now been transferred to Juventus, news of which had not then reached Desirade, which shows how out of touch they are.

Desirade hasn't even got a football pitch, and I looked everywhere, which makes Henry's success all the more remarkable, but I can vouch for the local ti punch. I had another, before we got the boat home. And I wasn't sick, either. Ti, by the way, is Creole, a shortened form of Petit. So what you are ordering is a small punch. So called, I like to think, in honour of the Arsenal midfield star. Famous footballers may not have many blue plaques, but it's nice to know that one of them has got a drink named after him.

GLENN'S HAIR, GAZZA'S TWITCH: FOOTBALL NEEDS THINGS TO MOCK

12 FEBRUARY 1999

I HOPE HOWARD WILKINSON STAYS IN THE ENGLAND JOB long enough for us to get to know and love his mannerisms and habits. I mean love in the sense of smiling at them the moment we spot them, enjoying it when he opens his mouth and is Howard Wilkinson, doing and saying the things Howard Wilkinson says and does.

Everything Hoddle did, his clichés, his grammar, his hair, his jaw, his mannerisms and affectations, became so familiar. We felt at home with him, like someone in our own family. You knew him with his back to the camera, could recognise his voice blind.

At the moment, Howard hasn't given us enough for us to go on to make caricatures of him in our mind's eye. There was a long shot of him in the crowd last week and I jumped up, my face pressed to the screen, saying who, where, which one, gerraway, that's not him, oh yeah, that's his thin face, his grizzled hair. With Glenn, I knew his whole wardrobe.

I'm still getting to grips with Wilko's quizzical look. It could be him thinking slowly, or thinking quick to hold back the remark he really wants to make. As an older, more experienced personage, he will probably give less away. Hoddle grew up and was formed with us, by us, and in the end gave everything away.

Television, of course, magnifies every mannerism, every black-head, but on the terraces, even in crowds of 40,000, we fans have always been able to identify the habits of our heroes. There's a bloke in front of me at Spurs who, the minute Darren Anderton saunters over to take a corner, is up on his feet, mimicking what dear Darren is about to do — ie, push back his floppy public-school hair with his foppy little fingers. The bloke himself is almost bald, another reason I always smile.

We know Dwight Yorke is smiling, even with his back to us, though I have a theory that it's not just his lovely, happy, smiling Tobagan nature, but his teeth. They are too big for his jaw. That's why you can always see them.

John Gregory, we know what he's going to do the moment he hits the touchline. His fingers will be in his mouth, whistling like mad. I spent years of my boyhood longing to be able to whistle like that. It seemed so manly, proved you weren't a girl's blouse. My mother did try to help me when no one was looking, carefully arranging my fingers, but I still couldn't do it. Does it run in families, or can you be taught?

I like watching goalkeepers who spit on their hands whenever they are about to take a goal-kick. For a penalty or a corner you would expect that, as their hands will be needed, but taking a goal-kick does not involve hands. It's a habit, something they can't help and are probably unaware of, like Darren when he's being a flopsy bunny.

I have a list of snot-blowers somewhere, and a graph of the incidents of snot-blowing. My researches show that it tends to take place after a missed chance, indicating that it is not a rush of snot but a nervous habit, a displacement activity, meant to cover the embarrassment of a missed chance.

We know the excitable players, like Ian Wright, who are all emotion, but I'm more fascinated by the emotionless ones who rarely smile, like Bergkamp, Anelka and Paul Scholes. Are they like that at home, in private? Anelka, from what I hear, is just as miserable off the pitch as on. What struck me about Man Utd's new young defender Wes Brown was his lack of expression. You expect a young newcomer to be nervous, but his look was blank and pale, as if all emotions had been drained. Andy Cole has gone through most of his playing life looking really moany and miserable, but now he's been in scoring form you often see his little teeth. Or is it the influence of Yorke beside him?

Gazza, in his early days, really did have a twitch. Watching him playing, close up, you could see his head shake, his eyes roll and I used to think, dear God, he's about to have a fit, or a stroke, let's hope we score before he starts frothing at the mouth or hits somebody. I think it was simply a case of hyperactivity, a spring wound up, ready to explode, which of course it often did. He is rarely hyper these days, and most of his activity is at walking pace, but you can still spot Gazza from 100 yards away.

On the management side, Big Ron is a case study in himself, a whole bookshelf of habits and mannerisms and speech patterns, most of which I suspect he has copied or perfected by watching himself on television, having been told, Ron, you are a character, Ron you are a one, Ron, do us your Big Ron imitation.

Brian Clough had even more mannerisms and he, too, became a caricature of himself. Big Ron took several years to be Big Ron, and in his early managerial life appeared to have very little personality, but Cloughie was a one off from the beginning, even in his playing days.

Has Howard Wilkinson got the job, however temporarily, because of his lack of mannerisms and strangeness, because he seems dry and boring and sensible, not off with the fairies like Glenn? That often happens when appointing new managers, just as it happens when appointing new popes, new party leaders, new headteachers. You go for someone not like the old one, who doesn't have the same faults and weaknesses. Or so you think. One of Glenn's big attractions when got the job was that he wasn't Terry Venables. Little did we know what was to emerge.

However long we have with Howard, I do hope he reveals something of himself soon, which we can mock and jump upon. I'm sure he will. We'll need all the amusement and entertainment we can get as England struggle to get to the European finals.

AN ENGLISH (SORRY, FRENCH)
GENTLEMAN SETS AN EXAMPLE

19 FEBRUARY 1999

I WAS AT THAT FAMOUS MATCH, YOU MUST KNOW WHICH one, where something happened that has not happened before in the past 140 years of English football. Arsenal – Sheffield Utd last Saturday, which Arsenal won 2 – 1, till Arsène Wenger agreed Arsenal had not played fair, so it is to be replayed.

I had arrived very early, by chance, not like me, as I believe punctuality is a vice. So I decided to walk round the ground, round the rectangle of streets that surrounds Highbury. Haven't done that for years, yet so little has changed. Walk around White Hart Lane and it's like a space station, with all the new stands, concrete giants, blotting out the sky. By comparison, Highbury is still in the 19th century, surrounded by terraced houses. But one thing has changed — the rise of the back-street entrepreneurs, many of them in the front rooms and gardens of little terraced houses, all selling Arsenal memorabilia.

It explained the recent survey in the magazine *Four Four Two* that put Spurs above Arsenal in the income stakes. Hard to believe, as Arsenal have done much better than Spurs these past few years and had bigger crowds. I now realise it must be because Spurs control more of their own merchandising outlets. At Arsenal, it's the geezers, not the club, flogging much of the junk.

I also did a walkabout because it was exciting, with so many Sheffield fans, in such good humour. Inside, they had taken over the whole of the Clock End. Not heard such away noises for years. Alas, they didn't have a good view of *the incident*, being at the wrong end. For those asleep that day, or on Mars, this is what happened. A Sheffield player was lying injured, so the Sheffield goalie kicked the ball out of play. When Ray Parlour took the throw for Arsenal, he threw it back towards the Sheffield goalie, to give it back to him, in the accepted manner, and therefore not gain any advantage. But an Arsenal player pounced upon it, passed to another Arsenal player, who scored, giving them a 2–1 lead, with only 15 minutes left.

Well, mon dew, quel drama. The whole Sheffield team went potty, as did their manager Steve Bruce. It took a while for the Sheffield fans to realise what had happened, but when they did, they went wild, trying to invade the pitch, fighting with officials.

For about eight minutes, it was chaos. Legally, it was a goal. There is nothing in the laws about such ungentlemanly conduct. When play resumed, the Sheffield fans were still furious. I heard shouts of "Fucking Arsenal, cheaters, scum, you are shit". All the usual stuff. But then they settled down into a dirge, a low but reverberating plainsong, which could be heard everywhere. "Shame on Arsenal, Shame on Arsenal, Shame on Arsenal". It was low key, understated, oblique, yet somehow eerie, creepy. I could sense it shaming the Arsenal fans beside me, and the players on the pitch, They knew they'd won by cheating. I think that chant had a lot to do with Wenger's decision to agree to a replay.

All week, there have been references to this long-standing 'British tradition' of giving back the ball when such a thing happens. I'd like to see the evidence for this. My memory is that it came from Europe, from Italy first.

There are people in Europe, probably all round the world, who do think it is part of the English 'fair play' tradition. And that's a laugh. The tradition in England is like anywhere else — you cheat as much as you can. The minute the ball goes into touch, you put your hand up to claim it, even though you know you put it out. Players dive, especially in the penalty area, hoping to con the ref. They push, pull, shove, kick, spit, abuse, intimidate. The only crime is to get caught.

English players are as bad as anyone else, though perhaps not as skilful or as subtle. Just like their football, in fact. Yet the myth persists that English players do practise fair play, because we gave the phrase to the world.

I was in Cameroon a few years ago. I went into a dressing room in a second division game and there on the wall was a notice: '*Le fair play c'est le respect de l'adversaire.*' It was a printed poster, put up by the football association for '*un sport sans violence et pour le fair play*'. Around the world, they know the concept of fair play is English. And think we are still the prime exponents. Some hope.

But we have accepted the unwritten principle of giving the ball back on such occasions. In fact, our players love doing it. The crowd always give them a good clap, for being so jolly sporting, and they glow in their own virtuousness.

So why did the Arsenal player not give it back? It was Nwankwo Kanu, who is a Nigerian. He'd not only just come on the pitch, but just arrived in England. He does know the tradition, but he hadn't realised what had happened. It was Marc Overmars who scored, and he should have been aware. We have to believe it was all a mistake. Arsenal would certainly not want to win by cheating, which was why Wenger offered a replay.

Would Alex Ferguson, say, have done the same? I'm not so sure. He might well have shrugged, said you have to obey the ref. Alan Hansen and others have said they think the result should have stood. A ref's authority has now been undermined. Where will it end? Will all 'unfair decisions' now be challenged?

Wenger has been rightly praised, though I suppose when your team are the champions, you can afford to be magnanimous.

It remains to be seen what happens in the replay on Tuesday, but there is only one clear, outright winner. Step forward, Mr Wenger, a perfect example of the traditional sporting, fairplaying English gentleman. Sorry, French gentleman.

A WEEKLY WAGE OF £20,000 IS A TERRIBLE STRAIN ON A POOR LAD

26 FEBRUARY 1999

OVER BREAKFAST WITH MY DEAR WIFE, WE WERE discussing various things, such as Iris Murdoch dying. I was wondering how many obits and appreciations Malcolm Bradbury had done about her, then wondering who will do them for him when he dies. Could be silence, as he's cornered the lit obit market. Then we got onto higher planes. Stan Collymore, I said. I feel really sorry for him.

"Who?" So I explained. "Aston Villa striker, cost £7 million, earns about £20,000 a week for playing, which he hasn't much recently, one of our footballing enigmas, innit. Last I heard, he was having treatment for stress, poor lad."

"Stress!" she said. "Footballers suffering from stress? Don't talk to me about stress. Just think of the stress your mother was under. Four kids, invalid husband, no money…"

"You sound like John Gregory," I said.

"Who's he?"

"Collymore's manager, that's who. He said much the same, though his comparison was with someone of 28 playing for Rochdale on tuppence a week with only three months of his contract left, a mortgage and three kids — that's stress, that is."

"Quite right," she said.

"Oh come on. Don't be so heartless. I expected you, being a woman, brought up on empathy, milk of human kindness, plus your cod liver oil, I thought you'd be really sympathetic."

"Why should I? Surely the whole point about football is to relieve stress…"

I had to think about that. She's right, in a sense. It's one of the pleasures, the shouting and screaming, the joys and depressions, the letting out of all emotions, cheap catharsis, regardless almost of what happens, otherwise how do you explain Man City still getting huge crowds. "True," I said, "but that applies to the fans, not the players."

"Yes, but when you played, you said playing relieved stress."

"That was park football, pet. And I did feel terrific after playing, win or lose. Been much more bad-tempered since I stopped. But that doesn't count. We're talking professional footballers. I really do feel sorry for them. Honestly. The ones at the top so rarely get any pleasure out of it. They come off the pitch with the most terrible headaches."

"I'm not listening," she said.

"The bigger the team, the bigger the salaries, the bigger the worries — about losing, being dropped, being injured, losing form. I remember doing a survey of the Spurs first team pool some years ago — almost all of them got more pleasure out of playing football at 15, when they were young and just beginning, than at 20 or 25.

A weekly wage of £20,000 is a terrible strain on a poor lad supposedly at the top of their profession. Today the pressures are even more intense."

"Boring, boring."

"They get screamed at by coaches and the management all week, criticised by the press, their bodies continually battered, yet they have to perform to their best all the time."

"Have you finished your muesli or not?"

"Imagine what it's like to be a footballer approaching 35. Not just your career, but your life is nearly over. You might have a million in the bank, but you're about to be nothing, nobody. Really, you're about to die …"

"My heart weeps," she said, stacking the dishwasher.

"Do you realise, football is one of the few activities where you get criticised while actually performing? Writers might get rubbished by the lit critics, but that's usually a whole year after they have done the work, and are on to something new. Nobody sits beside them while they're writing, shouting in their ears, 'What a load of rub-bish, gerrimoff, what a wanker'. Ditto film stars. Footballers have to take stick, there and then, on the pitch. It can devastate, break them, ruin them, especially when their own supporters turn against them. Think about that."

"I'm thinking about going to work now."

"Fans get upset when their team gets stuffed, but they come home, kick the cat, put the wife out, and get on with their life. Players can't. That *is* their life. Are you listening? There's no escape. So I honestly think they deserve all the money, for what they have to suffer."

"Spare me."

"Will it end tomorrow, that must always be at the back of their minds. What if we get a new manager and he doesn't like me? Are they about to buy somebody better, younger, or just cheaper? God, their heads must be in a spin. No wonder it's win or lose, out on the booze."

"That's British players. They don't do that abroad, or so you've told me. Ours are pretty stupid, if you ask me. . ."

"No, it's being brought up in a hot-house. Only one part of their personality has been developed. It's not their fault their education has been limited. They're quite intelligent, really. They have to be, to understand all the modern tactics and formations, instructions and directions. They can't play their own natural game, the way they would like. No wonder they get stressed and need someone to help them."

"David Lodge," she said.

"You what? He can't help Collymore. Right city, but Stan needs a therapist, not a retired professor of English with a dodgy haircut."

"I mean when Malcolm Bradbury dies. David Lodge will do the literery obits."

"Of course, why didn't I think of him? At least we've solved one problem."

I KNOW MY WAY TO WEMBLEY,
EVEN THOUGH I'M A SPURS FAN

19 MARCH 1999

SPURS ARE ON THEIR WAY TO WEM-BLEE BUT, BEFORE MY knees get all trem-blee, here's a question. When Spurs won their first ever Cup Final in 1901, how many London players were in their team?

It's my hands that are all trem-blee, having paid £48 for one of the cheapo seats. It's turnstile G, block 245, row 12, seat 94, wherever that is. My ticket for the 1966 World Cup Final was turnstile K, entrance 36, row 9, seat 37. That cost £5 and was one of the best seats. I still have the ticket stub, probably worth £20 now, judging by the prices realised by Christie's for football memorabilia.

I love going to Wembley and yes, I do know the way. If another Arsenal fan makes the same jokes, I'll thump him. George Graham will have to sit at the front of the Spurs coach as he's the only one who knows the way, ha ha. It is true that Spurs have not been there for eight years, but I have been twice in the past five years — with Carlisle United. The Auto Windscreen Thing. They won it in '97 and were runners up in '95. I still have my plastic sheep somewhere. I took it first time but got so exhausted blowing it up I couldn't be harished next time.

I always park near Finchley Road Tube station, then get the Tube to Wembley Park. I love walking up Olympic Way, observing the rival supporters in such good humour, so pleased with themselves. I love seeing the twin towers, then climbing all those brutal steps, round and round, in and out, till that first glimpse of the startlingly green grass leaps up, as if I behold a rainbow in the sky. As Wordsworth said. He wasn't a football fan, but he loved ice-skating. He considered himself a dab hand, though behind his back De Quincey said he was 'like a cow dancing a cotillion'.

I love the history of Wembley stadium. It was built for the

1924–25 Empire Exhibition, a miracle of the age, made of ferro-concrete. A whole battalion of soldiers were marched in and marked time in the stands to test it out.

The stadium was one of dozens of equally impressive buildings put up for the exhibition. All except the stadium were disposed of afterwards. The Palestine Pavilion became a laundry in Glasgow. The East Africa building was turned into a jam factory. Several cafes were taken away and re-erected as Bournemouth and Boscombe FC's grandstand.

The stadium itself will be going soon. I plan to make a bid for the towers, as they don't seem interested in preserving them. Not sure if they'll fit in my back garden.

I became so interested in the history of Wembley that for ten years I collected Wembley stuff, trays, teaspoons, postcards, stamps. As all philatelists know, the 1924–25 stamps were the UK's first commemorative stamps. Now they get issued on the hour. I sold my Wembley collection a year ago. Not quite sure how much I lost.

Going to Wembley, breathing in Wembley, thinking of past Wembleys, I love that. What I hate is sitting there. The seats are so uncomfortable, set so far back, you can't see a thing. I'll sob when the towers fall, but a new, modern Wembley is long overdue.

Naturally, I'll also cry if Spurs lose on Sunday. It's only Leicester. If we can't beat them, it's a poor do. Under George these days, we don't normally look as if we're going to get stuffed, which is the biggest improvement he has made.

Ian Walker is the most improved player, but then he had become so bad I feared Sol Campbell would walk off the pitch in disgust. Stephen Carr has got better, as has Sol himself. The defence as a whole is much more solid.

In the middle, Sherwood and Freund are good additions, though the arrival of Freund seems to have had a bad effect on Nielsen, whom I've always liked. He's got worse, if anything. So far, it's hard to see any improvement in the three strikers, Ferdinand, Armstrong and Iversen. None has hit a run of form. Ginola, kissy kissy, is the loveheart of all Spurs fans, and gloriously hated by all opposing fans. Deep down, I suspect George is not totally, absolutely, altogether convinced by him.

As for Anderton, George has done little there. I can see no improvement, no change or extension to his game. But at least he doesn't spend all week in the sick bay.

One thing to look out for on Sunday is the number of English players on show—Walker, Anderton, Campbell, Ferdinand, Armstrong, Edinburgh, Sherwood, Sinton and Luke Young. Carr is Irish, though he's been at Spurs since he was a boy. The foreigners are Ginola (French), Freund (German), Vega (Swiss), Iversen (Norwegian) and Taricco (Argentinian). Of the starting line-up, I expect at least seven to be English. That's a lot these days, when you think how teams like Chelsea are almost wholly foreign.

So what was the make-up of the team in 1901, before aeroplanes, the Bosman rule and millionaire mercenaries? The answer is— there were no London players in that Spurs team. Today, there are four—Campbell, Ferdinand, Edinburgh and Young, plus Sherwood, born in St Albans, and Walker, born in Watford.

I owe the fascinating fact about the 1901 team to a reader, John Baxendale of Sheffield. He tells me that Spurs that day consisted of five Scots, two Welshman, an Irishman and three Northerners. The final was held at Crystal Palace before a crowd of 110,802. Spurs drew 2–2 with Sheffield United. Spurs won the replay 3–1. Mr Baxendale is a Blades fan. That's why he knows. And that's why he's never forgiven Spurs.

HOW SOCCER'S NEW RICH
NEGLECTED A GRAND OLD MAN

2 APRIL 1999

TWO INTERESTING THINGS HAPPENED TO ME AT WEMBLEY which I'd like to share. It was Spurs' first time at Wembley for eight years, so when one of my Spurs friends suggested lunch beforehand, I said yeah, why not. We haven't had a lot of fun in recent years.

Normally on match days, I go on my own, since my son left home. I arrive as late as possible, sit on my own, swear and curse on my own, leave the very second the whistle blows, dash for chips, drive home, listening out for Carlisle's result, all on my own. Sad, really. My football following is a solitary pastime, but of course I am surrounded by 33,000 fellow communicants, plus several million in my head, whom I like to think are with me round the globe, not forgetting several billion in the past, who have been there before and whose spirits linger on.

Arriving at the Hilton Hotel beside Wembley Stadium at 12.30 I was clearly not going to be alone. Dozens of heavies in dark glasses and flash suits were keeping back the throng. Stretch limos about the length of our street were pulling up, letting out even flashier blokes in flashier suits. The Hilton had apparently been taken over by the Football Hospitality Industry. No one was being allowed in without a ticket. I didn't have one. Richard had mine. All I knew was that our lunch was to be in the International Suite, but I didn't know with whom. I failed to get in by saying I was meeting some-one inside. I then retreated, watched for another limo arriving, and walked in behind them, holding up an old envelope.

In the suite were about 100 people, all very overexcited, hugging each other, and that was just the men. I blame these foreign johnnies coming into football. Even the supporters have picked up these pansy ways. Bill Nicholson and Eddie Bailey would certainly not have stood for such emotional nonsense.

It is said that the middle classes are now flocking into football, but this gives the wrong impression. I do have an Arsenal friend who is a judge, and turns up wearing his red bobble hat on match days, but I never hear him shouting. The shouts and accents you hear, at both Arsenal and Spurs, are the new middle class-garage owners, financial traders, people with their own businesses who have done rather well. It's their children who have the traditional middle-class accents. They are cash-rich people, prepared to pay whatever it costs, or whatever ludicrous sum Ken Bates says a season ticket is going to cost, plus all the assorted executive fripperies.

We sat down at tables for a very good three-course tuck-in, with wines and goodies. Richard's wife and son, who is a chef, were there, plus two other families. Jolly nice people, and I enjoyed the chat — but the noise, my dear.

At one end or the room was a giant TV screen showing Aston Villa – Chelsea live. Then as the meal progressed, every table got louder and louder. My head was aching, with the noise, drink and food, and the match seemed to be receding. I began to wonder: where am I? All these years of enjoying football quietly on my own, I had forgotten about this enormous industry linked to every Big Club. At Man Utd, Newcastle, Chelsea, even West Ham, they do this all the time, marathon meals which cost a fortune and last for, hours. You end up feeling knackered — before the match even begins.

It was a relief to get out and be walking into Wembley Stadium. Then came the second interesting thing. As I walked up the concrete steps to turnstile G, I could hear the crowd ahead shouting someone's name. Not Gee-no-la, which I'd heard a million times already. "Billy Nicholson" they were shouting. Spurs' greatest ever manager, creator of the Double winning team.

By chance, I caught up with him — and introduced myself. I hadn't seen him for 25 years. He's 80 this year and was obviously struggling with the steps. On the step ahead was his daughter, holding his stick. He took my arm and together we got up to the top — where he announced he wanted to go to the lavatory. I said I would take him, as I go on the hour myself, and bring him back to his daughter.

I didn't know which daughter it was, as he has two, but I do remember him telling me, back in 1972, that he had cried at his daughter's wedding. When I'd asked him why, he'd replied, "Because I never saw her growing up". He said that was his other daughter, who now lives in the USA.

As we worked our way to the lavatory, I feared he would be knocked over by the crush, but once he was recognised, people stood back, wanted to shake his hand, take his photograph. It was remarkable how loved and admired he clearly is. Football fans don't forget. Tribal memories live on.

He did his best to smile and charm, though desperate for the lavatory. As a dour Yorkshireman, he was rarely seen showing any emotion, though I can see in my mind a tight-lipped smile as he stood in the Spurs dressing room, on his own, after a victory.

Bill gave his whole working life to Spurs, from the age of 16 as a ground staff boy on £2 a week, as a player, then manager. His name still appears in every Spurs programme. "Club president — W E Nicholson OBE."

So what was he doing struggling up to one of the cheap seats? Why wasn't he with the directors, or in the royal box at least, getting the sort of help and hospitality he deserved? "Oh, they forget things," he said, with a thin smile.

There was a third interesting thing that day. Spurs won. A dreary game, the details of which I've now forgotten.

YES, FOOTBALL FANS ARE NASTY.
BUT IT'S ALL IRONIC, INNIT?

26 APRIL 1999

THE OTHER WEEK I TUNED IN TO SOME TENNIS. CAN'T remember why. Probably I'd been searching for live football, anywhere, any level. Sad, I know. I did catch England schoolboys in a friendly against Turkey schoolboys and that was quite good, if you're desperate, suffering from deprivation. I even made notes, writing down likely names to look out for in the future, if I'm still here, if they ever grow up, so I can say, yeah, I remember him in nappies, always thought he'd do well. Turkey had this very small kid in midfield, ever so quick, ever so skilful, called Circec. Think that was his name. Can't read my writing now. More than sad. Pathetic.

Anyway, the tennis was Greg Rusedski against Jim Courier in the Davis Cup and it was really, really exciting. Britain had to win to move on to whatever the next thing is they have to win, so I shouted to my wife, come quick, this is really exciting, Greg looks like winning for Britain.

He's not British, she said, I'm not watching him. Yes he is, I said. He's become a citizen and anyway his Mam came from Pontefract or Batley or somewhere. Don't care, she said. He's still not proper British. Sometimes, I said, you sound more and more like your Dad. That silenced her. But she still didn't come and watch.

So I was there on my own, cheering on our lad. Apart from about 10,000 people watching in the flesh, in some aircraft hangar in Birmingham. Greg was all sweat and emotion, his heart on his sleeve, his feelings slopping about all over the shop, terribly un-British, or half un-British. He was rushing things, getting himself in a panic, and in the end he gave it all away. Courier was an automaton.

The most interesting thing of all was the crowd. They have

stayed in my mind ever since. They were so clean, well dressed, civilised, ever so polite, waving their sweet little Union Jacks as if they were at the last night of the Proms. A few equally cleanos were waving sweet little Stars and Stripes.

No one booed. That was what I couldn't get over. No one hissed, jeered, sang rude personal chants about Courier's sex life, drug life, mother's life, wife's life or personal habits. If, of course, he has any. Even at a vital moment, such as getting ready to serve, they stayed silent.

In their sweet little minds, the Brit fans were clearly willing him to make a mistake, yet no one went "Aaaaaahhhh, you're shit!" the way we do in football when the rival goalie is taking a goalkick. No voices tried to drown out or abuse the Yank fans when they did their bit of cheering and waving. As we do in football.

Now why is this? Why are we in football so horrible, while in tennis they are just so, well, nice?

Social class, that might have something to do with it. We football supporters are working class in our roots, apart from a few recent arrivals. That's how we were brung up at our sec mods and comps. We don't know any better. Tennis, like cricket, was always for poshos.

Tradition, that's another reason. We shout those chants, or similar, because our fathers did, or similar. "I'm forever blowing bubbles" has been sung at West Ham for about 70 years.

So we have been conditioned. We can't help how we react. Just like Julie Burchill or Germaine Greer can't help how they react. They rubbish sex or men because they have no sex or men in their lives. That's the environment in which they live. You have to feel sorry for them. They can't help their views, poor petals. Now where was I?

There is a blind prejudice in football, stupid loyalty to one's club, which hasn't got a counterpart in tennis. We love one team, ergo we hate the other. I don't think tennis fans identify with one player to the extent of actively hating the rivals.

Then there are the players themselves. That's a vital factor in explaining the crowd difference. In football, players on the pitch are nasty to each other, abuse each other, wind each other up. That's what you are expected to do. God knows why Le Saux and Fowler got punished for such normal, healthy, routine, manly behaviour. Fortunately Robbie only got a £30,000 fine, ie, about three minutes' wages.

It's also a physical contact sport, unlike tennis. You push, shove, kick, try to hurt, try to weaken. And you cheat, given half a chance, claim things you know are wrong, pretend injury, pretend fury, do sly, cruel things. It's little wonder that football crowds are nasty. They pick it up from the players.

Yes, we are pretty unpleasant people, vulgar in our chants, stunted in our emotions, violent in our hatreds. There is little help for us, oh Lord.

Except that complete beginners, arrivals from another planet, might not be able to interpret the anthems, understand the rhythms. It's a joke, most of it. Cheap irony and rough sarcasm.

Look at the faces as they chant the songs, waving their arms, stripping off their shirts on the coldest of days. It's a laugh, innit? When the other lot retaliate, that's even more fun. "You're not singing any more" or "It's all gone quiet over there" are desperate appeals, wanting the enemy to abuse us even more.

Most of all, it's an outlet, a safety valve. We get rid of our nastier, pettier emotions, just as the players do. You have to feel sorry for those tight-arsed, buttoned-up tennis fans, sitting there prissily, silently, when Greg got stuffed.

"Aaaaaahhhh, you're shit!" I shouted, all on my own, when bastard-face Courier won. And felt really good for the rest of the evening.

THIS COULD BE THE END OF CIVILISATION
AS WE KNOW IT

3 MAY 1999

THIS IS THE TIME OF THE YEAR THAT IS HEARTBREAK FOR some, the end of civilisation and Saturdays as they knew it, who have supported the Reds, Blues, Stripes, Pinks, Pansies through thin and thin, who stood on the terraces when they were knee-high to FC Grasshoppers, in the days when you could buy two full-backs for a fiver and still have change for a glass of Woodbine and a packet of Bovril.

I see these outpourings. Take in the first paragraph. Understand the pain. Recognise the agony. Then I turn the page, sharpish, thinking boring, boring. What does relegation to Notts Forest, Blackburn, Charlton or Southampton mean to me? Or Bristol City, Oxford or Crewe? Lincoln or Macclesfield? Bugger all.

I happen to be sitting here worrying about Carlisle United. Now that I've told you, do feel free to skip. I will understand. No hard feelings.

Being chucked out totally from the Football League, which has looked more than likely for most of the season, would be tragic for Carlisle. I take that back. Very sad. OK, let's get it in proportion. A pity. Cumbria, the second largest county in England, would then be without a league team. Workington dropped out in 1977. Barrow departed in 1972. All Michael Knighton's boasts and promises, wheeling and dealing, will have been in vain. That lovely new stand will be a mockery.

He has done a good job keeping the club solvent, when you think of all the clubs, much bigger, much more famous, that have ended bankrupt or near bankrupt. He was quoted recently in the *Cumberland News* as saying that it would be better to be demoted and solvent than stay up and be bankrupt. Discuss. Morally, intellectually, financially, you could chew the cud on that for ages, but emotionally, no fan will give it one second. Staying up, that's all that matters.

The other team, in an equally dodgy position at the bottom of Division Three, has been Scarborough. It's noticeable how often remote teams—ie, stuck in remote towns—tend to do badly. You might imagine that teams like Walsall, Bradford, Tranmere and Brentford, who are in the middle of big conurbations, surrounded by much bigger clubs, would have it harder than Carlisle or Scarborough. Yet if they show the slightest bit of success, they have it easier. They get the fans who can't get tickets for Man Utd, Liverpool or Chelsea, and they get the players who haven't quite made it with the local big teams, but don't want to move away from the area, or at least their wives don't. Carlisle, like Scarborough or Torquay, are always going to find it hard to tempt stars at the end of their career, or youngsters still hoping to make it. Carlisle has always employed players who refuse to live in Carlisle, commuting instead from Lancashire, Tyneside or Scotland. Which doesn't help dressing-room bonding.

Long-distance fans like, well, me and Melv, who mouth support for our hometown team, hardly help much, either. Don't you find, friends, that many of us have a Carlisle in the corner of our lives? How often, I wonder, has Alastair Campbell seen Burnley this season?

I've seen Carlisle four times. And got the programmes. But I've also got Spurs to support, while dear Melv follows Arsenal. I do have a friend, Charlie, who has also lived in London for many years, yet who manages to be a True Blue, resolutely refusing to acquire a London club. He travels to Carlisle matches as often as he can. His kids wear CUFC kit. Well done, Charlie.

We have had our Glory Days. If you blinked, you probably missed them in the First Division, but they were there for one season in 1974. I have the front page of the *Evening News*, on the day they went up, framed on my wall. It's growing a bit yellow at the edges. But then aren't we all. They even topped the league after three matches -beating Chelsea, Spurs and Middlesbrough. I've also seen them at Wembley twice in the past four years for the Auto Windscreen. Winning once.

So we've done good, for a small, remote club. Which leads me to think well, if you have winners, you have to have losers. Going up means going down. Must be far worse for Blackburn if they go down, after spending all those millions.

And what about poor old Scarborough or Hartlepool? They must have thousands of equally passionate supporters, who have followed the club all their lives. They will be just as upset, just as worried about what is likely to happen. Come on, Hunt, be fair.

It's also good that clubs like Cheltenham now have their chance to play in the football league. Good for football, not just Cheltenham. Be fair.

Cheltenham? From the affluent bloody deep South-west? I never knew they played football in Cheltenham. Isn't it all Georgian houses and horse racing down there? Why do they want a football club anyway? What do they think they're doing, taking away *our* football from *us*?

In fact it's not fair at all. Bloody Cheltenham poshos. Don't they know how much it means to a remote town like Carlisle?

As for Scarborough, they're johnny-come-latelies. They didn't get into the Football League until 1987. Absolute newcomers. What does it matter if they go down? Carlisle have been in the Football League since 1928.

So no, I'm not going to be fair and sensible. It will be a bloody disaster if Carlisle go down, the end of the civilisation, etc. So come on you blues.

WE HAVE UGLY PLAYERS, BUT WE DO
GET STYLISH FOREIGN ONES

10 MAY 1999

"YOU FOLLOW FOOTBALL, DON'T YOU" SAID MY YOUNGER daughter Flora, coming through the front door. Rhetorical question, as I have done so all her life, and longer, but I nodded sagely as I walked into the kitchen and opened the fridge. Then I thought "sage", it must come from the French for wise, not the plant, though perhaps there was once a connection. Sage is meant to have healing qualities, which wise persons were perhaps meant to know.

"Are you listening?" she said. "I've got a question about football for you." I had now opened the fridge and was getting her a drink, trying to disguise the shifty chardonnay that I bought on special offer in Safeway's last week before discovering it was medium chardonnay, yuk. Language and tastes have moved on so quickly in the wine world that medium now equals sweet.

"I'm not having that," she said. "You tried that on me last week. I'll have your good stuff, if you don't mind." She comes round here for supper every Sunday, the petal, and brightens up our lives. So what's the question?

"Why are British footballers so ugly?"

A few weeks ago she'd switched on the telly and found there were two live football matches on, plus some rugby. She gave all three a few minutes of her precious attention, before recoiling in horror at the sight of so many ugly blokes. Then by chance she switched to Channel 4 and got the Italian football. She watched that right to the end. Parma and somebody else, she thinks. No idea of the score. But the blokes, well, most of them, were surprisingly attractive.

"Compared with British players," she said. "So tell me, as you watch football non-stop, why are they all so ugly in Britain?"

I've never rated them that way. Though yesterday, watching Rio Ferdinand, I thought what a mistake, having all his hair off when he's got such a pinhead. Someone should have told him.

I then started whizzing through various teams in my mind. In the Arsenal defence there's Adams, Dixon, Winterburn, Bould, Keown. Hmm, none of them exactly male models. Alan Shearer, England captain, probably the kindest description of him would be plain. And Butt, Scholes, Sheringham: all at the back of the queue when looks were given out. Robbie Fowler, he'd probably run away with the Premiership's Mr Ugly prize. No, not many natural pin-ups come immediately to mind.

"Beckham!" I shouted. How could I have forgotten him?

"He's not a man," she said. I wonder if Posh knows this? "And he's got horrible, cheap hair," she continued. "You'd think as he can afford a Ferrari, he'd find a stylist and get himself a decent haircut. Ugh. Those nasty highlights. Looks as if he's been down Archway to some cheap barber's ..."

"Then what about Jamie Redknapp?" I said. "All the girls are said to love him."

"Not the ones I know. But Chris fancies him." Chris is a bloke, and gay.

"Ginola," I said. "You can't possibly say he's not attractive."

"I suppose he is, though I don't like his clothes. But he's not British, is he?"

She'd got me there.

It is interesting how foreigners generally tend to be more stylish, but I suppose you would expect that. We get the best, the intelligent ones, the ones keen and capable of settling in a foreign country, who make the most of being over here. Emmanuel Petit is currently moving to a house in Primrose Hill, showing excellent taste. Klinsmann, when he was over here, had a house off Hampstead High Street. Vialli lives in Eaton Square. If you are going to play for a London team, you might as well experience the best of London.

Homegrown players live in horrible mock-Tudor houses miles out in nowhere places.

Does it matter? Of course not. It might indicate a more interesting personality, but not a better player. Football doesn't work that way, not with managers. If your personality, clothes and lifestyle are thought interesting, you might get on better with your team-mates, but it would never influence a manager. Or would it? I poured myself another drink, of the rubbish stuff. Someone has to drink it. Not wasting it.

If you were an attractive, friendly, well adjusted bloke, it might be a consideration for a manager who's thinking of signing you. He wants someone who will fit in, be easy to deal with. But if he thinks Mr Ugly can do the business better than Mr Pretty, despite his bad breath, unfortunate habits, boring house and nasty clothes, Mr Ugly will always get picked.

Where being attractive matters is with the marketing men. The ones thought pretty, such as Beckham, make most money, though he does have a very good agent. They swooned over George Best, who had everything, looks and skill. Not many of those around in British football today. Gazza had skill. Shame about the looks.

I suppose Flora does have a point about Italian players. They always seem to look more stylish. In every sense. But so what? Didn't Man Utd stuff Juventus and Inter this season? And they'll be meeting Bayern Munich in the big final. It could be the Battle of the Uglies, who just happen at present to be the two best club sides in Europe.

"You haven't answered my question," she said, pouring herself another glass of the good stuff. "I asked why British footballers are so ugly."

"Dunno."

"Well, it's obvious. It's because British blokes are so ugly."

1999–2000 SEASON

*Beaten up at Wembley, generous in
Namibia, crying at Euro 2000*

TO BE A GOOD MANAGER, YOU MUST
BE ABLE TO THROW TEACUPS

13 SEPTEMBER 1999

"WHAT DO MANAGERS DO, DADDY?" THEY MANAGE, SON.
"Like grandad manages?" Yes, like that as well.

There are two meanings. In the executive sense, a manager is in
control. In the sense my father-in-law used it, he wasn't in control.
Whenever I asked him how he was, he would say, "managing",
which meant he didn't have control, but was somehow coping,
getting by, still with us, which he was till he was 96.

By the time you read this, we'll know how Kevin Keegan is managing. That game against Luxembourg was a joke, a country of 50
million playing a country of 50,000, Man Utd against a non-league
team. What could that possibly prove? Poland should show us how
Kevin is managing.

Bobby Robson, for the past eight days, has been the greatest, most
loved, most admired manager in the history of managing. He could
probably have remained so, but alas Newcastle have to play a game
on Saturday. Shame, really, just as he was doing so well. Harold

Macmillan used to say that running the country was a doddle, awfully easy, except for one thing. Events, dear boy, events.

In the case of a football manager, events mean injuries, loss of form, chairman going potty, all those events over which they have no control. Now there is a new thing over which they have no control. Their players.

Players are being carried away by their own importance, egged on by their agents, blinded by the thought of someone else getting £80,000 a week. They now make impossible demands, require ridiculous perks. Frank Clark, the former Nottingham Forest manager, tells a story of a star player wanting the club to re-lay his living-room with wood blocks as the fluff from the carpet was annoying him. Poor diddums.

Alex Ferguson and Gérard Houllier were going on about this problem last week, saying how tough it is, handling the modern player, people just don't understand. They each suggested that the media, the supporters and the players all 'need to show managers more respect'. More diddums.

So what do they do, what does it take to be a manager? Being a bastard, that seems to be a help, but a fair bastard, consistent, so all the players know where they are. Throwing teacups in the dressing-room, that seems to help as well. It did Fergie no harm.

There is no point in a manager trying to be personally popular. That's a sure sign of weakness. It rarely works in the real world, either. When I was a boss, of sorts, managing a little team of 20 people, I tried to be popular, keep them all happy—and failed. They all hated me. When I was chairman of the governors of our local primary school, I got that wrong as well. After our first meeting, I treated them to champagne, as a sort of bonding, so they would really, really like me and work awfully hard. One bloke, a Tory councillor, said he only wanted to be a governor for his CV when he stood for parliament. He wasn't coming to another meeting. He did become a Tory MP. Even got knighted. And I wasted my champagne on him.

The only way a football manager will be popular is by being successful. Then everything is forgotten. So how do you become successful? It pays to be able to identify people who can play football, that does help, but getting them to play well and consistently, that's harder. Some do need a good kicking, some a good cuddle, some are fragile flowers, some nutcases.

It takes cunning and cheap psychology to handle them. Fergie, in his autobiography, describes this process very well, learning how to pretend you are decisive when you're not, how to let them down lightly, when to give reasons for your actions.

One mistake managers make is to believe that if they put in the hours, success will come. Most do work too hard, rushing around the world to look at players, often unnecessarily. Videos these days give good clues to potential signings. You need a network of contacts whom you can trust to tell you the truth, about who's a boozer, a druggy, a lazy sod, hated by everyone, always late for training. But all that can be done on the phone.

When teams get stuffed, or perform appallingly, managers will often bring them in next day and make them do extra training. This rarely works, except as a punishment. During a long, hard season, extra training is not what they need. Talking it through with the senior players, and being honest about each other and the team's tactics gives a better chance of identifying problems.

But managers think that practice, practice, practice will do it. It does for individual players. David Beckham did not wake up one day able to make a perfect cross. Dwight Yorke wasn't born with the brilliant ball control he has today. It took them years of doing the same things, over and over, mostly on their own.

Getting a unit to function better is different. The problem and the solution are often abstract, and can't be prescribed beforehand or explained afterwards. So much depends on timing, chance, dynamics, events. Why did Dalglish do it at Blackburn and not Newcastle? Why has Graham Taylor done so well with Watford yet not with Wolves? Who knows? Except that the ones who survive can manage in both senses. They are in control when things are going well, as Fergie is today, and also able to cope, to manage somehow, keep alive, when things are not going so well. Which is what Fergie did in his first five years. He managed to manage.

BIG SLOW AND TALENTLESS?
YOU TOO COULD BE A FOOTBALL STAR
20 SEPTEMBER 1999

I SWITCHED ON EUROSPORT THE OTHER DAY, HOPING FOR sport of a footballing nature, anywhere on the globe, and saw a sight I have never seen before in a lifetime of seeing sights. Someone was playing in shades, well, playing while wearing some sort of sun specs. Quite remarkable, as David Coleman would have said, is probably still saying, somewhere or other.

It wasn't just any old footballer but a top player, Edgar Davids Juventus, a world star whom Man Utd supposedly failed to sign. He was playing for Holland against Belgium, neither of whom has to go through all this qualifying nonsense for Euro 2000 as they are there as joint hosts. But it was a proper game, nonetheless, very exciting, very competitive, and Davids scored a brilliant goal, weaving his way through the defence as if he had X-ray vision or second sight.

We then got a close-up afterwards and I could see that he was wearing rather trendy wrap around plastic shades, with a blue tint, but a bit heavier than the norm. What a poseur, I thought, copying those American sprinters, who wear shades as fashion accessories, to look superior, intimidating or just cool.

We've had every permutation of hairstyles in football, including perms — remember Kevin's and Bryan Robson's? I bet their children burst out laughing when they see those old pics. We've also had a variety of body jewellery, such as ear-rings and necklaces. As Edgar Davids is so well regarded, shades are now bound tb be the next thing for footballers with attitude. They are such copycats. What next? Strikers playing in baseball caps, worn back to front, goalkeepers in kilts with sporrans, wingers in sarongs as worn by Becks?

That's what I was thinking, when there was an even closer close-up of Davids. This time I could see his shades were more like goggles, a bit heavy to be fashion items. Then I thought, oh my God, I've been horrible to him, accusing him of posing when they're obviously for some medical condition. I hope he didn't hear me.

Later on I found out that Davids suffers from glaucoma, a pretty serious condition, and this is part of his treatment, so no more silly remarks, please. But that led me on to thinking about why football is so popular right around the world, among all sorts and conditions of people. And the reason is that all sorts and conditions of people play it.

Anyone can join in, have a go, regardless. You need very little equipment, but most of all, you don't have to fit a certain physical type, as in many other human activities. Sprinters, for example, all look the same, as do people running the 1,500 metres. With football, people with totally different body weights, heights, widths, ages and talents can still take part.

And we're not just talking about Sunday morning park football. Would anyone, for example, looking at Gazza in the buff, think wow, there goes a superb physical specimen, he must be a soccer star? No chance. Or gaze at, say, Pat Nevin and think, what a hunk. Of course not. Michael Owen is so titchy it's hard to think what other game he could have done as well at. As for Zola, he wouldn't get a game with anyone, at anything. You'd send him back, no ends of the litter today, please, chuck him out if you got him in a bag of new potatoes as being too small to eat. Or what about Niall Quinn? So tall and gawky, his mum must have thought no, we won't buy him some football boots, what's the point, we'll just use him as a clothes pole.

In any line-up of football teams, at Premier level or international level, I always love it when the camera goes down the line, seeing the vastly different heights, which usually catch the cameraman out, and he has to juggle it. I study all the different physiques, the different phizogs, the different expressions. I always think, my God, who would ever have chosen that lot to be star footballers, if it had been solely dependent on choosing ones who supposedly looked like star footballers?

It's not even a matter of having skill. That comes in all forms as well. You have no ball control, you're very slow but big, then no problem, you can be goalie. You are small, but with few skills, no problem either, we'll get you fit and teach you how to kick people and you could be full-back for Arsenal for, oh, the next decade.

Which brings us to actual disabilities, as opposed to lack of natural talents or physical gifts. Davids is now showing us that you can still be at the top while suffering from a worrying eye complaint. Gary Mabbutt showed us how to play while suffering from diabetes. Paul Scholes has asthma. So has Matt Jansen.

I started watching Scholes carefully, once I learnt that, as I had awful asthma most of my early life. He has his inhaler in the dressing-room and usually takes a puff before a match. You can see him not talking when he comes out, because you can't or shouldn't talk after the Ventolin, or whatever it is he uses, if you want it to get deep into the lungs. People with asthma, particularly young people, are embarrassed, want to pretend they don't have it. I think this explains why Scholes is one of the most silent, retiring players in the Man Utd dressing-room. At England level, Keegan says he can't get a word out of him, either. Poor lad.

So hurrah for Edgar Davids, showing not just all footballers but all of us the way to overcome the handicaps that either nature or other folk place upon us. Amen.

OOH-AAH CUMBRIAAH,
AS WE SAY IN LONDON

ONE OF MY FAVOURITE FOOTBALL MAGS IS 'HIT THE BAR', which I've been reading for 25 years. It comes out every six weeks and is usually 80 pages long. Three things about it would immediately strike any football fan reading it for the first time.

First, nowhere in its pages will you find a mention of Man Utd. Or Liverpool, Arsenal, Spurs, Chelsea, Rangers, Celtic or any big flash club. Second, the lack of bad language. I don't understand this, as it did used to have the odd 'fuck', lots of 'crap', quite a bit of 'bugger this', 'bloody that', the sort of stuff you expect in footer fanzines. Now you could let your maiden aunt or Ann Widdecombe read it.

Third, it's all devoted to one club—Carlisle United. *Hit the Bar* is the magazine of the London branch of the Carlisle United Supporters' Club. There are around 60 such supporters' clubs in London, still loyally following the fortunes of their home-town clubs. When I become depressed about the state of soccer (oh, I sometimes do, often for minutes on end) as I see the likes of Man Utd turning over £100 million a year or Chelsea's international glamour stars, each taking their pulling power for granted, I think of all the little clubs with no players anyone has ever heard of, which still manage to have devoted followers trekking the length and breadth of Britain to watch them play, get stuffed, then trail all the way home again.

Are they sad gits, losers or what? You can understand why each week coach-loads of Man Utd fans set off from Carlisle and Torquay, Hartlepool and Shrewsbury, not giving a bugger about their home-town club, wanting instead to share in the success and glory of someone else's team. Not much fun supporting Carlisle this season. Or last, despite the incredible escape.

The London supporters had their first meeting on 16 November 1974. CUFC were at that time in the First Division — blink and you missed them. They asked three Cumbrians to be honorary vice-presidents: Derek Batey, ex-Border TV, who used to be famous on television for *Mr and Mrs*; Melvyn Bragg-what happened to him? — and me. Our three names have appeared on the masthead all these years, although recently Melvyn has been replaced by Peter Beardsley, MBE.

I still have the honour, despite never having been to a club meeting, but last Saturday, I made it. I went to Brunton Park to see Carlisle play Brighton, a match sponsored by the London supporters. They paid £1,500 out of their hard-earned club funds, for which they got a pre-match finger buffet in the sponsors' lounge (yes, they do have one), good seats in the stand (well, there's not a rush for them these days), a full-page advert in the programme and a chance to pick and meet the man of the match. Man Utd and Chelsea get hundreds of thousands from match sponsors, mostly business firms, who can write it off as advertising, publicity or hospitality. CUFC London supporters did it out of pure love. Ahhh.

A total of 46 London-based supporters made the trip. As I looked around the sponsors' lounge, I tried to see a common denominator. Average age 37, with wives, partners and children. No sign of any sad gits. They all seemed to have good middle class, white collar jobs.

Malcolm Fawcett, who edits *Hit the Bar*, was there with his three children, one of whom was mascot for the day. He comes from Seascale, down the Cumbrian coast, and is an accountant, now working, for Conoco, the big American oil firm. In his current editorial he apologises for various bits missing in the mag, saying he had to chair a conference in Moscow, and then a girl spilled coffee over him on the Tube.

He was a founding member of the club. Editing the mag takes up a whole week of his spare time every six weeks. I wondered why, with his skills, he was not doing something more worthwhile, saving the planet, finding a cure for cancer, rather than helping a little football club. He has asked himself that. He thinks it does help. It gives exiles in London a focal point, sometimes finding them a job and a place to live.

In the 1980s the London supporters' club nearly packed up, when it was down to 36 members and could manage only three people at a committee meeting. Now it is thriving and hopes to reach the 400-member mark this season.

A quarter of them live in the London area, inside the M25, while the rest are elsewhere in the UK, plus abroad, in countries such as Fiji, the Philippines and Japan. They have several Internet sites and had a club tour of Germany this summer. It's a social thing as much as a football thing — people from Cumbria keeping in touch with each other when they've left home.

Their 25th anniversary committee meeting is on 17 November. It will take place at the House of Commons.

"The meeting follows and slightly overshadows the state opening of parliament," says the announcement in *Hit the Bar*. Present will be Carlisle's MP Eric Martlew and also, so they hope, the MPs Tony Banks, Joe Ashton and David Clark. Well done, lads, keep up the good work.

On the absence of swearing in the mag, I did ask him that. It was a deliberate change three years ago. Lads who met in the pub, 25 years ago, did rather let themselves go in print. Now in their middle years, with families, they want their children to support the Blues, as members of the Junior Blues, so the language has been cleaned up. And I should think so too.

BEATEN UP IN THE TOILETS AT
WEMBLEY — FOR BEING A FAN

I NOVEMBER 1999

I LANDED LUCKY, COMING BACK TO LONDON WHEN I DID.
At least I thought I was lucky, until something rather nasty
happened to me at Wembley.

The good luck first. I returned for the Manchester United home
game, what a victory. That was on Saturday — Spurs' first Saturday
home league game since 28 August and the last till 22 January 2000.
Tragic how Sky has ruined the social life of the nation, upsetting a
tradition of Saturdays established over a hundred years.

My half season ticket for Arsenal has also turned up some excellent fixtures. By half, I mean the one I share with a friend who is an
Arsenal supporter. He has two, but his son is away at college and he
didn't want to give it up, so I pay half and get it for certain months.
It's coincided this time with the two European Champions League
games in a row at Wembley.

It was strange going to Wembley for an Arsenal 'home' match.
Usually at Wembley, for things such as cup finals, the crowd is
equally divided and awfully well tempered, pleased with themselves
for having got there. I didn't see or hear any Barcelona fans at all. It
appeared to be 100 per cent Arsenal, as I suppose you might expect
for a midweek game.

Barcelona were brilliant, two ahead without hardly trying, so
fluent, so confident, so lithe, while Arsenal appeared lumpen.

Around me Arsenal fans were muttering, "That's it, Seaman's
finished, our defence is crap, it's finally going to fall apart, old
age has caught up with them". Seaman did look dodgy and very
nervous, right from the beginning, unable to direct the simplest
clearance. Tony Adams was falling over his own feet.

I went to the lavatory at half-time, hoping that Arsenal would be
better in the second half. I rarely do that at half-time as my Spurs

seat is in the middle of a row. I can't get out so I sit tight, legs crossed. The queues were enormous, about 300 blokes pushing and shoving to get into the lavs while at the same time 300 were trying to get out. This was in the North Stand, turnstile F. It's the same all over Wembley. I'll be sad when the old Wembley goes, and the twin towers are no more, but the facilities are archaic.

I got in OK, and was just coming out, my mind miles away, when this bloke aged about 30 grabbed me. He pushed me up against a wall and started punching me.

"Tottenham wanker!" he shouted. "I know who you are! You're a Spurs fan!"

Others took up the cry and started pushing me as well. The first bloke grabbed my hat, just a brown woolly thing, and pulled it down over my head so I couldn't see.

"That's how you want to watch the second half, you Tottenham cunt!"

It happened so suddenly, out of the blue. I couldn't think what to do or say. I got mugged once in Kingston, Jamaica, my own fault, getting lost, and it was some time before I realised a kid had pulled out a knife and was slashing at my shirt.

This time, I wasn't hurt. I was just pushed and banged, and eventually got free and returned to my seat, quite shaken.

I don't know how I was recognised. It's not as if I'm Melvyn Bragg, to whom I had been speaking, as he was in the row behind. I wasn't wearing, a Spurs scarf. Not that daft. Just my usual scruffy going-to-football clothes.

It is true that I have written various articles over the years about being a Spurs supporter — and also written about going to Arsenal matches. Rather stupidly, which I now bitterly regret, I did once say in passing that "I go to Highbury to see Arsenal get stuffed". It was inflammatory, I was being a big mouth, showing off, very silly. And it's not actually true. I don't go hoping to see Arsenal beaten, unless of course they are playing Spurs.

Football is what I love, ahead of any individual club, though for 39 years now, Spurs has been my first team. But I honestly go to a football match, any football match, to see good football players performing at their best. I take pleasure in watching Arsenal doing well, as long as it's not against Spurs. And that night I really did want them to do well against Barcelona.

It's a strange thing, football loyalties. Love for a team should simply mean love for a team. It doesn't work that way, not in football. You also have to hate, whichever is the other team one is supposed to hate. And when you haven't got a traditional hate team, then you make do with Manchester United.

I don't hate Man Utd either. But most fans do. You get otherwise sensible people, who help old animals across the road, are kind to dumb women, who always want Man Utd to get stuffed in Europe.

Few football supporters understand how anyone can regularly watch two rival teams. It is hard to explain. It defies decades of football logic and traditions. I didn't even bother to try, when confronted by those blokes at Wembley. For the Fiorentina game, I'll be going in disguise. If asked, I'll say I'm Melvyn Bragg.

THOSE FOOTBALL STATS ARE JUST
A DAFT AMERICAN IMPORT

22 NOVEMBER 1999

IN WEDNESDAY'S ENGLAND—SCOTLAND MATCH, THERE WERE 12 attempts at goal by players whose surnames ended in N, 45 throw-ins taken by players with aunties living near Troon, 112 headers by players wearing red, white and blue jockstraps, three strikers had a tattoo saying "Tracey" on their private parts, there was a total number on the pitch, including subs, of 3,456 ginger pubic hairs, possession was three parts of the Denis Law, and shots on Scholes came to 13. Cole was disallowed thrice and the Opta Carling Faffing Around Index indicated 3,214 on the Karl-Heinz Riedle scale.

I'm making all of this up, as it's Tuesday and the match hasn't taken place yet, but we're bound to have stuff like that, or similar. I have newspaper stats covering the whole living-room floor for last Saturday's Scotland—England game, giving ratings for everyone and every little thing, telling me the exact percentage of headers on target, off target, chances in the penalty area, total passes, total passes completed, shots on goal, blocked shots, goals-to-shots ratio — oh gawd, it gives me a headache just looking at them.

In ye olden days, when I was a lad, we were quite happy with saucepans instead of computer games, banging two tin-head Jerries together instead of Gameboy. We cut out photos of our heroes from the Pink 'Un and stuck them in old exercise books with paste made out of flour — oh, very environmentally sound.

We made our own fun, in them days, as Hoddle would say; made our own lists of how many goals our hero had scored, and we was happy, as Hoddle would also say. You got the league tables published once a week, and that was that. No need for anything else.

Now there's acres and acres of statistical analysis as newspapers compete to think up new ways of dissecting games and making them more meaningful. Or, in most cases, more meaningless. Why is this, you ask?

First, I blame the Americans. They have done this for decades with baseball and other kiddies' games, creating new sciences, new areas of study, with their own languages, all devoted to dopey records. It's a bit like economics. Basically common sense but if you tart it up with enough complications, new words and some fancy graphs, you feel awfully clever, awfully knowledgeable. And you've given yourself a job for life.

This passion for sporting stats has hit Britain in the past couple of years as football has exploded in mass popularity. Papers now have so much space for football, every day of the week, and are desperate to fill it, especially on days with no games, which are now pretty rare.

You'll notice that the broadsheets have most of these potty lists. The reason is that they're cheap. They can't pay Alan Shearer £2,000 for three minutes on the phone — for writing his own exlusive column — which the tabloids can easily afford. All the broadsheets can afford is £4.95 an hour, plus a canteen lunch, for some football-mad drip with a first in computer sciences from Cambridge to sit and create some statistics. Unless they can get this for nothing from a PhD student in theology from Durham doing work experience.

Computers have obviously had a big influence on football statistics. Shove in a mass of assorted information, twiddle them about, and you can easily pull out any variations you fancy.

Commercial influences, that's another reason. There really is a Carling Opta how's-your-father statistical service, which the London *Evening Standard* always seems to use.

It's like research. You have primary, secondary and tertiary sources. There is so much commercial, advertising and marketing money chasing football these days that all the primary sources have gone, been bought up, such as Dwight Yorke's left thigh, or David Beckham's right buttock. So you throw your money at secondary sources, such as sponsoring shirts or having your company's name on the lavatory at the Kop end.

If all this has gone, and you can't actually get close to anything to do with real football players or matches, then you are forced to sponsor facts about football. Fantasy football is a good example of tertiary involvement.

The middle class, that's another reason. We've always had anoraks, but with the arrival of the middle classes into football, we have a new and growing breed of young middle-class anoraks, most of them damn clever.

They have all the *Rothmans*, bought by Mummy and Daddy when they were little, all the computers and a lot of time on their hands as they don't want no boring professional-type career. They work for a pittance for a football fanzine, or one of the ever-growing football monthly mags, thinking up daft football stats, surveys, questions, lists—in order to amuse other daft lads, just like themselves.

The saving grace in Britain, unlike the States, is that we are already into a postmodern, ironic stage. A lot of the stats, especially those to be found on the Internet, are larky, rude, taking the piss. Something called Sporting Index was taking spread bets for the Scotland–England match on how many times David Seaman would touch his moustache or push back his floppy hair during the game. Brilliant, don't you think? You'd have to be really clever to work out the odds on that.

YOU'LL NEVER WIN ANYTHING
WEARING A HEADSCARF

WATCHING CHELSEA GET STUFFED BY SUNDERLAND LAST week I began thinking about body language. Chelsea were four down at half-time, so their body language was pretty clear and simple: help, help, help, get me out of this bloody mess. Poyet was frantically head-clutching. Vialli's lips were so tight they had disappeared. Zola's little head, bless him, was almost on the ground

In the case of Chelsea, we are mostly observing the body language of small bodies. Strange, isn't it, that they have so many titchy players? Oft when I'm watching them I think: who's been eating my porridge? When I'm really, really bored, I get out my record books and look up the heights of Wise, Ferrer, Zola, Deschamps and Morris, just to see who's the tiniest.

A small body doesn't necessarily mean you give off the language of a small body. Wise never does, nor does Batty of Leeds, nor in ye olden days did Johnny Giles or Billy Bremner. They were big inside, just packed into small outer cases. The problem of a big physique in football is that it does give off the wrong signs. The right signs, if you are Vinnie Jones or Tommy Smith, hoping to intimidate the opposition, but it does mean the ref has got your card marked.

If I were a manager, having signed a thug, complete with monster thighs, ten-day beard, piss-holes-in-the-snow eyes and Oscar winning scowls, I'd send him to charm school. I'd teach him to say "yes sir, no sir" to every referee, "how are you today, can I carry your whistle, how is the good wife, oh, did my elbow really do that, I'm awfully sorry". It's like being caught by a traffic cop. The first thing any sensible guilty person does is get out and apologise profusely, smile and look abject, your majesty, your highness. Yet what does your average football thug do? Argue back. You can clearly see them mouthing "fucking hell", then they lumber off, making stupid gestures, pointing to their head, indicating the ref is bonkers, which makes things worse. They lose, because their concentration is broken, and the ref will remember. Such body signs should be worked on in training to eradicate them.

Other body signs show depression rather than aggression, often very subtly, which only their coaches and managers can detect. They know by the stoop of a shoulder, the cut of the jib, the hunch of the back, whether a player has bottled it or not. Dwight Yorke, for example, slaps his thighs when he's having a poor game or feeling cheesed off.

As for the body language of managers, that can be harder to interpret. I am at present fascinated by Harry Redknapp's facial twitch. Even when nothing much is happening, and he's just standing silently, his face is twitching like a camshaft, whatever that is, his jaw and eyes darting all over the place. I can't tell if he's wondering whether to have another piece of chewing gum, bring on Joe Cole or if he's having a heart attack. Gazza used to have a similar nervous twitch, though in his case his whole head would jerk wildly from the neck. It's faded with age. As have his talents. Perhaps such twitches are a reassuring sign. Proves they are alive.

I should mock. My wife maintains that my mouth always moves when I read, which I'm not aware of, though I do sometimes have to cope with some awfully long words since these players from Iceland arrived. When walking, I'm constantly humming, so she says. A really tuneless hum, so she says. Then I have acquired a leg twitch, when lolling on my sofa of an evening, stretched out with my drinky-poo. She shouts at me to stop my feet moving. So I do have sympathy with Redknapp. I can at least do my twitching in private.

Clothes are a form of body language. What you choose to wear reveals the person you are, or would like to appear. It happens even in football, despite the uniform strips. Cantona put his collar up, a style copied by Yorke, as a way of saying I am original, I am special, I am an artiste.

Consider the return of gloves in football, now that the bad weather is here. Traditionally players from warmer climates used to wear them, from Africa or the Caribbean, though that did not apply when they were second or third generation, brought up here. Desailly was wearing them in that Sunderland game, and so was Babayaro. And a lot of good it did them. What was strange in the Leeds against Spartak Moscow game, the one in Bulgaria, was seeing players on both sides wearing gloves. You'd have thought Moscow players would be well used to the cold. And Leeds players. If this catches on, some smart sponsor or marketing whizz will be selling advertising space on gloves.

The most worrying sign in that game was Darren Huckerby. He's a talented, quick player, liable to break down the toughest defence with a bit of magic, or run straight into the billboards as he hasn't looked up. There's definitely a problem there, and I think what he wore in that game gave it away. He was wearing a headscarf. Honestly. Check your video. A sort of broad, woollen headscarf over the front of his head, like what my mum, and everyone's mum, used to wear during the war. Presumably he was wearing it to keep his ears warm, the petal. But it was an item of bodily language which I'm sure gives a clue to his real self. Huckerby is a big girl's blouse.

THE TELEVISION COMPANIES ARE
JUST RIPPING OFF THE FANS

20 DECEMBER 1999 – 3 JANUARY 2000

I WAS LOOKING FORWARD TO THE THREE EURO MATCHES, all on roughly at the same time, involving Arsenal, Newcastle and Leeds, wondering which Sky would choose. I wanted them all to win, but had no real favourite. I like Bobby Robson and David O'Leary, as human beings, and as managers, so I wanted them to do well. I go to Arsenal and know their team well, but they were easily ahead on the first leg, so their game didn't sound so exciting. Any road up, hurrah for a bit of live football, around which to organise my evening, my work, my life.

So was I spitting when I turned on Sky and found that Sky Sports 1, 2 and 3 had no live football. What a swizz. After all the money I pay Cable London. I got out my last bill and it clearly says: "All Sky Sports — £27.99." I rang cable and screamed at a poor bloke with a nice Scottish voice sitting in some electronic battery farm, probably in the Hebrides. He said: "Ah yes, but we don't provide Sky Extra." I said surely "All Sky Sports" must include Sky Extra? "No sir, they don't let us have it." I slammed the phone down and rang Sky. Screamed at them as well. Then I rang ONdigital, whom I hate for its poncey capital letters. It's currently offering a digital box free, but no, they didn't have any of the three Euro matches either. Oh Gawd. I hate them all. Hate, hate, hate. Each call took for ever, listening to idiot messages and music.

I will break soon, I really will. I can only take so much of being manipulated, being treated like a halfwit. They have no real interest in football. What happens is that some potty channel or TV company you've never heard of pays a fortune for the rights to certain matches, purely in order to make you subscribe to their stupid service or buy their horrible dishes or hideous boxes. You're then landed with a year's sub for loads of shite programmes you're never going to watch. Then when the next big match comes round, they haven't got it. Some other chancer has nicked it.

I rang our two nearest pubs. One didn't have it, but at the other a barman said yes, they did have football on, it looked like the Arsenal game, just started. I grabbed my coat and ran like hell. It was the Dartmouth Arms, just one street away, but I have been in it only once in 36 years. The last time was ten years ago, when I went to watch Wally Fawkes play his clarinet with his trio. Could be playing in heaven now. But not Wally. He's going strong, cartooning away — as Trog — for the *Sunday Telegraph*. I often see him in our street with his shopping.

The pub has changed since 1989. Gone all modern — ie, all old fashioned. None of that plastic nonsense or jukeboxes or blokes with beer bellies standing at the bar. It's thirty-something women smoking and laughing at the bar, battered leather couches, shelves full of books, nice fire, wood-panel walls, veggie dishes, amusing Italian bread. The TV was a small one, high on a shelf. I ordered a cappuccino and a whisky and got a seat in front of the TV. After ten minutes, my neck was killing me with looking up. I moved back a bit. Which made it hard to watch. Close ups I could see. But not the rest.

The bar was only half full, and most people were ignoring the TV. When Arsenal got a goal, no one cheered. Strange, as Arsenal is geographically the nearest club. A young bloke in front of me on the couch with his girlfriend made a face at the TV. The girl was practically on top of him, but I could tell he was trying to watch the football. I like a chap with the right priorities. Arsenal got a second goal, by which time the girl was almost down his throat, but he turned round towards me and groaned. "Fucking Arsenal."

I looked around. Nobody else seemed to be watching. A couple of girls at the bar had glanced at it from time to time, but they were mainly talking and laughing. At half-time, I asked the barman if perhaps he could change it to Leeds or Newcastle, to see how they were getting on. There were obviously no Arsenal fans present.

"She is," he said, nodding towards one of the girls at the bar.

"No, she's not," I said. "She's been standing gassing. Anyway, she's just one girl, what does she matter?"

"It's not just one girl," he said. "She's the boss ..."

Oops. Sorry I spoke. So that was that. I finished my drink and went home. My neck is still stiff and my eyes sore from straining, and I'm livid about the state of football on television.

It's chaos at the moment, and it's changing all the time, with different deals, different languages, so complicated and confusing. There should be some sort of tracker system, the way they do with unit trusts or shares. I'd pay a fee to someone to move my subscription around, find the best deal with the most games, without me having to bother about keeping up with all the latest scams, weaselly words and tricksy offers.

If our football authorities had any sense, instead of being blinded by short-sighted greed, they would not have allowed any of this to happen. There should be one dedicated sports channel, showing only football, and it should be owned by football—by the FA, the Premier League and the clubs together. They would run it, control it, take all the profits. They already make a fortune from TV, but don't tell me that Sky and cable and ONdigital and the rest of them are not making even bigger profits, purely on the back of football. Otherwise why are they doing it?

Once again, we fans have been caught in the middle. But I suppose we deserve to get conned. We're all stupid, when it comes to football.

ALASTAIR CAMPBELL SAT NEARBY,
SO I EAVESDROPPED

6 MARCH 2000

I WAS A GUEST AT WIMBLEDON LAST WEEK, FOR THEIR match against Man Utd, going there with my dear friend Joe Kinnear. It was almost a year to the day since Joe, while manager of Wimbledon, had a heart attack before their match with Sheffield Wednesday. It happened to him in the tunnel, and the medical people were able to get to him in seconds. He's now fit and well, fully recovered, raring to return to football management.

He must be potty. Imagine wanting to go back to that mad way of life. But, at 53, he feels he's got ten good years still in him and is dead keen to manage another club. That day, before he left his house, there were 30 calls on his answer phone, offering him assorted jobs, opportunities, engagements. About half were from Deep Throats, saying they were intermediaries for X, Y and Z clubs. Football these days is full of money and chancers.

The day was also a big day for Wimbledon. Not just the visit of Man Utd — which is always a sell-out — but also the end of Wimbledon life as we have known it for the past 23 years. Sam Hammam, who dragged the club up from the Fourth Division to the Premier League, something it's impossible to imagine ever happening again — had decided to sell his remaining shares. We got there at one o'clock, just in time for lunch in the boardroom. What a tuck-in we had: best wines, best food. Well, I tucked in. I am certainly not on a diet or watching my weight, which Joe now is.

While there, I was ticked off by a Wimbledon director for not wearing a tie. I don't wear a tie, or a suit, but I thought I had made an effort, wearing my smart new black cardigan. I had noticed that my Directors' Box ticket said "No jeans or trainers". They have standards, these football folks.

But they were awfully hospitable and friendly, which is often the way at the smaller clubs. I talked to Sir Roland Smith, chairman of Man Utd plc, and he said that, yes, Wimbledon was one of the friendliest. "I don't know about the food, though. Bobby Charlton keeps a list of the Premier League's best food and wines."

I think I'll be a football director when I grow up. I could have been a director of Carlisle United — well anybody could really: all it takes is a few washers, but I think I'll stick to the Premier League. It gives such social status, being a Premier director, such popularity among all classes, all ages. Sam is going to miss it.

Fergie came up into the boardroom, just before kick-off, and sat deep in whispered conversation with another guest — Alastair Campbell, spokesman for the political classes.

I thought you were a Burnley fan, I said to him, after Fergie had gone. He is, and showed me his Burnley, scarf, but one of his sons is a mad-keen Man Utd fan. I asked what he was talking so intimately about with his old friend Fergie. He wouldn't tell me, the rotter.

I sat with Joe during the game, which was most illuminating, although it was a bit annoying having Alastair Campbell in front of me, constantly on his mobile or his pager. Hmm, must be ringing Tony, I thought, or making anonymous, menacing calls to Ken Livingstone. It turned out that he was ringing someone in the crowd at Burnley's game who was supposed to be ringing him with the latest score but hadn't got through.

Wimbledon's team is basically still Joe's team, the team he created. He pointed out that Carl Cort was playing out of position, not as a central striker, more of a wing back. Joe also pointed out when free kicks and set pieces went wrong and what should have happened. I would always like to watch games with an expert such as Joe, so I hope he doesn't get a job too quickly and I can go with him again.

Egil Olsen, the new manager, has introduced zonal marking at the back. Joe always preferred man-to-man marking. "OK, if you have world-class players, clever and skilful, then zonal marking is fine. Otherwise, it's better to stick man to man. You give each one their instructions, so they know exactly what they are supposed to do." And if they don't do it, you stand on the touchline and give them a bollocking. As Joe did, sometimes for 90 minutes. I don't think I've ever seen such an involved manager. After every game, it took him two days to get his voice back.

After the game, I got a lift home with Alastair, because he lives near me. I asked him again what plots he and Fergie were hatching. Fergie is a known socialist and Blair supporter, which may not always endear him to the more right-wing Man Utd directors. But he still wouldn't reveal anything.

But he did tell me about the time he went to Carlisle as a teenager, on a supporters' coach from Burnley. In the excitement of Burnley scoring a goal, he lost a shoe. It just came-off, fell under the crowd, probably rolled down the terraces. At the end, he waited till the crowds had cleared, but couldn't find it. By which time the supporters' coaches had left for Burnley. Alastair was forced to hitch-hike all the way home, wearing only one shoe. Bless.

I promised that the next time I'm at Brunton Park I'll have a look for it. Michael Knighton, the Carlisle manager, must have found it by now. He did have an idea for a football museum in the stadium, so it could be an interesting exhibit. Early Example of Spin-Doctor's Shoe, as used for Kicking People. Unless he's sold it. CUFC does need all the pennies it can raise.

I WAS A USELESS LEADER,
AND FERGIE WILL BE A USELESS MAYOR

20 MARCH 2000

WHAT DOES A CAPTAIN DO? IF HE'S A STRIKER OR FORWARD player, norralot. A striker is selfish, temperamentally more concerned about his own game than anyone else's. He has one basic function, which is finishing — quite an important function. OK, *the* important function, which is why strikers are so expensive and so well paid. He plays up field and can be out of the game for long stretches, cut off from the rest of his team. Hence it always strikes me as potty when they make a striker the captain.

I think Alan Shearer has been a pretty useless England captain. So was Kevin Keegan, ditto Gary Lineker. In their case, the job was ceremonial, a reward for being the star or senior player, admired by all — like the way a headmaster makes the most boring, most sensible sixth-former the head boy.

Ideally, a football captain should be a defender or midfield player — either involved in all the action or watching all the action happening in front of him. And he needs the right personality and the right sort of football brain, both of which, though not always, come with experience.

Tony Adams is clearly the best bet for England captain when Shearer hands in his armband in the summer. He is a leader on the pitch, a screamer and shouter, director and motivator, excellent at urging them on. If, that is, he's fit. That's the only doubt hanging over Adams.

Sol Campbell is not ready for it yet. He has matured over the past couple of years and become more of a leader, but he is still too quiet, too reserved, not nearly dominant enough. On the other hand, I can't quite remember Bobby Moore giving people bollockings. He led by example rather than by his personality. Gareth Southgate leads well, and has a good football brain, but he's not sure of his England place — which is a bit of a handicap.

Dave Mackay was the best captain I ever saw. The modern version is Roy Keane, the best of today's captains. He is the heart of the Man Utd team, without whom they never tick as well. You don't have to be the best player to be captain, but it does help.

When Alan Mullery was captain of Spurs, he was not all that popular with the rest of the team, nor particularly admired as a player, but everyone agreed he made an excellent captain. Martin Peters, when he took over, was greatly liked, hugely admired as a player, but as captain he was rubbish. Completely the wrong personality.

Oh, isn't it fun making these huge generalisations, but then that's the point of being a football fan. No qualifications needed. Just open your mouth and away you go.

Could *you* be captain? Could I do it? I never thought I was cut out to be a leader of men, though I was a patrol leader in the Boy Scouts. Hawk Patrol, 17th Carlisle Church of Scotland Troop. Now you remember. I was never a prefect at school, partly because I changed schools so often, but when I got to Durham I was, to my surprise, voted Senior Man of my college, which was what we called the president of our junior common room. I rather liked that. You got a better set of rooms and a sherry allowance.

My next incarnation as a leader of men was as a leader of women. I was, for a time, editor of the women's pages on *The Sunday Times* — the best fun I ever had in journalism, and the longest lunches. Just a small team, hand-picked, no factions, no arguments, we all got on well. I liked it, they liked me. Later, I was made editor of the colour magazine — a much bigger job, with more people, more departments, terrible problems, awful arguments. I was useless. They didn't like me. And I disliked being unpopular, which is a terrible weakness. So that was my life as a leader. One thing I didn't like was having to listen to people's boring moans and groans about their expenses, their status, the size of their bylines, the size of their desks, and having to keep a serious face when I didn't give a toss.

Leading on the pitch isn't quite the same as leading in real life, but a club captain or national captain does have certain off-the-field functions to perform. He becomes a quasi union rep, going to see the management on behalf of the players, involved in decisions about the team's perks, which can be pretty tedious.

Do good captains make good managers? Bobby Moore didn't, but Kevin Keegan did, well he's still employed as one. George Graham was never a captain, and as a player was far from a model professional, on or off the pitch. I never saw Alex Ferguson play, but from his autobiography he appears to have been a bit of a loner, and was virtually elbowed out of Rangers. George and Alex, with age and experience, have turned themselves into leaders of men.

One of the dangers of having proven man-management skills in one particular area is to assume that it can be transferred. Fergie would be a useless Mayor of Manchester, which is now being proposed, and would be bored rigid by the job. So don't do it, Fergie. And don't do it, Manchester. Stick to football.

I CONQUERED AFRICA,
WITH MY MAN UTD WRISTBANDS

17 APRIL 2000

FILL IN THE GAP IN THE FOLLOWING WELL-KNOWN CHANT, "******* is the greatest team the world has ever seen." It's a strange chant, which you can hear being sung by the supporters of each of our 92 league clubs. Strange, because it doesn't rhyme and, for at least 99 per cent of our teams, it isn't remotely true; yet, I've heard fans from Carlisle to Colchester lustily belting it out as if they truly, sincerely, madly believe it.

It's a tribal chant, traditional grunting, received posturing, which nobody takes literally, and nobody stops to think about the words. A bit like, "We hate Nottingham Forest, we hate [etc]". Now that is totally meaningless. I mean, who could muster the energy to hate Notts Forest? One of the most boring teams the world has ever seen. There is, however, one team that can make a claim to being the greatest the world has ever seen: Manchester United.

Bugger it. In an instant, I've lost 80 percent of any possible readers. From Carlisle to Colchester, via Chelsea and Charlton, just the mention of Man U makes your average Brit fan not just switch off, but scream and shout: "Oh, not them again. The telly loves them; the papers love them; advertisers love them; even the refs love them. Give us a break."

They are not the world's greatest team. How can they be, when we can't even agree on the terms? Do you measure a club's greatness by the size of its crowds? In that case, Barcelona is miles ahead. Do you measure it in transfer fees, in who can pay most for a star player? In that case, there are about six clubs, in Italy and Spain, that have paid more. Man Utd, the club, is the richest on paper, now worth a billion pounds; but given that so much of its income is generated by merchandising, this is an unfair comparison. A club like Barcelona does not stoop to such vulgar, moneymaking methods, being too proud to sell its soul or shirts to sponsors.

Man U's best claim to world greatness rests mainly on armchair followers. Hard to compute how many there might be, but it's usually assumed that Man Utd has around six million fans in the UK, most of whom will never see the tearn in the flesh. They can't get tickets. Around the world, the estimate is 20 million fans, who can only ever follow them from afar.

In the past three weeks, I met two of these far-flung fans. First, there was Andy in Botswana. I was there visiting our daughter Caitlin who is married to Ron, and they've just had a baby called Ruby. (Since my return, I've met two babies called Ruby. Is it something in the air? Do mothers of a certain age, certain type, even 10,000 miles apart, get brainwashed into thinking they have chosen a totally original, unusual name?)

Last Year, Caitlin happened to mention that the mechanic who services her car was a Man Utd fan. I sent her a signed photo of Dwight Yorke, whom Caitlin had never heard of, but she reported that Andy was now the most envied mechanic in Maun.

So when we set off for this trip, instead of taking beads for the natives, as we did in the old colonial days, I took some Man Utd sweatbands — you know, those things in your club colours that you put on your wrists. I was coming out of my dentist's in Archway and was passing a charity shop when I saw them in the window. A bargain at only 30p each. I bought the entire stock. Just the thing for any poor people I might meet in Africa, having had a baby up a tree, or homeless after the floods. Bound to cheer them up.

And it was true, more or less. Andy was knocked out, made up, over the moon when I gave him a Man Utd wristband. He would have serviced my car free for life, or longer, if only I'd had my car with me. He was aged about 40 and had fallen in love with Man Utd as a boy, at a time when they were not doing very well. He knew the name and life story of every player who had ever turned out for the club in the past 20 years. Botswana is an ex-Brit colonial-type country, once called Bechuanaland, even though it didn't have white settlers, so you might expect some residual relationships with Britain. But we then moved on to Namibia, a country with no British connections, formerly a German colony.

We went on safari on the edge of the Namib Desert where our guide up a sand dune was Isiah, a Namibian aged about 30. He grew up speaking his own tribal language, plus Afrikaans, then had to learn English ten years ago, when Namibia went independent. He was a Man Utd fan as well. In a Wilderness Safari camp, stuck out in the back of beyond, the staff are isolated for three months at a time, with no radio, TV or newspapers. Following football, or showing your allegiance, is therefore rather limited.

But last year, while at home in Windhoek, Isiah did watch the Euro final, shouting all the way through for Man Utd. Sitting beside him was his younger brother — shouting for Bayern Munich. I presumed that this was due to the German connection, from their country's colonial past. But no, said Isiah, his brother's team is in fact Leeds Utd, and his favourite player is Lucas Radebe. Now that was interesting. It showed that the Man Utd syndrome we have noted in England — whereby every football fan who doesn't support Man Utd hates them — has spread round the world. There was a Namibian, who happened to be a Leeds supporter, reacting like any good Leeds supporter anywhere round the world: wanting Man Utd to get stuffed.

I gave Isiah two sweatbands, one for each wrist, just to annoy his brother next time he is home on leave.

MAIL OR INDY? MAN UTD OR CARLISLE? LIFE IS FULL OF CHOICES!

8 MAY 2000

IMAGINE A BOY CALLED DARREN. HE IS A BRILLIANT 16-year-old footballer. He's still at school, but now has no interest in school work, although he could have done well, almost as well as his older brother and sister. He's played for his home town, Carlisle; his county, Cumbria; North of England schoolboys; and has also been capped once by the national under-18s, despite being only 16.

Scouts have been hovering at his back door since he was in nappies. One recently climbed through the lavatory window. Or he might have been an agent. He's still in hospital, unable to speak. But Darren's pet Rottweiler is recovering well.

One club, which can't be named because we are talking readies, has promised his dad, who is a cracker packer at Carr's, £5,000 plus a car of his choice. Another club has promised Darren's mum a new semi. She quite fancies moving to Stanwix, Carlisle's most desirable suburb, as Raffles is now a bit rough, not to say a no-go area. Most of their neighbours have been boarded up — the occupants, as well as the windows. A third club has offered his dad a new woman of his choice, or a season ticket for Man Utd/Chelsea/Newcastle — all of which are harder to get and more expensive than a new woman.

Darren is determined, hard-working, well adjusted, but a bit small and light for his age. All the clubs have done their homework. They know the weight and height of his dad at this age, and now look at him — enormous (and it's not just because of the crackers). With professional training and a strict diet, they know that, at 19, Darren will be six foot tall and will weigh 11 and a half stone. Same as Becks. Man Utd has now made a definite offer. The *Cumberland News* led with the story. Four years ago, Darren said that he wanted to play for Carlisle United, but who could have known then that he would keep on developing. Manchester City, currently of the First, but bound for the Premier, has also made an offer, lining up just as many treats as Man Utd. They are promising a first-team chance within a year. Carlisle United would put him straight in the first team, and probably make him captain, manager and give him all the shares, if only he'd sign.

What does Darren do? Which club does he sign for? He's not really interested in the money, although he knows that the average Premier League player now gets £409,000 a year, a First Division player gets £109,000, while at Carlisle, if they manage to stay in the Third Division (which is still in doubt), he would be lucky to get £37,000 a year.

While Darren decides, let's pop over to Durham, where his big brother Steve is a leading student activist. He fancies a political career, but doesn't care which party. If he goes Tory, he could be on the back benches, out of government for decades. If he goes Labour, he'll be in government; but with so many other MPs, many of them from Oxbridge, how will he shine? Go Lib-Dem and he could be a front-bench spokesman in four years, if he works on his rural accent.

Meanwhile, at Oxford, Darren's big sister Zoe has just won the young student journalist of the year award. Both the *Daily Mail* and the *Independent* have offered her work. The *Mail* money is mega, plus huge expenses, a picture byline, foreign trips and lots of fun stories. She's a bit worried by 'fun stories', suspecting that they mean girlie or human-interest stories. The *Indy* is offering a quarter of the money, no expenses, though possibly her Tube fare now and again. It promises her 'off-the-wall' stories. She suspects that they will turn out to be girlie and/or human-interest stories. She knows that the *Indy* won't worry about bad language. 'Fuck' will be fine, if the story calls for it. Even if it doesn't. The *Mail* has made it clear that she might get away with 'damn', at a pinch. Otherwise it's '*****'.

A friend has told her that the *Mail* has 93 bright young things, all earning a fortune. A shame that most of them haven't had a piece in the paper for seven weeks. On the *Indy*, she's told, anything you write gets in, because they are so short-staffed. By joining the *Mail*, she'll have a deposit for a flat in a year—on the other hand, her name might well be meaningless to anyone, even back in Carlisle. On the *Indy*, her name is bound to have been seen and registered by every editor in Fleet Street, wherever that is, even though she's still sleeping on her friend's sofa in Kentish Town. What does she do?

Back to Darren, who gets Matt Jansen on his mobile. Matt, also from Carlisle, turned down Man Utd when they came along. He decided he wouldn't make the first team for years, if at all. Instead, silly sod, he went to Crystal Palace—what a mistake, a club in chaos. Then he went to Blackburn—another mistake, another rubbish team, going down. The moral seems to be: you just can't tell how life, football, the universe, will work out.

So what did they all do? Steve graduated with a 2:2 in History and is now doing a law course. He has worked out that, as a barrister, he could be on £400,000 for 20 years as opposed to ten as a footballer and bugger all as a politician.

Zoe joined the *Mail*. The thought of the sofa must have put her off the *Indy*, especially as her rasta boyfriend is six-foot-four. She also found out that the *Indy* would take her later, even if she got nothing in the *Mail*, just because she'd worked on the *Mail*.

And Darren? He's joining Spurs. The money's very good, his Dad won't get his legover, but the car's quite nice, plus there's a free Amstrad. Darren knows that he's bound to shine in such a middling rubbish team sadly lacking in decent young players.

WHAT WE NEED IS GERIATRICS
AS BALL BOYS AND NO OFFSIDE

22 MAY 2000

FIFA HAS AGREED THAT A CHANGE IN THE RULES ABOUT free kicks can be tried next season, just to see how it works. It will give the referee the power to move a free kick ten yards further forward, should the defensive wall be mucking around, encroaching, delaying, generally playing silly buggers, which they have always done, since the year dot com.

I'm not quite sure how many times the ref will be able to move the kick forward, if an offence keeps on being repeated. It could happen that one side is moved right off the pitch, into the stadium, back into the dressing room, out into the car park, into the coach, up the High Road, on to the motorway and home. It would be a good way for players to avoid all the post-match traffic and make it to the pub or the club before anyone else. It is well overdue. Buggering around at free kicks deserves to be penalised; it is so petty and annoying. FIFA has seen it working well in rugby. Worth a try.

I think the sin-bin idea is also worth borrowing from rugby. This is when someone committing an offence is sent to sit on the bench for ten minutes. I like watching their faces. Some look pensive, some pissed off, dejected or resigned, head in hands, hands in face. It certainly cools them down.

A red card could still be issued for something really nasty, and the player would be immediately off for good, but ten minutes in the sin bin could be used instead of a yellow. Very often, a red card is the result of two very piddling yellow-card offences, neither brutal, such as swearing or kicking the ball away. The sin bin would be sufficient punishment for such offences and not cumulative.

Not arguing with the referee, that's something else that could be imported from rugby. It's remarkable how obedient they are in rugby — union or league. It could be something to do with all the money now at stake in football, although I suspect it's more historic. Traditionally, rugby players did not go in for all that celebrating — which today means cuddling, kissing, punching the air, nor did they go mad and emotional when things went wrong. Public school chaps did not do that sort of thing, unlike those unwashed working-class soccer players, unable to control themselves.

What else? I would still like FIFA to contemplate reducing the number of players on the pitch from eleven to nine. Now that all players are so much faster and fitter, pressing and harrying for 90 minutes, many games become totally congested in the middle of the pitch, with no space or time to build up moves.

I would also like to see the abolition of the offside rule. This is the most controversial law in football, which always leads to arguments. It has been in existence since 1867, so purists will say that it must be retained, but it has been altered over the years. Early on, it required three of the defending team between the attacker and the goal to play him onside. Then, in 1925, it became two defenders. Now one dozy defender can play an attacker onside. I think I've got that right. I can understand its spatially, when it happens, or doesn't happen, but it's hellish to put into words. I've just looked it up, rule 11 of the 17 laws of the game, and trying to work it out has given me such a rotten headache. The Campaign for Plain English should have a go at rewriting it. What is the point of it? I presume it was to stop goal poachers — players just hanging around in the opposition's goal mouth, the way we used to do in playground football.

Defenders would have to rethink their tactics totally if there were no offside rule. The effects might be negative, with certain defenders made to stay rigidly at the back, never allowed to go forward, in order to guard against goal hangers. On the other hand, it could lead to more exciting, more open, more positive play, stopping the *coitus interruptus* that occurs when a brilliant move, resulting in an excellent goal, is then deemed to be offside.

I would like to see referees given proper watches. At the

moment, they are all working on watches that add on more time at the end of the second half than at the end of the first. Oh yes they do. I've been keeping count. A second half can go on for five extra minutes, for no apparent reason, whereas the first half usually ends on time. Why is this? Is Sky to blame, wanting the half-time ads to start on time? Or is it because the ref is dying for his half-time cup of tea?

I'd like to see gloves banned. I mean for outfield players, not goalies. No reason really. It just annoys me. I now boo every player wearing gloves, especially if he is a native-born Brit and should be used to our weather. Becks can wander around half naked in a thong, yet in the winter he insisted on wearing his little woolly gloves to keep his little pinkies warm. Diddums. ("Is it a shit-slicer?" I heard one little boy ask his mum when he saw an illustration of Becks in his thong.)

It's good to see female refs coming through, if only one or two at the top level, and it's also good that team mascots, the little kid who gets to walk out with the team, can be either a boy or a girl.

But there is one diabolical unfairness I'd like to see changed. It's dreadfully ageist, probably against the law. Why can't mascots or ball boys be oldies? Why have they always got to be kids? We have an oldie of 67 managing Newcastle United, still full of pep, and all his hair, so why not ball oldies? It would keep a lot of overactive oldies off the streets, out of the strip clubs and the saunas.

Perhaps FIFA could get working on this in the close season. What am I saying? It doesn't exist any more. Traditionally, after the Cup Final, the lads had two months off. Not no more. Football, like the poor, is always with us. But I'm off for two weeks. Back in time for Euro 2000.

EURO 2000 IS HERE — AND I'VE GOT AN AWFUL FIXTURE PILE-UP

12 JUNE 2000

I GOT MARRIED ON 11 JUNE 1960: WHAT A MISTAKE. Getting married, dearie me no, that was certainly not a mistake. But the date. What a stunner.

I became president of Cumbria Wildlife Trust five years ago, or it could have been six, anyway, the late Brian Redhead rang me up one day and said would I take over from him as pres of Cumbria Wildlife Trust. What a mistake. Not agreeing to it. Just not realising that the annual general meeting, which every year I have to chair, takes place in June. This year it's 10 June. Oh lor. What have I done? The first matches in Euro 2000, as we all well know, just look at all the supplements, take place on 10 and 11 June. And I'll be otherwise engaged.

If only I'd been really, really clever when we walked into the Oxford Register Office in 1960 and said: Hold on pet, how about holding on pet, till let's say, I dunno, mid-August, when there's no football? That would have seemed sensible 40 years ago. Nowadays, it would be stupid. That's when the new season has already begun.

Today, anyone getting married, any time, in any month, or agreeing to do anything, any time, well ahead, will always find that the random date, agreed to with a clear head, a good heart and an empty diary, will turn out to be the same day as an absolutely vital match which can't possibly be missed. Parkinson had his Law. I hereby decree that the aforementioned observation is Hunt's First Rule of Football.

Of course, I'll be celebrating my ruby wedding, the full treatment, with 40 roses, a real ruby necklace and a night at a posh hotel near Windermere, Linthwaite House, where I've already inquired about their television reception. The AGM of the Wildlife Trust is also in Windermere, quite near a few pubs; so, with a bit of luck, a bit of ducking and diving, a bit of I must go and check the lounges, see a man about Peter Rabbit, I should at least catch the goals, if any, in the opening game, Belgium *v* Sweden, as well as Turkey *v* Italy and Holland *v* Czech Republic on Sunday.

Then it's whay hay the lads, I'll be back home, in our Lakeland house in Loweswater, on Monday for England's first game, against Portugal. I have the wall charts pinned up, the glossy supermarket kiddies' books opened at the first pages and the pullout sections from every newspaper carefully laid out.

Look, my petal, if it's vital, tell me now. If not, hold your tongue, I'll be incommunicado until 2 July. Come on. I did buy you roses, they don't grow on trees, and those guaranteed 100 per cent kosher rubies, they weren't cheap. I could have had the goldfish or the coconuts, but I was thinking of your pleasure.

So, I'm all ready. To be totally, utterly, completely depressed by England's performance.

It was jolly clever of Kevin to tell the lads to play like shite in their final warm-up against Malta to fool the spies from the other Group A teams. Malta are roughly the level of the Carlisle and District Sunday league, division ten, and the world at large expected England to hammer them by, oh, something stupendous, like 1–0. But I saw through the bluff and double bluff. England *were* shite because they *are* shite.

When they drew against Brazil, which was truly astonishing, even though Brazil were strolling, hands in pockets, looking the other way, one foot tied behind the other, I joined the national euphoria, clamouring for a dukedom for Kev, a Nobel peace prize for Michael Owen for his wonder goal. Then when we hammered Ukraine, who couldn't even get to Euro 2000 and probably didn't give a toss, I was over the moon, chuffed to bollocks, etc.

The Malta match, that did bring us all down to earth. And reality. I'm now in the right frame of mind for Monday. I'm ready, and also resigned. I wish Kev was.

Kevin has clearly no idea what he's doing, what his formation will be, or his tactics, let alone his players. It was bringing Kieron Dyer on as a sub in the Ukraine match, when he'd already told him he wouldn't be in the final 22, rather than giving a run-out to a player who would be going, that finally convinced me Kev is off with the fairies. Whatever his motivation — to confuse the press, to stop Kieron crying — it was completely potty. In all three warm-up games, on the very eve of the Big One, he used different tactics, different players, showing his lack of resolution. Alf Ramsey had his faults, but dear God, he knew his own mind.

So how do you feel, Hunt, resolution-wise, as you are so awfully clever?

I'm pleased by the state of Shearer, which I wasn't a few months ago. Ditto Ince and Scholes. They'd be in my team. Barmby has at long last fulfilled the promise he showed at Spurs all those years ago. Owen is in, not just for that wonder goal, but because he suits the big occasion. Heskey is still too raw, too naive. In the midfield, our strongest area, there is a relatively rich choice. I'd have both Beckham and McManaman, even if each can be a luxury, along with Barmby, Ince, Scholes.

That means three at the back. It's where there's little choice, as our defenders are currently about the poorest, least-skilled, worst passers in the western world, so we might as well have three useless players as opposed to four useless players, all liable to make mistakes. So bye bye to the Neville brothers. Which leaves Adams, Campbell and Keown.

In goal, I'd have Martyn. I've watched Seaman very carefully this season for Arsenal and, despite that controlled air, that confident air, I think he's blown it. Not just his barnet, but deep down he knows his best days are behind him. Alas, ditto England, I fear.

WELL, AT LEAST WE CAN BEAT THE WORLD AT WRITING CLICHÉS

3 JULY 2000

SO WHAT DID YOU THINK OF IT? ENGLAND'S IGNOMINIOUS exit'? I thought the lads played a blinder, incisive, direct, no messing around, got the boot in where it hurt, took no prisoners. Yes, a great victory once again for our glorious media. The football experts who know it all, especially afterwards, have been on top form all week, telling us exactly what's wrong with England.

My favourite was a *Sunday Times* pundit who suggested that English schoolkids should no longer be driven to school, but should go on their bikes, as they do in Holland. Dutch kids weave in and out of traffic, live on their movement, live on their wits, hence, wait for it, they grow up to be Bergkamp and Overmars. Brilliant, huh?

Others blamed the government, cutting school sports, thus kids come home and play with their computers instead of growing up to be, well, Dennis Bergkamp. Funny how Bergkamp, after a couple of good games, became a role model. Would you want your kids to grow up scared of flying and with a perpetual scowl?

It's too easy to say "Sack Keegan"—very few have said that so far, it's hard to spin it out for 1,000 words—and it's far too obvious to say "England are Crap". We've said that for, oh, must be 30 years. After every humiliation, every stuffing by the Faroe Isles, every time we failed to get through the qualifying rounds for a World Cup or European Championship, we've had breast-beating, soul-searching, cliché-clutching. We must teach our kids proper skills and technique. We must renounce up and under. We must copy Johnny Foreigner's training methods, diets, sexy shorts, slipper boots, command of English, great haircuts.

Whatever happens, "we must learn from this". How often have we heard that phrase? Said not just by the clever clogs on the back pages, but by the great brains of the FA, the officials and coaches who always promise, after every débâcle, that things will be different next time, that changes will be made. And what happens? Nothing. Only the blame changes. Being out of Europe, that was fashionable for a decade. Now it's Europe being over here, that's the real trouble: too many bloody foreigners in the Premiership, stopping our brilliant young talent from coming through.

I prefer the obvious explanation for England's early exit: they were crap. We have defenders who are middling to good at defending, such as Keown, Campbell and the Nevilles, but useless at anything else. So they thump it forward to midfielders with only marginally better ball skills, who can't control it, so back it comes. The best form of defence, they say, is attack. That's not quite true. The best form of defence is possession. Then pass it to someone, preferably in the same colour shirt, who can attack.

Why can't we do that? Why don't we have players in every position who are comfortable on the ball? I don't have clever clogs, just cheap ones for the garden, but I am willing, like everyone else, to lay blame for this on our boring, blinkered coaches.

But I'd also blame our blinkered players. In the end, they have to perfect their own skills, teach themselves to kick with either foot from the age of eight, practise on their own each day from the age of 14 even if they are in so-called academies of excellence, not tell themselves they've made it and have no need to practise any more just because they've got to 18 and are in the first team on a million a year with everyone telling them they are brilliant. They let themselves down. Not just us.

We've known it, seen it, commented on it for years—their lack of ball skills. What was more surprising and worrying was a lack of confidence. Never thought I'd see English players with their heads down, scared of the ball, with so little self-belief. Under Hoddle, you often saw them looking confused, because Hoddle's mind and methods were often confusing.

But Keegan is the ultimate optimist, one of nature's cheerleaders, who told them they could win, and appeared to mean it. He looked round the dressing room, saw big names, and convinced himself that this meant big winners. So why did their heads drop, morale seep away, despite having a manager like Keegan? It could be that, after 30 years, it's at last got through to English players. They now *know* they are crap.

So perhaps this will be the real turning point, when lessons will be learnt by the people who matter most: the players. They will now arise and heal themselves. Or possibly, no I can't bear it, I've already got a headache thinking back over their three games—things will get worse. Before they get even worse.

One more game and I can bin the charts I have lived with these past three weeks, vacate the chair I have grown into, clean up the apple gowks [cores] on the floor, the dirty mugs, the whisky glasses. And end with some cheerful thoughts.

Almost every armchair punter got it right, whether in the street, down the pub or up on the fells. Three weeks ago, I wrote down on one of my charts—oh god, it's faded in the sun—what three local sheep farmers and our two regular postmen had all told me—the last four teams would be France, Holland, Italy and Portugal. As for the experts, in the back pages and on the telly, only half of them got it right. Mainly because so many tipped Spain and England—yes, even England—in their last four.

Among the TV commentators, Barry Davies in the end annoyed me most. He now appears convinced that he's too clever to be a common or garden football commentator and should really be at All Souls, or working on the human genes thingy.

Unlike our own dear Big Ron. What a treasure. I'll miss being in his Wide-Awake Club these past three weeks.

2000−01 SEASON

Boo to Keegan, hurrah for Sports Report and a trip to Spain.

I WAS SO VERY DEPRESSED, BUT THEN SAW TITUS FROM IPSWICH

11 SEPTEMBER 2000

WELCOME TO THE NEW SEASON. WELL SPOTTED. IT BEGAN four weeks ago. You could argue that there's been no new season. If you blinked and missed a few hours sans footer from about half past midnight one night in July, it would appear to have been going constantly and seamlessly since this time last year. Or, if you prefer, since 1863, when the FA first opened up shop.

Before that, well, I wasn't here. But it must have been pretty grim in 1862, tuning in at five o'clock for James Alexander Gordon and the football results, only to hear bloody bugger all except stuff about Bismarck becoming leader of Prussia, Garibaldi trying to seize Rome and cotton famine in Lancashire. I got those dates from my *Pears Cyclopaedia* (1978), which I have next to my *Rothmans* (1985), both on my desk here in Lakeland for emergencies, such as sudden attacks of total, utter boredom.

I haven't been able to face the new season. Until now. Euro 2000 pissed me off, so deflated and depressed me that I thought: that's it,

I'll go back to stamp collecting, you know where you are with stamps; Penny Blacks and Tuppenny Blues, they don't let you down — not like Penny Beckham and Tippy Shearer.

I did watch the pre-season games played by some of our so-called leading clubs, such as Man U, Arsenal, Liverpool, and had to look away in disgust. It was impossible to believe that they were playing the same game, pursuing the same sport as Real Madrid and Barcelona.

Then George Graham sold Ginola. More depression. All that money on a new season ticket and he's got rid of the only person in the squad worth paying to watch. Rebrov, well, only seen him on the telly so far, and the Gordon Drury is out as regards to that one, at this moment in time.

Carlisle United began the season as they ended it, cowering at the bottom with Shrewsbury. What is the point, I thought, giving all these hours, all this mental and emotional energy, to people who don't deserve it, who don't even know how I cross my fingers every Saturday at three, willing them to win, twiddling the knobs, trying to pick up the latest on their own goals, send-offs, dodgy penalties, diabolical refereeing.

But hey, as I write, CUFC is zooming up the league, blasting their way almost to the halfway mark in Division Three, only 80 clubs now ahead of them: my heroes, come on you Blues, praise the Lord and Eddie Stobart. I got quite excited for Chelsea's sake when they signed Hasselbaink and beat Man Utd in the Charity Shield, thinking that should fettle Man U's chances this season. After which, nothing. Did he sign or did I imagine it?

I have liked the look of Ashley Cole of Arsenal, playing for England's Under 21s. And also Michael Carrick of West Ham. Two likely lads to watch, so that cheered me up. And to amuse me up, I was pleased by the arrival of Titus Bramble when he came on for the Under 21s. I was so delighted that I shouted out to my dear wife hey, new kid here, come quick, got a really brilliant name, bet you can't guess where he's from. Don't say it, I was being geographist. Why should it matter where he's from, etc. I know. I know. Just slipped out. What's his first name? shouted back my wife from her desk. I forgot I'd tied her there. When I told her it was Titus, she said he's either very, very upper class or from Notting Hill. Ipswich, actually, pet.

And so to the international games — time to resume hostilities, futilities, utilities. By then, I was feeling a bit more chipper, more able to cope with a new season's old disappointments. Scotland scraped a jammy win against Latvia, but their supporters were in fine voice. I spotted the first rendition of a new chant that we'll hear for the next two years, destined to replace "Wembur-lee, Wem-bur-lee". "Que sera", etc, then it finishes with "We're going to Toe-kee-oh". The Irish Republic were brilliant against Holland, and should have won. So that was very cheering. When the Irish do well, or the Scots, they are one of us, so our little chests puff out.

But the most cheering was England against France, the world chumps. Such an interesting game — because England didn't play like England. They were like one of those small to piddling foreign countries we play every season and from whom so little is expected because they are so far away, so foreign, not in the major league of soccer nations, like what we are — ha ha, in our dreams. I'm thinking of Georgia or Latvia or Iran, countries that surprise us by being, well, surprisingly good: able to pass the ball quite well, considering they don't speak English; show good technique, considering they don't have any GCSE's; create some good moves, yet not one of them drives a Ferrari. For 30 minutes, we patronisingly think, hey, we've underestimated these Johnny foreigners from the Faroe Islands... hold on, where's my programme... from Baffin Island. They're not as useless as we thought; they don't just thump the ball upfield, they could give us a game.

That was England. That was how they appeared. And that was how France treated us. Surprisingly good, you could sense them thinking, for a third-world, rubbish, crap, useless, far-flung foreign country that has won rien. Honestly, I was well pleased. I was not ashamed of the midfield, and I hardly closed my eyes when the defence had the ball, apart from Keown. One can't expect total miracles overnight.

There was no penetration up front until Owen came on, despite all the neat and pretty passing stuff. I fear it's bye bye Andy Cole, for ever. But hey, I'm feeling much better. Ready at last to face life, the universe and a new season.

MYSTERIOUS MOUTHFULS AND
EVERYDAY BOLLOCKS

18 SEPTEMBER 2000

WHAT DOES IT ALL MEAN? NOT LIFE, POLITICS, THE universe and all those piddling mysteries. Or even the middling mysteries, such as why does the *Independent* insist on telling us at the bottom of the front page of the *Review* section to now turn to page eight. That makes me so mad, so mad that I never ever read the end of their main feature, just to spite them.

I'm thinking today, friends, of some major mysteries, phrases that occur every day, every moment, in football life, but whose meaning is not always clear. Here's one I wrote down last week while watching *Match of the Day*. It was Newcastle *v* Chelsea; commentator, Tony Gubba. "That would have been goal number 201 for Shearer, who became a father for the third time only a week ago."

It was a unique sentence, so that was interesting, one never to be repeated, and you don't get many of them in football. If Gubba ever attempts such gobbledegook again, one of its three variables at least will have to change.

The mysterious part was why did he come out with such a mouthful so early in the game? I suspect it was panic. He had these two incredible, amazing facts written down in front of him, amazing to him, but yawn-making to every Newcastle fan, probably every football fan. He was determined to work them in during the game but, like many a player, he stabbed at it, went in with both facts blazing before he could help himself.

Now these are harder, do concentrate.

- "The level of defending in the Premiership is very poor," said George Graham, the manager of Spurs, last week. Why did he say that? He must have been criticising himself, surely, because he is very proud of having improved the defence of three Premier clubs.

The answer is Penguin psychology, the cheap paperback edition. He was in a competition to sign Sergei Rebrov from Ukraine, who was sorely tempted to go to a decent team in the Italian or Spanish league. George's clincher was that he would score more goals here than there. Nice one.

- Christian Ziege appeared with bleached hair last week. Why? You noticed, did you, and been pondering it ever since. I would suggest it was not a fashion statement, which would be the obvious explanation, but, first, a nationalistic one. He was saying "I am not a boring, dreary, identikit German defender".

  Second, it was a football statement. Hur-bloody-ray, he was proclaiming, thank the Lord I am out of that crap team at 'Boro who are going to win nothing. Now I am with Liverpool, who might also win nothing, but will score goals, entertain, please the fans and be fun. Hence I am a new man with new fun hair.

- That stuff on the chin of Robert Pires of Arsenal, what is it? Slime. He got spotted by a Highbury pigeon. Next.

- Who is Reg Vardy? Pass on that. Unless he's an old music-hall comedian currently sponsoring Sunderland.

- EDS on the Derby shirt, who or what does it mean? Stands for Everyone in the Derby team Stinks.

- "He'll be disappointed by that." Which gets said by commentators who are creeps, or hoping to get invited into the players' lounge after the match. When said by managers or coaches, it means the player is utterly useless, playing like a total wally, I wouldn't pay washers for him, who was the eejit who bought him, oh, ah, could have been me.

- "I never saw the incident." Another example of manager-speak and cherished by all fans who assume it's bollocks, a complete lie. That's the accepted wisdom, but it's wrong. The manager did *not* in fact see it, for the simple reason that he had no need to watch. All week they have practised clattering the opposition's star striker, pulling his shirt off, kicking him up the backside, grabbing his balls, trying to break one of his legs. The manager was therefore able to look the other way, pick his nose, make notes, then say "Hospital? He's gone to hospital, oh dear."

- "Players today are becoming too greedy." Another favourite utterance from our leading managers, hoping to make themselves sound pious and virtuous. What they miss out is the end of the sentence. "But not as greedy as me."

- Players, if they are lucky, manage to be greedy for ten years, max. Managers, the ones supposed to set an example, can coin it in for decades. They will leave a club for a bigger whack, just like a player. They'll sell their names and souls to advertisers, if the fee is big enough. They'll capitalise on their privileged position, which gives them inside information on famous players, and will tell all, at once, without having the decency to wait, if a publisher offers a big enough advance. Yes, I mean you, Fergie, and you, the Blessed Hoddle.

- "Crikey." Now which manager, still alive, is fond of saying that? You've got it. Graham Taylor of Watford. But why has he picked on an archaic, 1950s *Dandy* expletive? Is it because he's an old fogey? No. It's because his wife gave him such a blasting for all those four-letter words in that TV documentary that, henceforth in public, he has vowed to talk like Just William.

- "They didn't show us enough respect." Words or grunts to that effect are used by hooligans to justify their actions. What they are saying is: "They didn't see us coming, so we got our retaliation in first, innit, jumping on the scum before they saw us, there was only two of them, 40 of us, we had bottles and they had scarves, so it was a fair fight, that'll teach them to show respect in future..."

ENGLAND NEEDS DRUGS NOW —
AND LOTS OF THEM

25 SEPTEMBER 2000

MY WIFE IS STILL MOPING AROUND, DISAPPOINTED THAT Mark Richardson is not in the Olympics, whoever he is. She has a working knowledge of so many sports, the leading players, their age, place of birth, marital status, career successes, awful setbacks — especially their awful setbacks: she is not interested in their times, records, medals, but just them, as human beings.

I follow only football, but I have been watching the Olympics — with amazement. Who are those blokes out of *Star Wars* with funny pointy heads and riding those plastic round things — can't be bikes — strewth, what has happened to bikes since I was a lad? Haven't spotted one Raleigh Lenton Sports so far, nor anyone with Sturmey Archer gears — God, they were hot, they were it, the envy of every school bike shed.

Then there are deformed young men and child women with no waists, shoulders the width of goalposts and feet the size of ham shanks, wearing strange all-in-one rubber suits. Are they going underwater diving, looking for Captain Cook's treasure? They can't be swimmers. Surely it is unfair, if not illegal, to cover your body in cling film just to make yourself go faster. Poor old Russians and East Europeans. You can spot them by their old-fashioned cossies. Nobody has told them about rubber suits, or they can't afford them.

Lots of east European wrestlers and weightlifters and the like are out of the Olympics because of drugs, just like your Mark Richardson, ha ha. Why do you follow him? No reason, she said, no logical reason. She just likes the look of him. She hates the gung-ho, flash git boasters, the ones who snarl and punch the air with their fists. Richardson has always struck her as fairly quiet and modest, which is why she is sad that he's not running.

But he took a drug, allegedly, supposedly, I said. One thing you can say about our footballers—they are not full of nasty drugs. Not while playing, anyway. Come over to football, pet. Forget these dodgy athletes.

Then I thought, is it true? Are our lads clean?

I can't think of a British footballer who has been found full of drugs—I mean, who has taken them to make himself play better. Apart from those with medical problems, such as Paul Scholes with a shot of Ventolin to help his asthma, or Gary Mabbutt injecting himself with insulin for his diabetes.

Off the field, yes, for purely recreational reasons, there have always been players who have abused themselves. Since football began, it has been littered with alcoholics, drinking all their money away, wasting their talents, ending up with nothing. In recent years, we have had a lot of druggies, on soft and hard stuff, not all ex-Arsenal, who have later told us all about it in lurid detail, once they have recovered, once they have seen the light, or seen the size of the cheque for their memoirs.

But on the field, they have been pretty drug-free. I suppose in team games, unlike individual sports, there is not the same pressure to improve personal bests. In athletics or weightlifting, there are constant measures to tell you how well or badly you are performing, how fast you are running, what weights you are lifting. In football, it doesn't work that way. You can't measure how well someone is doing in training. Even in matches, who played well is often a matter of opinion.

In football, speed and strength are important, but not as important as skill. There is no drug, as yet, to make you score goals. Alas. Why not? Surely, by now, there are drugs that can help players to play better? First, we need a drug to speed up reactions, to make players mentally and physically sharper. We could certainly do with that at White Hart Lane. Sol Campbell is too often beaten to the ball these days by smaller, slighter, but nippier players.

British defences in general could do with this drug, because there are far too many dozy buggers, ball-watchers, who stand there bemused, confused, when these foreign johnnies start running and passing through them. And we need it quick, before the German game. Double doses, please, for Martin Keown and Gary Neville.

There must also be a drug that gives self-confidence, makes you feel and play like a winner in every game, regardless of who you are playing against. Chelsea could do with some of that, bucketfuls of it — during the past two years, any crap team has been liable to give them a hammering.

Perhaps Claudio Ranieri has brought a few packets of it, stuffed inside his Guccis. Any leftovers could be given to Andy Cole. He would be advised to overdose on it if he ever gets picked for England again.

An aggression drug would be useful, too — the sort that Vinnie Jones and Roy Keane were supplied with naturally in their mothers' milk. Then we would have no more fairies in the Premier league. Darren Anderton would soon be punching the air, yelling: "Bye-bye sick notes, hello testosterone." My wife would certainly not approve, but the rest of us would.

So come on, Boots. Start working on it. Our lads need you to come up with something to enhance our chances in the next World Cup. England managers are supposed to act like psychological drug-dealers to their players, creating artificial highs, instilling that 'never say die' spirit, psyching them up so that they'll run through walls, or at least the Faroe Islands' ace defence. That doesn't work any more. So bring on the pills. Anything, really, that will enhance performance.

LET'S HEAR IT FOR THE FANS: TEAMS COULDN'T DO IT WITHOUT US

2 OCTOBER 2000

THERE'S A NEW THING ON SKY DIGITAL THIS SEASON THAT is quite interesting. Don't worry if you haven't got Sky or Digital, it's still quite interesting.

It is called Fan Zone. You flick the appropriate flick and, instead of hearing Martin Tyler and Andy Gray doing their smooth, professional commentary, you get two geezers, chuntering on. Each is a fan of one of the teams, and they cluck away, uninterrupted, unled, all on their own, throughout the game, making any half-witted, half-formed thoughts and observations that come into their totally biased minds. Just like the rest of us, really, as we sit and watch a game — although there must be some sort of direction, because I haven't heard many swear words yet, apart from arse.

It's rather refreshing to hear their amateur, unreconstructed, un-PC thoughts, so unlike the safe, obvious and totally uncontroversial thoughts that get trotted out by most of the so-called experts who rarely say what they really think. Their most daring, critical comment is always "He'll be disappointed by that". But the fans groan and moan, rubbishing their own side as much as the opposition. And if their lads are doing well, they get very excited, shouting and cheering.

They argue among themselves, which makes interesting listening. In the Man Utd *v* Newcastle game when Keane was sent off, there was a heated exchange about whether it was deserved or not, with each fan taking a different view. You can guess the Man U reaction. No one likes us ... we do care ... it was out of order.

Fans are also funnier and ruder than professional commentators. In that particular match, there was a sudden close-up shot of Peter Reid, the manager of Sunderland. "Is that a chimpanzee in the stand?" asked the Newcastle fan. You won't catch a pro commentator saying that sort of thing.

In the Leicester *v* Everton game, the Leicester fan specialised in being rude about his own team. Impey, he said, "cost £1.5m, which means he was overpriced by £1.6m". He had it in for Guppy: "He's only got one weakness — he can't tackle and he's only got one foot." He rubbished all their strikers, "who couldn't score in a knocking shop", which naturally meant that, two seconds later, they did score. I'm amazed he got away with saying that "Heskey goes down quicker than a cheap whore". Perhaps Sky hasn't got round to a digital ten-second button yet, which would enable it to cut out the more offensive pensées.

The downside to the experiment is that you can tune in and find dead silence, so you think, heh up, I've flicked the wrong flick, the sound's gone wonky, is there wax in my ear, or what? There's also a lot of chat that is little more than "Come on you Blues".

I don't intend to watch it again. Not because of the offensive remarks, but because Sky insists on flashing stupid e-mail comments across the bottom of the screen. So annoying. I also happen to like Andy Gray and Martin Tyler. If they have done their homework, and are on form, what they say can be illuminating. The fans illuminate themselves, and their prejudices, which is amusing, but in small doses.

A combination of the two would be worth trying — a pro commentator and a fan working together, especially for all these European games. A fan of the foreign team would be able to explain the background to their players, their history, personalities, how they are rated, what obscenity the crowd is chanting and why. Our Brit commentators often show total ignorance of foreign teams.

The experiment is interesting because it shows how the game is developing. At long last, the views and feelings of fans are not being totally ignored. Several clubs are currently working on ways to give fans a voice on the board. Disabled fans are being better catered for. Some clubs are cutting back on season-ticket seating to give the fans who can't afford a huge annual outlay the chance to get an occasional seat.

But on the whole, fans are still treated like shite. Oh yes we are. We are fodder. Our purpose is to be fleeced. But any club chairman with some sense knows that we play a part. We can win several points a season, just by roaring our heads off, getting behind the lads — if, that is, they deserve to be roared on, if they are really trying, really determined.

We can also make life hell for a team or player, chairman or manager, even hound them out. It was the crowd at Man City that turned against the team's former captain Richard Edgill and got him on the transfer list. I suspect that the Chelsea crowd's lack of enthusiasm for Deschamps last season hastened his end. Perhaps the worst crowd victim was Perry Groves. His life at Arsenal was total misery once the fans had gone off him.

Oh yes, we can influence our club, even if we have nothing like the muscle of the merchandising and marketing people, the sponsors and TV companies, the agents and the players who are now kings. And there is a strength that we haven't tried yet. It is called direct action. If agricultural workers can man the barricades, and truckers can block the motorways, it would be very simple for a hundred fooball fans to disrupt the next live match on TV and lose the clubs concerned millions of pounds unless they give in to our demands. All we have to do is lie down in the middle of the pitch at kick-off and refuse to move. Or, even easier, block access to the car park, so that the opposition's team coach, or the home players in their Ferraris, can't get in. That would fettle them.

Oh, there is much we can do if we fans start flexing our flex. Not all of which I will reveal at this moment in time. But the clubs have been warned.

JOE WANTS TO BE A MANAGER AGAIN.
SO HE MUST BE POTTY

9 OCTOBER 2000

THAT'S IT THEN. NO MORE FOOTBALL BOOKS. DONE, GOT the signed jockstrap. My portfolio is now complete. I created this ambition for myself many years ago, back in 1972, when I did a book about a year in the life of a team. One day, I said, I'll do a book about a player. After that, I'll do a manager. Then I'll hang up my Sporting Amstrad.

But for 27 years, other things happened, such as life. Until last year, when I did the biog of a player, Dwight Yorke — remember him? Great story, very interesting life, but hell to do because I got messed around. I was kept waiting for hours, he hardly concentrated when I was with him, and Man Utd gave no help, even though it was officially a Man Utd book. The buggers. But I did achieve my second ambition. Having got inside a top team, I had been with a top player, watching his life while he won the treble.

So how to line up a manager? It is hard to engineer such things if you are outside the football-reporting fraternity. Not easy to make new contacts, living half the year in Lakeland, finger on the remote control. My opening came on 3 March 1999, at an evening match between Sheffield Wednesday and Wimbledon. Joe Kinnear, the Wimbledon manager, went out on to the pitch with his team for the warm-up. He felt his throat go funny, sweat was pouring from him, he couldn't breathe, his left arm went numb — the classic signs of a heart attack. If it had happened on the motorway, he would probably have been a goner. But Wednesday's club doctor was on hand, and a specialist heart unit only minutes away. It was life or death for 24 hours, intensive care for two weeks, followed by months sitting at home, bored out of his mind. Which was where I came in.

When I wrote *The Glory Game* in 1972, Joe was my best friend in the Spurs team. He was a bachelor, with afternoon time on his hands, although he did have a girlfriend, Bonnie (now his wife), who, by chance, I already knew. She had a men's fashion shop in Hampstead Village, where I bought the odd bit of men's fashion. Bought nothing since. Waiting for it to make a comeback.

One of the things I asked the first team pool of 18 was if they wanted to stay in football. Almost all said: "Not bloody likely, I'd end up in the loony bin, I've seen what it does to Bill Nick." (Bill Nicholson, their manager — do concentrate.) Yet eight of the Spurs players became managers, with varying degrees of success — Martin Peters, Alan Mullery, Graeme Souness, Cyril Knowles, Steve Perryman, Mike England, Phil Holder and Joe Kinnear.

Back then, Joe was one of the few who said he couldn't imagine a life outside football. He hoped he might be a coach one day. It took some time before he arrived at Wimbledon as reserve team coach in 1989. I kept in contact with him over the years. I would often ring him just to hear his latest answerphone message: "If you want tickets for the match, then piss off, but if you're ringing from Barcelona or Milan, I'll ring you right back." When he became Wimbledon manager, I was occasionally invited into the directors' box, usually when they were playing Spurs.

So, naturally, I rang him when he was ill, sent one of my lovely books — a biography of Robert Louis Stephenson — which, naturally, he still hasn't read. And, as therapy for him, and to pass the time, I began taking down his life story. It was a perfect project for me, because he lives just 15 minutes from our London home — that's the sort of travelling I like — and, because he had time on his hands, I got his full attention, unlike what's-his-face, Dwighty Baby.

As Joe recuperated, he often did nothing for days, except take his grandson round the garden. But one day, when I said that it must be so boring, Joe, poor old you, he said, not really, Vinnie Jones picked me up yesterday, went to see him on the film set with Brad Pitt, then it was a party in the evening with Madonna. These modern footballers, eh. As he got stronger, the phone started ringing, with Deep

Throats from Celtic and Blackburn saying that there could be a vacancy soon, possibly might be. Was he available? But keep shtum.

While I was writing the book, Joe did get several offers—but from clubs with money problems, wanting him to work the miracle he had managed at Wimbledon. For eight years, he kept that team high in the Premiership, despite lousy crowds, buying cheap in the lower divisions, polishing them up, selling them on. The whole Wimbledon story, their rise from non-league, is indeed miraculous. I can't see it ever being repeated.

Trailing to all those lower-league games meant 18-hour days, thousands of motorway miles, mountains of chips and burgers, plus gallons of Guinness. All fans saw how Joe had ballooned—especially the opposing fans. But now he is slimmer, as fit as anyone his age, and he wants to get back into football management, if the offer is right. I think he's potty. It was football that contributed to his heart attack—the stress plus the lifestyle. Why go back? It's a drug, innit? It's all he knows. He's only 53, much younger than Uncle Fergie and Grandad Bobby Robson. Still time, so he says, for another decade in the dugout.

If he does pack it in, and takes one of the many media jobs on offer, it will be football's loss. He has been one of the most successful, best-loved managers of the past decade. There aren't many such large, very English characters like him in top management today. OK, he is Irish-born, but he has spoken Watford Cockney since he was seven. Very soon, the Premiership will be filled by emotionless suits from France and Italy who never swear, and who look and speak like accountants.

OF COURSE KEVIN WON'T
RESIGN. DON'T BE DAFT

16 OCTOBER 2000

I WAS SO LOOKING FORWARD TO ENGLAND–GERMANY. I GOT such a lot of work done in the morning, knowing the treat I was going to give myself in the afternoon. And I lined up such an array of goodies for the match itself. A huge slice of homemade ginger-bread, two pears from my garden, and the last of my excellent apples, now not so excellent, as the wasps have got at them. Enough to keep me going till half-time, when I can open the Beaujolais in celebration.

Beside me, just for luck, on the arm of my favourite chair, I had my 1966 Wembley World Cup Final programme—I've kept it well clean all these years, just the odd gingerbread stain—and my reproduction copy of the first Wembley Cup Final of 1923. About 20 years ago, I was offered an original for £90 and I said, get lost, no one will ever pay that. Last week, at an auction held by Sports Progs, I bid £650 for one—and failed.

I do love reading this 1923 programme, or anything to do with Wembley. "This vast Stadium, the largest in the world, the most comfortable, holds more than 125,000 people. In area it equals the Biblical city, Jericho." How did they know that?

As it got near three o'clock, I wondered if I should have a hankie at the ready. Just in case it all became too emotional, or I needed to mop up the tears of joy.

The first worrying sign was Richard Keys, Sky's presenter, who exclaimed just before kick-off. "It doesn't get any better than this!" Hold on, Rich, I thought, do contain yourself. Then I thought he might inadvertently be right. His words could also mean that this, now, is the best it will be, when nothing is happening. When it does, it could be rubbish. Nah, no chance. Inger-land. Wem-ber-lee.

Bobby Charlton appeared in a stupid Puffa jacket over his suit

jacket. What a wally, how out of touch, how clumsy and old fashioned compared with the suave, neat, disciplined-looking
Beckenbauer in his fashionable raincoat. Will England be equally
uncomfortable, and Germany similarly well organised?

In the line-up, I looked into Michael Owen's eyes. How dark
they are for a young man. Is he ill, has he been up all night, does he
know what's coming?

The English crowd booed the German national anthem. Hey ho.
Not just disgusting and pathetic, but so uncool. One of the things
about Premiership crowds today is their sense of irony, their ability
to mock themselves. At England games, the lumpen think with
their beer-guts. Why didn't they stand up and cheer the German
anthem all the way through? That would have scored house points
and totally confused the Germans.

I saw the German goal coming. I did. I was screaming at our
defence, as they stood around like dozy buggers. My wife, who was
listening quietly to the radio in the conservatory, jumped up in
alarm, thinking I was having a seizure.

After that, England were total rubbish, sliding on their back-
sides, as pathetic as their fans, who started singing, in their witty
way, "Stand Up If You Won the War".

I hate England fans. I hate the England team. I am hating this
match. I am just so full of hate. And that includes Nationwide.
"This international is supported by Nationwide," blared an advert
on the screen the moment the halftime whistle blew. So it's their
fault. I'm cancelling my Tessa.

At half-time, I went for a quick walk through the fields. Four
cows watched me over a dry-stone wall, their heads following my
every move. What are you lot looking at, you stupid arses? I'll fight
every cow in this field. Down at Crummock Water, I threw some
stones into the lake. Take that, you horrible water.

The second half wasn't quite as bad. More the normal, useless
England team. How could Kevin on *Football Focus* at lunchtime

have talked about going all the way — winning the World Cup? He must be potty, or totally deluded.

It's Wembley's fault. Wembley should have been blown up in 1966. I never liked the place: nasty concrete, shitty food, smelly lavs. How could I have been fascinated by Wembley all these years, collected all this stupid memorabilia? I'm the potty one.

I had such a headache when the final whistle blew; I just grunted when my dear wife came in to find out the score. She then started chattering on about this really good Radio 4 programme she'd been listening to, old people talking about places in their lives, part of *The Century Speaks* series, really interesting.

Shurrup, I said, I'm watching Kevin. He was walking straight down the tunnel, on his own, never seen him do that before. Managers normally stand at the side of the pitch waiting, commiserating or congratulating each player as he comes off. Very strange, not like our Kev.

Do you think he'll resign, asked my wife.

Keep quiet, woman, you don't know anything about football. If I want an inane opinion, I'll ask the Herdwicks. Of course he won't resign, not now. Don't be daft. After Euro 2000, that's when he might have done, should have done. Not now.

Look, I'm switching this thing off. I'm not watching England, ever again. In fact, I don't want to talk about football, or Kevin Keegan, not any more. Don't tell me any football news. I don't want to hear. And if I mention the word Wembley again, just shoot me.

Now I'm going to duff up those cows. I may be some time.

BACK IN TOWN: A NEW ROUTE, A NEW SEAT, A NEW MATE

AND SO BACK TO LONDON, HEART OF THE EMPIRE, HEART OF the matter, after five months in the provinces, living as a provincial. Oh what bliss it was to be alive up there and not having to read about Ken Livingstone, beginning to believe he never existed. The only thing I ever truly miss in Lakeland is the *Evening Standard*. and even that I don't miss very much. When I got back and rushed for my first copy, it was to discover, oh no, they've still got Brian Sewell.

There is always a re-entry period, three days to get my bearings, get up to speed, assume my hard London face, my pushy metropolitan demeanour, my city-slicky attitudes, till I'm able to bustle about, elbows out, effin and blinding, carving up others at the lights, knowing that the weak are suckers who get left behind.

All of which meant that, by last Saturday, when I strolled up Tottenham High Road for my first of the season, it was like I'd never been away. And nothing had changed. I walked behind two blokes who were saying they hoped Derby would beat us, so that fucking Graham would have to resign.

I got there by a new route. After 30 years, I've given up the hell of Turnpike Lane. During that time, I'd memorised every sari in every shop window, every Indian butcher, every Cypriot club, every abandoned car, every boarded-up window. Thirty years ago, I used to do it in 20 minutes. Last year, it took an average of one hour.

Saturday was also another first for me. I have a new seat. For the past five years, I've been driven mad by a family behind me. He's a geezer, or similar, while his three boys, aged between ten and 14, are all at some potty fee-paying school. They talk in loud voices all the way through. They're the ones who shout, "The referee's a virgin". At the end of last season, I couldn't stand it any more and asked for a change.

I knew from the plan where my new seat was, just one row in front, but further along. In my absence, *in loco parentis*, my son had been using my ticket. He'd told me it's a brilliant position, really good, but he hadn't mentioned what my new neighbours were like. I might find them more objectionable than the ones I've left behind. What if they are screamers and shouters, idiots or nutters, racists or bruisers? Fat or smelly? The seats at Spurs are so tight together, being a tight club, that you can end up in the lap of the next person.

It turned out to be excellent. Bang on the halfway line and at the end of a row, which is what I had requested.

Then, oh no, as I sat down, I could see that the bloke in the next seat was smoking. I hate smokers. And he had a kid of about ten with him who was stuffing his face with chocolate while clutching two plastic carrier bags containing enough emergency rations of sweets and horrible drinks to keep him going till he's 21. Probably at a private school as well. What have I done?

There is an etiquette in football stadia. People have the same seats for generations, know each other, have a history, even if they never meet apart from at the match. I was the newcomer. So I didn't say nuffink. I thought it might take a few games before he realised I was the new season-ticket holder, as opposed to a one-off punter. But, at half-time, he said that Stephen Carr done well, innee, the only player who's got better under George Graham, the rest have got bleedin' worse, innay.

I thought he was speaking to his kid, but the boy was busy on his 15th Mars bar. The wisdom was being addressed to me. I said yeh, spot on, couldn't agree more, always liked Stephen Carr, for years, since I first sat ... but he was on to Ben Thatcher before I could drag in my provenance. Thatcher turned out to be his No.1 hate, bleedin' hell, cost five million bloody quid, our cat could do better. So nice to have a decent, adult, intelligent conversation for a change. My dear wife does her best, bless her, but she gets all her opinions from the back pages of the *Independent*. Up in Lakeland, our copy hardly ever has last night's scores, never mind last night's opinions.

When Anderton got a little itsy scratch on his forehead, and reappeared with a monster bandage round his head, I said to my neighbour, watch this, when he takes a free kick, he'll still try to push back his floppy hair. And it came true.

Together, we loudly cheered every half-decent pass Ramon Vega made. He has taken over the Ronny Rosenthal role, a vital one in every team. This is the person who makes all fans groan, but, with time, the groans turn into ironic cheers when it's clear that, however useless he might be, he is at least trying, unlike some players we could mention whom we now really really hate.

For half an hour, that was the whole Spurs team as they let Derby back into the game. Immediately, the crowd was shouting for Graham's blood. Not a pretty sound. There is always something malicious, nasty, when a crowd turns against its team. Yes, it upsets the players; yes, it makes the manager bitter and twisted about so-called loyal fans; but this is the nature of modern football. Big fees, big wages, big fame, mean that fans have big expectations and low tolerance. Even at Man Utd, there is hate lurking underneath the love for certain players.

But Spurs won. My neighbour didn't smoke during the game itself. Which was good. I'm now back. With a new best friend.

HOW I STAYED IN WITH RUBY
AND FLORA, AND LOST £60

20 NOVEMBER 2000

I HATE WASTE, HATE EXPENSE — IN FACT, I HATE SPENDING money. I can lash out on big things, such as going to the Caribbean in January, but would never get a taxi, even if it was pouring down. I don't buy new clothes, always get the cheapest shoes and steam stamps off envelopes if they haven't been franked. And yet, and yet, I've done something so wildly wasteful that I'm bound to go to the badfire. That's what my mother always said, unable to use the word 'hell'.

It was Tuesday evening, the night of the Spurs home tie in the Worthington Cup against Birmingham. I told myself all day that I was going, did lots of work, got ahead, washed my Thermos out in preparation — goodness, doesn't it get cacky and pongy if you don't rinse it?

Our elder daughter, Caitlin, had just arrived with baby Ruby, all the way from Botswana. They are with us until Christmas, and I still intended to go to the match. I do have my priorities. Am I not a loyal supporter? Don't people such as George Graham and Roy Keane depend on people like me? I have never knowingly eaten a prawn sandwich. And I have paid £795 for my season ticket.

But as it grew dark, the rain came down. Outside began to look so miserable, while inside Ruby looked so lovely. Can I really drag myself through boring old Crouch End, horrible Hornsey, turdy Turnpike Lane, all those places I hate to hate, just to watch a team I am beginning also to hate?

I'll be giving away four hours of my short, but so far very exciting, life. Four hours that I could spend with my loved ones — less, say, 90 minutes max watching the live match on the telly. Yes, I had suddenly noticed that it was on.

It would also mean I could have a proper supper with the family, drink without worrying about driving, play with Ruby at half-time — perhaps even during throw-ins, if it's boring. So I didn't go.

Next evening, it was Arsenal at home to Ipswich in the Worthington Cup, which I planned to attend, thanks to my half of a £778 season ticket. All day I told myself I was going, laid out my knapsack, quite forgetting it was the birthday of Flora, our younger daughter, and she was coming for supper. Could I really rush off just after she arrived?

I did get to the front door, but my hand got stuck in my pocket. I won't be able drive, will I? Won't be able to read the programme. I know: I'll just stay at home, I'll open another bottle — for Flora, naturally. All right then, might as well watch bits of the game on the telly in my room upstairs. You lot don't want me down here, all women together, chuntering on.

So I didn't go to either match. I willingly, wilfully threw away extremely desirable tickets worth £60. Perhaps more. I reckon my Spurs season ticket probably costs me £40 a game.

I could have given each ticket to a poor person. Yes, I know the government doesn't want us to spoil them, wants us to walk past them in the gutter, not give them anything, but I could have gone down to Kentish Town Tube and said, "Here, poor person, do have this ticket for Spurs, but please don't swap it for drugs, poor person." And what would they have said? "A ticket for Spurs? Up your arse." And they would have been right. Both Spurs and Arsenal got stuffed. So I missed nuffink.

But the point of it all is this: I predict that, eventually, there will be so many live games on television that it will have an adverse effect on gates.

It's hardly happened yet, not over a season, but I did notice lots of empty seats at the two matches I watched on TV. And at both games I didn't go to, crowds were down by around 10,000. At Arsenal, currently in good form and playing a top Premier team, the gate that night was only 25,105 — compared to 37,679 for the next home game against bottom-of-the-Premiership Derby.

But ah, that was on the Saturday. Saturday afternoon is when God intended us to go to football matches. It was His plan, His wish, back in 1888 when He created the Football League. "Let there always be Saturday afternoon games," He said. "Let rattles be rattled, but Bovril can be optional and may be replaced in due course by prawn sandwiches." (Where did Roy Keane get them from? Never seen a prawn sandwich at a football game, not even at Carlisle United. Smoked salmon bagels, yes. Shitloads of them at White Hart Lane.)

I don't think I would ever give up the chance of a Saturday afternoon game. Not even for a brilliant live match on TV at the same time—which, needless to say, they'd never allow (they're not that daft). But on those increasingly frequent Saturday afternoons without a game, I never know what to do. I am distraught. Might as well go to bed. Yet I have two teams to watch. The normal fan has one.

Each season, we lose more and more of our Saturday afternoon games as they bugger about, changing games to Sunday morning, Sunday afternoon, Monday evening, just to suit the television companies.

So far, the clubs don't care about the gaps on the terraces for midweek games. Ten thousand not turning up is meaningless to them, because we have all been tricked into buying season tickets. They've had our money, months and months in advance. If we then waste our tickets, that's our stupidity.

But as football life goes on, with more and more games on television during the week—by which time, most of us will also have been tricked into having those stupid digital channels—it will become less and less attractive to drag ourselves out to watch a run-of-the mill evening game. More hands will get stuck in more pockets. And eventually, what you'll get at some games is total silence from a totally empty stadium. That'll larn 'em.

JAG, THE MAN WHO HAS READ THE RESULTS FOR NEARLY 30 YEARS

27 NOVEMBER 2000

ON SATURDAY A FEW WEEKS AGO A NATION HELD ITS breath. For a moment, it seemed as if one of our national treasures —the unflappable, the inimitable. James Alexander Gordon—was going to stumble as he read out the football results. But then, phew, he recovered, and on he sailed. I touched wood, prayed that it was only a minor cough, a passing itch, not something nasty. How awful it will be when James Alexander Gordon reads out for the last time the immortal words:

"Forfar Athletic ... Four.

East Fife ... Five."

Mere words on mere paper cannot possibly hint at the subtones, the undercurrents, that he puts into his reading of the results. We know and love his inflections so well that we tell ourselves we know where they are going, can guess what comes next.

These days, most of us are aware of the main scores well before James Alexander Gordon clears his throat at 5pm. So many radio programmes do ball-by-ball reports, so many round-ups, so many people on mobile phones. My friend Ian, who sits beside me at Arsenal, has a transistor radio earplug in one ear and his mobile ready at the other. While watching the game in front of him, he nudges me with news I don't want to hear: "Spurs are one down", usually followed by "Spurs are two down".

In the early days of *Sports Report*, which means 52 years ago, the nation relied totally on its reading of the football results. The march *Out of the Blue* must be one of the most recognised signature tunes in the English-speaking world. OK, apart from in the US. I still shiver in anticipation when it strikes up, then smile in pleasure at the thought that, out there, at this very moment, I am bonding with millions of my fellow fans, all of us waiting for James Alexander Gordon.

When I was a boy in the Fifties, my father would demand absolute silence the moment the first note was heard. No one could move or breathe until all the results had been read. As the eldest child, I had the pencil, the *Daily Express* folded with the fixtures and a copy of my dad's treble-chance predictions.

It was my job to catch every score, correctly, then to check if we had become millionaires. One mistake, and I was for it. My father was an invalid during most of my formative years, marooned in bed with multiple sclerosis. Even at the end, when he was dying, we still went through the same five o'clock ritual every Saturday. In my mind, James Alexander Gordon was reading the results. Michael Palin, in a new book called *British Greats*, writes about his memories of *Sports Report* and gives the impression that he, too, heard James Alexander Gordon reading the results, back in the Fifties. Surely some mistake. That would make him about a hundred years old. We must have imagined it, believing that JAG — great initials — has been with us for ever. So I decided to ring him, inquire about his cough, try to find out who he is, get the facts behind the voice.

He lives near Reading, and retired from the BBC staff ten years ago. As a freelance, he still comes in each Saturday to read the results. He's never missed a day through ill health since he first started in 1972. No, not 1952. But, all the same, well done James.

Quite a young chap, in fact: not 65 till February. He comes from Scotland, born in Edinburgh — as his accent suggests — but his real name is not James Alexander Gordon. Just as Tony Blair, another honey-tongued, Edinburgh-born person, should not really be called Tony Blair, so JAG should not be JAG. In James's case, he was the one adopted. (In Tony's, it was his dad.)

James knows his real surname, but won't reveal it. "I had a lovely childhood, with lovely adoptive parents. I wouldn't like anyone to step out of the woodwork after all these years.

"When I was a boy, I used to listen, with my old dad, to *Sports Report*. He was always complaining that the results were read out too quickly. I am supposed to have said: 'I'll read them one day.'"

This didn't happen for a long time. He went into music first, playing the piano and clarinet, then into music publishing. One day, he had to write a little piece about music for the radio. When he handed it in, they told him to read it out.

"By an amazing bit of luck, the then head of presentation, Jimmy Kingsbury, heard me and asked me to meet him. 'Your accent is Scottish?' he said. Which was well spotted. He said they were wanting to change the image of the BBC by getting different accents. They hadn't got a Scottish one yet, on the national network. Would I like to apply?"

James got the job and did newsreading, trailers, the weather forecast. One day in 1972, he was told to do the football.

"When I first did the weather forecast, I made a point of finding out where all these places were. I wanted to understand what I was reading, and so be able to communicate better.

"With the football, I decided I would communicate better if I was in sympathy with the listener. So, for example, if Arsenal have lost, I always try to put some sympathy into my voice when I say: 'Arsenal ... one.' I'm then more upbeat when I say: 'Manchester United ... two.' If it's a draw, then I don't alter my inflection. My voice is the same for both sides. You may think this is completely batty ..."

Not at all, I said, fascinating stuff, almost forgetting to ask him about his cold. "Oh, I didn't have a cold. Something went wrong with the air conditioning in the studio. Kind people from all over the country have been sending me cough sweets ever since.

And quite right, too.

SO IT MAKES YOU RICH, BUT IS IT
WORTH THE YEARS OF PAIN?

4 DECEMBER 2000

I PLAYED FOOTBALL WELL INTO MY FORTIES, PARK FOOT-ball, on Sunday mornings, till I couldn't play park football any more, could hardly walk any more, could hardly get up in the morning. I was in treatment or in bed all week, only staggering up in time for 11 o'clock on Sunday morning in order to go out there, get knackered, then go through the whole process again.

Yet I was supposedly a sensible, mature, grown-up person, with three children, two houses, lots of commitments, oh so much more in my exciting, fulfilled life than piddling park football. So why did I keep going for so long, when my body was clearly screaming at me, "Time's up, Hunt"?

I still can't believe that, after a cartilage op at 42, and recovering from it, I continued to play for another five years, until I had to have another cartilage out, from which my right knee never really recovered. Potty or what?

Hence, I have great sympathy with those stupid, dopey young footballers — the real ones — who, when they are injured and can hardly move, willingly accept some dodgy painkiller (or dodgy advice) administered by a grizzled physio whose qualifications are as dodgy as the painkillers, purely in order to get out there and get stuck in. Only to give their body another clattering. It's their job, they tell themselves. Get injured, and someone else will take your place. Bottle it, refuse to go out when carrying an injury, and you will soon be on your way, son.

They have nothing else in their lives, poor things. It's all they've ever known, all they've wanted, so they ignore what their body tells them, mouthing clichés about "I'm doing what millions would love to do, lucky me, getting paid to have fun".

The truth is that the best fun in football is playing it for fun.

Those Sunday mornings were sheer pleasure. Playing it professionally — that's very rarely fun. Mostly, it's physical grind and mental stress. Players come off with raging headaches, not just aching limbs. But when they're young and fit, thinking they will always be young, and fit enough to recover in time for the next match, what they don't want to hear is some research figures just released from Leicester University.

Half of our pro footballers will end up with arthritis. One in three will need surgery. One in six will be registered disabled. Frightening. Not that any young footballer will ever be frightened. No more than smokers fear smoking by thoughts of what's to come.

Nowadays, every time my arthritis plays up, when my knees are absolute agony and I can't get out of bed, I think: oh God, you fool, why did you carry on when you knew you were crocked'? You knew you'd have to pay for it. Yes, I know, I might have got arthritis anyway, but I didn't help myself, did I?

It is, in fact, OK at present, thanks for asking. I've kept it at bay with a brilliant drug called Sulphasalazine. I hope, touch wood, that I'll never need surgery. Unlike poor Tommy Smith. You would have thought the sight of him hobbling around would scare the shit out of any of today's players.

Which is why I honestly, sincerely, deeply believe that players deserve whatever they can get. The transfer system is ridiculous, out of control, going to ruin football, should be altered, and soon will be. But a million a year for regulars in the Premier League, while stupendous compared with days gone by, seems to me pretty fair, all things considered.

Consider their short working life — ten to 15 years — plus an early death or a crippled old age. Top barristers can earn much the same, but they can stay at the top for 30 years and don't need handfuls of painkillers to get off the bench. Editors of national newspapers might get the push, but the pay-offs are big, and all they get from sitting at their desk is a fat bum as opposed to broken bones.

Film stars, if they are male, can go on for ever—even baldies such as Sean Connery—with no one kicking them off the ball or up the arse.

In TV, the only possible damage is to your ego, not your shins or your fib and tib. Des Lynam's got a contract for £5m, plus £5,000 extra for working on a Saturday. He does so little over the year, presents so few progs, then talks for hardly more than seven minutes max, that his only fear must be sleeping sickness. No doubt he's got that covered in his contract. Falling asleep through boredom probably means he gets penalty payments.

If Brooklyn Beckham ever grows up and decides he can't do accessory modelling for his parents for ever, then he'd be mad, given a choice of careers, to go into football. Now, *talking* about football, that's much safer. Or if he does well at Eton, gets some half-decent grades in ancient history and environmental studies, he could go into public relations. No chance there of being booed by the crowd, ridiculed in the tabloids, stalked by halfwits, hounded by the paparazzi.

The clubs, needless to say, don't care. They are experts in taking one game at a time, living for today, with no thoughts for the long-term good of their charges. They aim to squeeze them dry, pound them into a pulp, then throw them away, buy some new models, and moan about the prices.

Is Rio Ferdinand getting £30,000 a week at Leeds? Does Roy Keane get £50,000 at Man United? I dunno. But I bet you one of them, at the age of 55, will think the money wasn't enough for what came afterwards.

THE FAT-FACED CURSE THAT
STALKS THE TERRACES

11 DECEMBER 2000

TO THE ARSENAL GAME. I TOOK MY THERMOS FLASK OF coffee for half-time, as per usual, carrying it in my new and rather bijou, chic, shiny rucksack, along with two tangerines and a packet of Strepsils. I haven't got a cold, but I find they're awfully efficacious for keeping the mouth active, the throat lubricated and the jaw engaged during those moments in the match when I might get caught with nothing to eat or drink.

Despite taking my own provisions, I bought a cup of tea the very minute I got there. I did look at the smoked salmon bagels, price £2.20, and the chicken mayo, only £1.70, but decided to stick to my own supplies and manage somehow to spin them out for 90 minutes.

I've already forgotten the score, but my record for spinning out one Strepsil during the match — which was against, hold on, I have it somewhere, oh yeah, Southampton — was 13½ minutes.

Then, before watching the Chelsea match on television, against another team, I had a cappuccino and a slice of home-made ginger-bread. That was just to get me upstairs and settled down in front of Andy Gray. During the match itself, first half, I had, now let me see, a pear, an orange, an apple and a plum, making them last about ten minutes each. Good job there wasn't much extra time for injuries. I'd have been well stuck.

At half-time, I went downstairs and had a glass of Chablis and some peanuts, my little refresher. I then took up with me a large glass of Safeway's Beaujolais, my favourite drink at the moment (hope Santa's listening), to get me through the second half. Well, it was a late-afternoon Sunday game. For an evening, eight o'clock kick-off, it's all of the above, plus a hot toddy.

Now why is this? Why do I have a compulsion to eat and drink all the way through a game?

First of all, I don't think I'm untypical. I remember years ago interviewing the writer Brigid Brophy and her husband Michael Levey, director of the National Gallery, neither of them football fans, and discovering that their weekend fix was *Match of the Day* while drinking whisky.

All round me at Spurs and Arsenal each week, I am surrounded by people stuffing their fat faces. The smells, the burgers and cheap tomato sauce, the nasty chips, the bottles of horrible fizzy drinks — yuk. I like to think the stuff I shove into my fat face is very healthy. All right, apart from the gingerbread.

Inside and outside Highbury and White Hart Lane, as at football stadia all over the world, there are fans stuffing their stupid faces with sweets and savouries, snacks and drinks. And nougat. That's what disappears into the fat faces in France and Spain. Disgusting.

When I first started going to Spurs in the Sixties, standing on the Shelf, there was this bloke who sold peanuts in little white paper bags. You'd put your hand up and he'd throw one to you, even if you were miles away. Bloody clever. Then you'd pass the money along, hand to hand. Very trusting. Wonder where he is now.

Going to Carlisle United, in the Fifties, it was Bovril and hot pies, yum yum. "Who stole all the pies?" That's the name of a fanzine, I think. They have always gone together, food and football.

Yet I despise myself. When I find myself watching the clock, rather than the match, to see if I'm due my next top-up — as I do like to spin them out — I think, how awful, how pathetic.

I used to criticise my sister Marion when she had a cigarette during a meal. Isn't one pleasure at a time enough, I'd say to her piously. Are you not ruining the taste of the meal by smoking at the same time.

At a recent *New Statesman* lunch, I sat next to Des Wilson. He asked me to pass him the butter. And I said no. The bread is delicious, I said, there is no need to put butter on it. Pass the bloody butter, he said. No, I replied. Butter is your enemy. You don't need it. He had to ask someone at the far end of the table to pass him their butter, and didn't speak to me again.

I don't know why I did it. Being silly, being stupid, being against the weakness that I myself suffer from. Doubling pleasures, when there's no need to. Or greed, as it's called. My greed seems to have trebled in the past year, which is why I bought myself the dinky little rucksack. At this rate, I'll soon need an Eddie Stobart truck to get me to each match. One pleasure at a time should be enough. If I say I love going to football, surely I can be content with that. Why pile on other pleasures?

Because I see others eating, all around me, is that why I follow suit? Not really. At home, I am watching and guzzling all on my own.

A nervous habit, perhaps? In some senses. I do twitch if I time it badly and there is a gap between Strepsils. But it can't be nerves brought on by worrying about the football. At Arsenal, I don't care who wins, yet I still eat throughout.

At Spurs, I am always nervous. That's why I have chips afterwards. I tell myself, during the match, I'll only have them to celebrate us winning. When it's clear we're not going to win, even if the match goes on for 90 days, I say, OK then, I'll get some chips, just to make up for losing. If it's a boring draw, I find myself getting a packet out of boredom.

In my normal, non-football life, I never eat between meals, so that can mean five hours with nothing in my mouth. But when it comes to football, I can't manage five minutes without something in my gob. I must have put on pounds this season already. What am I going to do? I can think of only one solution. Anyone like a rather chic, silky, bijou rucksack?

HE WAS BECKS'S BEST MAN, BUT
GARY IS STILL THE WEAKEST LINK

26 FEBRUARY 2001

I WAS LOOKING FOR SOME FOOTBALL, LIVE OR DEAD, HIGH-lights or lowlights, on any channel, anywhere on the globe. I wasn't fussed. Spanish football is about the best to watch at present, and I do like that Spanish bloke in the studio. His English is so good and his clothes so bad. On English TV, the experts dress up for the studio, often in very expensive flash clothes that strobe so much you have to put on sun specs. But Guillam (as it seems to be pronounced) dresses from Oxfam.

No luck, though. I was just about to switch off and do some work instead when I came across this quiz programme called *The Weakest Link*. Very easy to come across, quiz programmes. If it's not cookery, it's bleeding quizzes. You can't, miss them.

I remember Anne Robinson when she was young and on the *Sunday Times*. They always had a silly young girl reporter who got sent on silly young girl reporter stories: oh, you know, dress up like a schoolgirl or a nun or Ann Widdecombe and ask for the morning-after pill in ten chemists' shops. The middle-aged male executives loved these girl reporters, gave them a big show in the paper. Much to the jealousy of the silly young boy reporters. We had to do boring stories about who might be the next Bishop of Southwark which never got in the paper.

Tina Brown was later one of the silly girls. I thought she, too, would be a silly person doing silly stories for ever. Like Anne Robinson, she turned out to be a real, talented toughie. Playing a similar role today is Victoria Coren. She'll probably end up DG of the BBC.

I watched *The Weakest Link*—nothing else to do—and Anne Robinson's acting is brilliant, but then you have to be a good actor to be a TV presenter. I loved the music, the lighting effects, the revving-up of the atmosphere. But the title is stretching it a bit. In the end, they are all competing against each other, not working together. It would apply much better to football. All the players in a team have to work as a unit, and are only ever as strong as their weakest link. So, while watching our lads in Europe last week — and didn't they do well; let's hope they're still in Europe by the time you read this — I found myself looking out for the weakest link.

With Man Utd, I thought at the beginning of the season that it might be Silvestre. He made soft mistakes, gave the ball away, but he has since improved. Wes Brown, as the newest regular, could easily have been the weakest link, but he, too, has got better over the season. Barthez has been lucky, doing silly things that could have rebounded. His weaknesses have yet to be punished. Could Beckham be the weakest link? In one sense he is, because so much is expected of him. He demands the ball, often when others are in better positions. His free kicks have been poor recently. And he can be petty, giving away daft fouls when he loses the ball.

But we are here today to eliminate the weakest player in the Man Utd team, the one most likely to muck things up.

Gary — you are the weakest link.

"Then how come Fergie always picks me?' mutters Gary Neville, walking away, shaking his head. "You've always had it in for me, just 'cos I was Becks's best man ..."

In the Leeds Utd team, Darren Huckerby, who has never knowingly looked up while on the ball, was the weakest, but he has gone to Man City. Jason Wilcox, another winger, once quite sharp, who now staggers up his own exhaust, is usually a sub these days, having already been identified by O'Leary as a weak link. The point of this exercise is to look at the players who are consistently in the first team and decide who is weakest. A sure sign of the strength of Man Utd is that, after Gary Neville, I would find it hard to chuck out anyone else.

With Leeds, there's quite a choice. I wouldn't have Danny Mills in my Leeds team, as he contributes little, nor Michael Duberry, unless I wanted someone clattered. Viduka has become a weak link by being so inconsistent. So much is expected of him that he often disappoints. But he can keep his place, as he is always menacing. Nigel Martyn could become a weak link, despite his sterling work. He is keeping Paul Robinson out of the team — who I think would make Leeds stronger. Having considered these possibles, I have no hesitation.

Michael — you are the weakest link.

"You wanna fight?" scowls Duberry, lumbering away. "I'll see you after the show."

With Liverpool, you might expect McAllister to be a weak link, at his great age, but his role is to fill in for the weakest at any given moment. He doesn't let the team down, is never weaker than the weakest link. Westerveld is currently seen to be weak, but he's their best goalie.

I think I can guess who Gerard Houllier considers his weakest link, yet he was a first choice when he first came.

Christian — you are the weakest link.

"Gott in Himmel, Donner und Blitzen," shouts Ziege, "vy did I ever shave mein hair ..."

In the Arsenal team, Luzhny is a lump, but he has not quite made it as a regular. Pires has, but is hardly worth his place so far. But it's another Frenchman I would give the heave to, because he is usually anonymous — except when giving away silly free kicks.

Giles — you are the weakest link.

"You're anti-French as well as anti-German," barks Grimandi, ringing his lawyer on his mobile as he leaves the studio. "Also, you can't spell. There's two L's in Gilles."

Now for Spurs. Oh no. If I start on their weak links, there won't be room for the classified ads.

THESE DAYS I'M JUST A HUMBLE
RESEARCHER FOR JULIE BURCHILL

12 MARCH 2001

THERE WAS A VERY SILLY OBSERVATION ABOUT DAVID Beckham the other day by a so-called football expert, one who has been writing about football for hundreds of years, goes to matches all the time, swears he loves the game. He suggested, rather smuttily, that the reason for Beckham's loss of form is because he and Posho are trying for a brother/sister for Brooklyn, aged two this month, so he's too knackered.

I don't suppose Becks lost any sleep over it, as he is the most written-about 25-year-old this side of the planet. With more to come. Julie Burchill is now working on a biography of him, once she's eased herself out of bed, once she's got to grips with what he does. She's been on the blower for help. I've faxed her a few technical details. Eleven-a-side, the white wooden posts are called goals, that round thing is the ball. If she doesn't give me a research credit, I'll be livid.

Salman Rushdie is doing a novel about him in which he falls to earth and turns into Angela Carter. Andrew Motion is finishing an epic poem about him. It's really about Andrew's old father, with some lovely memories of his Brylcreem jar, but he's got Becks in the title and the *Guardian*'s panting for it.

The silly person was me. And I take it all back. Loss of form is a very serious condition that should not be mocked or made little of. Normal people, going about their normal work, don't suffer from it. Only those whose work depends on skill or artistry know what it's like when it deserts them.

Poets, so the myth goes, perform best when young. Their loss of form comes quite suddenly, and the muse moves on. Hence it's vital for poets to die young, like Keats and Shelley, and be considered geniuses for ever. Don't hang on or you'll be laughed at behind your back, like Daddy Wordsworth. Novelists can keep going longer, but then fashion rather than age catches up with them, and their form goes, becomes out of date. When I used to interview famous novelists, I'd ask them for their best own book. It was usually the one least regarded by the world at large. Artists, you see, often don't know what it is they have. And can't understand it when it goes.

Footballers are much the same. They're training just as hard, driving the Ferrari the same route to work, putting the jock strap over their head in the same order, so what's gone wrong, they cry. Why have I lost form? Most of what they do is instinctive. Trying a certain shot from a difficult angle is as much a spontaneous reaction as it is down to training. In the condition known as loss of form, none of these instinctive reactions seems to be working.

Even worse, when loss of form arrives, players find themselves unable to do the simple things that they've practised doing all their lives. The most obvious example is their first touch. With loss of form, their body tenses, their limbs stiffen, and instead of cushioning the ball and immediately controlling it, they lose it. They lose it because they've lost it. Whatever it was.

We're not talking here about loss of form through carrying an injury or recovering from an injury. We're talking in the abstract. A touch which, out of the blue, out of the air, has dematerialised. Yes, it's connected to lack of confidence, but confidence goes after form has been lost. Making them both return, that's the hard bit. It's mystified football managers for 150 years. I'd be emeritus professor of football theory at the University of Leicester if I knew the answers, not just a humble researcher for J Burchill.

I remember asking Bill Nicholson what he did. His answer was three words — work, work, work. That was all he could ever think of doing. Back to the training ground. Work the buggers till they dropped. More recently, I asked Joe Kinnear. What he often does is rearrange the team formation, give the out-of-form player a slightly different, less onerous role, until his confidence returns. Or he might rest the player—but keep it dead secret, pretending he has an injury—thus removing him from the limelight before it gets worse and the fans get on his back.

Beckham's recent loss of form is not apparently connected with any injury, as in the case of Fowler, Owen and Kewell, though he did say he'd had the flu a few weeks ago.

Individual loss of form is often connected with a team's loss of form, but not in Beckham's case. Man U are now so ahead of the pack, they're out of sight. Nor is it connected with any personal loss of status. Being made England captain was clearly a matter of great pride.

On paper, most things could hardly have been going better for him this season. Even the *Daily Mail* has come round to him, seeing him as an excellent father, good husband, upholder of family values. I now expect a grovelling apology from anyone who ever suggested he might be a spoiled brat who wears nancy clothes. Even the jokes about his IQ have become affectionate.

Perhaps he needs something to go wrong, to be attacked and jeered at again. It was remarkable how he recovered from being sent off in that England game, blamed for everything, then for months afterwards he got booed at every away game. The boy done well, surviving all that. Perhaps Fergie should drop him, or Eriksson not pick him for the next game. That might shake him up.

Or is he just confused? Confused about his best role in the team, wondering whether he should play wide, in the middle, go forward, stay back? Or confused about his role in life. He has given off some strange signals about his sexuality over the past year.

I've suggested this to Julie. She says she's already on to it. Got 50,000 words on the subject, even before she's struggled out of bed.

NOW THE RUSSKIS SING AND SHOUT
LIKE THE REST OF US

19 MARCH 2001

FOURTEEN YEARS AGO, MY WIFE AND I GOT INVITED TO Russia by the Russian Writers Union. They wanted a writing family to have a holiday with Russian writers and their families at Pitsunda on the Black Sea. We took our younger daughter. Flora, then aged 12. The hotel was an awful concrete block, with awful food, and the day we arrived Gorbachev banned alcohol. Did I moan.

We also had a week in Moscow, which was fascinating. They'd asked in advance what we'd like to see. I said definitely no opera or tractor farms. What I wanted most of all was to go to a football match. So they arranged it, even laid on a Chaika limousine to take us there, one of those monster black numbers that leading comrades ponced around in.

It was Moscow Spartak against Moscow Torpedo in the Lenin stadium. The programme was only ten kopeks, about 10p, just two sheets, printed on what looked like wartime lavatory paper. I still have it. One of my football treasures. A memory of one of the weirdest games I've ever witnessed.

The military were everywhere, watching every supporter, in case they got out of line. There were no scarves, no singing, no cheering, just a bit of clapping for a good bit of play and whistling in derision for any mistake. At the end, we all filed out slowly, section by section, watched suspiciously by the military, while a giant screen showed a comedy cartoon. I presumed this was to distract the fans and keep them quiet.

Fourteen years later, I was really looking forward to watching Moscow Spartak again. As I walked to Highbury, I wondered how many of their fans would turn up. Must be pretty expensive, getting from Moscow to London for a match.

I was at Arsenal's two previous European Champions League games at Highbury. The fans of Bayern Munich, about 5,000 of them, were brilliant, sang all the way through, often in English, good-humouredly taking the piss out of the Arsenal fans.

There were just as many French fans for the Lyons game. They were also terrific, really got behind their team, but didn't sing quite as loudly as the Germans. And they stuck to French. So badly educated, these Frogs, not like our cosmopolitan Arsenal fans. Oh yes, they often sing in French. "*Tee-erry onree, Tee-erry onree.*" There, that's four French words for a start.

I caught sight of my first Russians about two streets from the ground. A Russian babe in her late thirties who looked like Pamela Anderson's poorer sister, only able to afford cheap cosmetic surgery, was tottering on high heels in the middle of the road. She held a camera and was taking a photo of her bloke. He was a heavy, aged about 50, in a camel coat, with a big cigar and Mafia-like leer. He had his fat arm around a policewoman who very sportingly was smiling for the camera.

At the ground itself, I was surprised to see a decent-sized queue for the away-supporters' entrance. There were about 500 Spartak fans, most of them wearing scarves, shouting and singing. Just like Germans, French, Brits or fans anywhere.

We all took some Russian lessons, 14 years ago. Flora was excellent, but I managed only a few phrases: thank you, hello, goodbye, your caviar is very good and where is the wine. The phrases are still in my head, but I can't remember what they mean.

I went down the queue and asked if anyone spoke English. A tall bloke of about 30 said he did, so we chatted away. He expected 2,000 Spartak supporters in all, half from Moscow, the others from France and Germany. He was from Moscow, where he worked as an office manager. He'd paid $600 for his trip.

As I was talking to him, a rather posh English bloke with a girl of about eight came up and started asking questions of my new

Russian friend. Do you mind, I said. Find your own rotten Russki.

"I am a journalist," he said. Same here, I replied. Ace football columnist for the *New Statesman*, so buzz off.

He was the editor of *Prospect*. It's a rather classy publication, but I don't think it has a football column. OK then, I said, you can join in.

As we got near the top of the queue, we could see that all the Russians were being searched on entry. Our Russian friend put his hands in his pockets and pulled out a four pack of Budweiser and handed them to me and the *Prospect* man. He was about to take one and I stopped him. You hold on to them, I told the Russian, you might be able to sneak one in. If not, you can get them back afterwards.

We all shook hands, wished each other the best of luck in the game. I walked over to the Upper West Stand entrance, expecting my Prospect friend to follow me. He said he hadn't got a seat. He lived locally and had just come out with his daughter to wander around, watch the crowds, soak up the atmosphere.

An interesting sign of the times. Euro games have become like street festivals. You wouldn't be scared to take along your granny. There is a camaraderie in football that gets forgotten whenever there's a nasty incident.

So it's been great this season, with all the Euro games. I've loved watching them, in the flesh or on the box. And haven't the English clubs done well? So far.

I am writing this on Monday, as ever, which is so annoying. Each week I think what a fool I'll look if Becks has a blinder, having slagged him off.

So as I write, I don't know whether it will be *dosvedanya* to Man U, Arsenal and Liverpool in Europe, but I hope not. Or whether *dosvedanya* means goodbye, hello or thank you. One of those, anyway.

THAT FAT BLOKE, WASSISNAME ...
GIZZA? WHERE IS HE NOW?

THIS IS THE TIME OF THE YEAR WHEN WE SAY THIS IS THE time of the year. OK, it's not quite the end of the season, but I'm getting in before all the real football brains give us the benefit of their wisdom.

Team of the Season Ipswich have done amazingly well with very little. Fulham also, but with quite a lot spent on them. But the team of the season has to be Leeds. Each time they progressed in Europe, I thought, that's it, they'll be found out now, it can't go on, they just haven't got the strength or class of Man Utd or Arsenal; then there was the court case, still with us, that might distract, if not derail, Lee Bowyer at least. But behold and lo, did not Leeds do well.

My Biggest Mistake Early in the season, I found myself moaning and groaning about D Beckham and G Neville, then groaning even more when sackfuls of letters from Man Utd fans poured in, mostly in green ink, mostly from south of Milton Keynes, many with prawn stains on them. I take nothing back about them. But I have to say I was wrong about Rio Ferdinand. I did think, at £18m, he was a waste of money. The lad done well. He's now Rio Grande, as we say in Spain.

Haircut of the Year Not awarded. Even I am so bored by the subject. They all look the same. As for Becks, I'd rather watch paint dry than watch his bum fluff grow again.

Forgotten Men That fat bloke, losing his hair, used to eat Mars bars, last heard of at Everton, now what was he called? Gizza? Gassy? Funny how household names can slide out of the back door, into the garden, over the wall and disappear. Then there was that very well-dressed manager, Scotch bloke, the one who didn't take a bung—am I making it up or was he really managing Spurs only a few weeks ago? I wonder where he is now.

Longest Leaver of the Season No competition here. Gareth Southgate has been leaving Aston Villa since I was a lad. Each week he was off, couldn't stand it any more, club had no ambition, open to offers, wants to improve myself, coats on the ground, satchels for goalposts. And yet he's still there, last time I looked. And still leaving?

Oldie of the Year Gary McAllister of Liverpool. What a bargain, at a cost of only nothing, and what a trooper, still fit, still keen, still sensible, still dangerous. Richard Gough is another oldie doing well. They both remind me of Gordon Strachan, who kept going while drawing his pension. There must be something in the Scottish blood, or the deep-fried Mars bars. Oh no, spare the green ink, silly joke.

Players a Pleasure to Watch Vieira, whom I have admired all season, along with Giggs, the most exciting for a lot of the season. Both are pretty obvious if you watch the English league, as is Henrik Larsson in Scotland. What a season he has had, after that long injury. In the First Division, I do like watching Matt Jansen of Blackburn Rovers, not just because he comes from Carlisle and has asthma, both of which help, but he has such flair. However, my milk token goes to Don Hutchinson of Sunderland. I'd pay money to see him. What am I saying? Do you want to know how much I've already spent, this season, on tickets for Spurs, Arsenal and Carlisle United, on programmes, on stuffing my face, on ONdigital in London and Sky in Loweswater? It must come to £2,500, which is more than Mark Bosnich earns in two minutes...

Least-liked Commentator I'm not mentioning Jonathan Pearce. I'm pretending he doesn't exist. So that leaves a vacancy on my allergy list. Ken Livingstone's voice is still there, Charles Dance's hair, Brian Sewell's face, Jonathan Ross's smirk, anything to do with Bridget Jones, but in the annoying football commentator list there's a gap at the top. Moving into it slowly is Barry Davies. He has become so superior and school-masterly with his "absolutely no need for that" or "oh dear oh dear oh dear". His most affected remark of the year was: "The referee declined to answer in the affirmative. "

Commentator of the Year I do like Andy Gray, but he's getting a bit earnest and I wish he'd stop saying "Richard" every time he pauses for breath. So, once again, it's the golden foot award for Big Ron, my all-time fave. I'll tell you what, he's been in the wide-awake club this year, though I was confused by one new Ronnism. "He's old-manned him." He said this after someone had got a dodgy free kick. I think, though I'm not sure, that he was suggesting that he'd pretended to fall over like an old man. Nice image. His best phrase was about Challinor of Tranmere. "Tell you what, he can throw the ball further than I go on holiday."

League of the Year No argument here, either. It's the Primera Liga in Spain. Once again, their teams have done best in Europe. Well done, McManaman, becoming a regular for Real Madrid, when initially he appeared out of it. And Figo now appears to have been worth the £40m, after all. I always smile when I see his name on a team sheet. Mr Fig, which is what his name means in Portuguese, makes him a figure of fun.

NOW I KNOW: JOHN SMITH IS
A SPANISH CLOTHES FIRM

14 MAY 2001

ALL SEASON I'VE BEEN WATCHING THE SPANISH LEAGUE ON Saturday and Sunday evenings on Sky. I have seen the quality, if not tasted the atmosphere. Easy to follow. 'Goal' and 'corner' are the same words. What has usually puzzled me are some of the adverts around the pitch. Is Caja Madrid, a shop? Where or what is Finisterre? Is Movistar something to do with movies? And who on earth is John Smith? Surely it can't be the English beer.

So I decided it was time for some first-hand research. My dear wife wouldn't come. All that way, just to go to a football match — you must be potty. Yes, but I'll have a short hol' as well, a bit of sun and swimming, which was one reason why I chose Mallorca. The other is their form. Mallorca are currently fourth in the Primera Liga, equal with Valencia, well above Barcelona.

I sent a fax to the club: awfully influential football columnist, writer for the world-famous *New Statesman*, please arrange press ticket, yours and much obliged. I heard bugger all. Probably wouldn't have worked in England, either. Some people are just so short-sighted.

So I got to the Son Moix stadium at four o'clock last Sunday afternoon, two hours before kick-off, and had it to myself. The whole of Spain is in hiding at that time of day. I walked round the stadium, which is a big new concrete affair, open on three sides. It's well outside Palma, beyond the ring road. Even one hour before kick-off, the atmosphere was nil. I saw only two stalls outside selling football stuff. At Spurs or Arsenal, the average is between 50 and 60 stalls.

Inside, it was all incredibly clean and tidy, with some dinky food stalls, but I couldn't find the club shop. I wanted to buy tat, I mean, treasures for my collections (I managed to buy some later at the airport). I did get my press ticket, though, with a bit of faffing, bit of flashing my BBC pass — it dates back to my Radio 4 *Bookshelf* days, a decade ago, so I had to flash it pretty quickly.

The press seats were at the very top of the main stand. They were ordinary seats, not separated, which meant that, minutes after kick-off, they filled up with families and kids moving for a better view. They'd hang you if you tried that at Spurs.

The programme was puny, just a little booklet with hardly anything in it, but it was free. Mallorca is not a big club compared with Real Madrid and Barcelona, but even so, it is in the Dark Ages as far as marketing goes. We might not lead Europe in footer, but by God we're ace at shifting merchandising rubbish.

Before the match, they played "Hey Jude", followed by "Yesterday", so I did feel at home. Then there was a minute's silence for the club's owner, who had just died. There was total silence apart from some solemn piano music. What well-behaved away fans, I thought, then realised there weren't any. Near me was a reporter from a Zaragoza paper, who said that 20 at most might have travelled to the match. There is no culture of away fans in Spain, he said. Distances are too long. Fans can't afford it. Matches traditionally take place on Sunday evenings, and they have to be up early next morning for work.

About 1,000 young Mallorca fans in the north stand managed to sing and chant constantly. The tunes sounded much the same as in Britain. When they were two goals ahead, they sang "We are North Bank/Hello South Side", just as fans do at Arsenal. There's never much swearing, so my friend said. Calling the ref a poofter is about their worst. At half-time, I looked around for the press room, desperate for a drink, only to be told that there was no hospitality room for the hacks. Bloody hell. They *are* in the Dark Ages. When I used to report matches, at White Hart Lane or Brunton Park, I always looked forward to my free whisky at half-time, a beer or coffee afterwards, plus hot sausage rolls. We do know how to treat the fourth estate over here.

In San Moix, I had to queue up with the punters and pay for my own beer — 350 pesetas (about £1.40). As I did so, I saw a notice saying "*Vomitorios — acces del 18 al 24*". What could that mean? A special place for vomiting? Now that's what I call civilised. I presumed it must be some sort of sickroom.

Mallorca beat Zaragoza 2 – 1, so kept up their chances of getting into Europe. The standard of individual play was about average for our Premier League, a bit like watching Ipswich or Leicester, but the atmosphere was poor. It was partly the result of there being no away fans, but mainly because of a huge running track round the pitch, separating the spectators from the action.

I went to the press conference afterwards to listen to the Mallorca coach, Luis Aragones. We sat in rows at desks, as if at school. In a close-up on TV a few weeks ago, I noticed that Aragones's false teeth fell out during an emotional moment on the touchline. This time, he hardly opened his mouth, grunting out a few banalities.

But I did notice on his tracksuit the words "John Smith". Turns out to be a Spanish firm that does sports clothes. Caja Madrid is a savings bank. Finisterre is an insurance firm. Movistar is some sort of telephone thing. So I didn't waste my time. It was a social and cultural experience. And I got a tan.

2001–02 SEASON

From England's triumph in Munich to World Cup departure

WHERE WERE YOU? ON THE NIGHT ENGLAND PLAYED Germany in Munich. What were you doing? Surely you can remember, will always remember. 'Twas a famous victory: that's what Old Kaspar remarked in that Robert Southey poem we all learnt at school—well, I did, being educated. It was on German soil as well, the Battle of Blenheim; Old Kaspar remembered it well, even if he couldn't remember the point of it all.

Southey, once poet laureate, would be so surprised if he came back now and found that, out of all the thousands of poems and dozens of books he wrote, he is mostly remembered for writing the original version of *The Three Bears*, for his poem about the Lodore Falls and for Old Kaspar's boring, banal observation about it being a famous victory.

In my lifetime, I can remember so many famous public events, such as England winning at Wembley in 1966, as I was there, and Kennedy dying in the year, er, whenever it was—that's about it, really. Until last Saturday. That should stay in my head for, oh, could be days and days.

We are in Lakeland, have been since May. Two months ago, my wife said what about getting three tickets for the Theatre by the Lake at Keswick for 1 September, for us and my sister, knowing she was going to be staying with us then. I said fine, good idea, go on, buy the tickets. Without looking in my diary. How could I have been so stupid? Yet for months I'd been counting off the days to the New Season and to the Big Match.

In June and July, I went searching the globe for anything foot-ballish, anywhere: under-14 games in Albania, South American cups in empty stadia, Asian exhibition nonsenses, Scottish Third Division warm-ups, even women playing women. Yes, it got desperate.

Once into August proper, the real stuff was with us at last, and I went mad and lashed out £60 for the pay-per-view season, even though we won't be here for most of it. That hasn't been a total waste of money. I now know that George Graham is still alive and looking even sleeker and smoother, with his hair turning darker with every appearance.

It's been dead good, these past three weeks, having real football games to enjoy, but what I was looking forward to most was the Big One. When I saw that in my diary for 1 September I'd written 'Skylight, Keswick', I could not believe it. I don't like the theatre anyway. And I certainly don't want to have to sit through some rant by David Hare. In fact, I'd pay good money not to. Which is what I did.

I drove them to Keswick early in the afternoon, dumped them in the street, shoved money into my wife's hand for the taxi back, and drove like mad over Whinlatter, getting back in time for Scotland's three o'clock game with Croatia. Didn't they do well, managing a draw, considering they have no decent players, but not as well as Ireland did against Holland.

I'd drunk most of a bottle of Safeway's Beaujolais by the time the England game started, telling myself I'll need something, to cheer myself up, this is bound to be depressing. Outside in the fields, I could hear what sounded like an oompah band, playing very loudly. The Jerries are already celebrating, I thought, then realised it was the wedding. A son of one of our neighbours got married in the afternoon and the do was at night, in a posh marquee, just two fields away.

I thought of the people there, not best pleased that a wedding had clashed with the Big Game, then after six minutes, when Germany got their goal, I thought, well, they won't be missing much. We could be in for a hammering here.

When it got to 5–1 to England, I was sure I was dreaming, or drunk. Even weirder, I found myself thinking that Gary Neville had played quite well, a thought I thought I'd never think, not in this lifetime. Beckham was brilliant, Owen was awesome, Gerrard was great. Those poor sods at the wedding, those saddos watching David Hare in Keswick — imagine missing such performances. I didn't mind witnessing it on my own. Or opening another bottle on my own. We all know what happened afterwards. Not to me. We won't go into that. To the world at large. It's been well documented.

Production in every office and factory in England went up next morning by 15.7 per cent, except in Liverpool, where it increased by 95 per cent. Sales of every newspaper have been 11 per cent higher, as Munich titbits were recycled all week, the FTSE has risen by 132 points, our gross national product for the month will break all records, 5,000 fans left for a pilgrimage to Sven's home in Sweden, 50,000 left for Rome to have him made a saint, the England medical team were all given knighthoods for services to Beckham's groin and Tony Blair called a snap election to cash in on the national euphoria. OK, I made up some of those things. But not the overall effects.

One effect on me is that I now have to acknowledge that

managers matter. Almost all those players in Munich were available to Hoddle and Keegan—except, perhaps, for Ashley Cole and Steven Gerrard. It was only last season that those two came through, became admired, got rated. All the others have been around and in the reckoning for the past three years. Yet Hoddle and Keegan buggered it up, couldn't fit the parts together, couldn't make the whole team work.

The other effect of last Saturday on me has been financial. I wilfully wasted a £10 ticket for a David Hare play, then forked out £23 for their taxi home. Sometimes I'm such a spendthrift. But 'twas money well spent.

I WANT TO SIT ON THE SUBS' BENCH:
NO WORK, NO STRESS, HIGH PAY

24 SEPTEMBER 2001

WHEN I GROW UP, I'D LIKE TO BE ON THE BENCH. NOT AS A judge, though that's quite a good job: no one argues with you and it's quite well paid these days. Last week, I had dinner with a QC who's working part-time as a circuit judge. "Must be losing money," I said, "compared with working full-time in your chambers." "Not at all," he replied. Judges can now get £120,000 a year. So he quite fancies it. Too late for me, I suppose. Forgotten all the Latin I ever knew and I hate anything on my head.

I mean on the subs' bench, needless to say. It's a very crowded place these days, for several reasons. First, each team is allowed to bring on three subs during a match. Then the top clubs have so much money, and so many vital competitions to play in, that they have two complete squads filled with top-class players, all capable of playing in the first team. They therefore have five subs, ready and stripped, sitting on the bench hoping to fill the three places, usually with another five behind, in their suits, looking awfully clean, glowing, affluent, but decidedly pissed off.

In ye olden days, with no subs allowed, and then just one, your first-team squad was quite slim. Even a top team would travel with only 13 players, leaving the rest of the club's professionals at home, playing in the stiffs. That was their role in life, lesser citizens, on piddling pay, doomed to the reserves, but at least they got a game each week. Now we have the situation at Man Utd, Arsenal, Chelsea and Liverpool where there are up to ten top-class players, at the height of their powers, physically honed to perfection, international stars, household names in football houses, earning £50,000 a week—and doing bugger all.

All they can do is sit there, week after week, thinking of their bank balance. There's little moral or financial pressure on them. No one makes them feel guilty about earning all that money while doing nothing. Often they've been bought for negative reasons (for example, to stop another club buying them), or for eventualities that no one expects will ever happen (such as all 17 of the club's first-choice strikers going poorly or Awol), or just as a warning, to make those playing play better.

So wouldn't you fancy it? All that money, yet no work, no responsibilities. The manager doesn't shout at you afterwards. You don't get criticised in the papers. You can go out on the town and not be hissed at by fans. You don't get dropped because of a loss of form. And you don't get injured. That's the biggest plus of all. Not playing must extend your career by about five years. As the money keeps pouring in, with managers buying everything that moves on two legs and can kick straight, we'll soon develop a breed of players who will spend their whole career not playing. You'll have to be good at 19, if not stunning, have every club in the world after you, then you sit back while your agent sells you on your video, from club to club. You'll peak financially at about 27, then for five years you'll go down the leagues, for less money — but what an easy life it's been. And you'll probably get a testimonial at the end. Tax-free.

Yes, I know there will be mental and emotional aggravation along the way. Subs do feel out of it, being there, but not being part of it, invisible men who never sweat, who stand at the back of the dressing room in their suits, don't get in the bath with the lads, find the top totty in the clubs looking through them. It's hard to keep your face straight and not punch the air when the team loses, tough not to look pleased when a player in your position breaks his leg.

In your mixed-up, fed-up state, you might even do the odd daft thing — I dunno, sue your manager for calling you fat and hire Cherie Blair QC to fight your case when all that's really bugging you is not playing. What's happened to Ginola, by the way? Is it true? Has it been settled? Must ask my part-time judge friend.

Robbie Fowler will get even more bitter and twisted this season if he remains a sub. And imagine being Andy Cole's partner when he comes home after a hard day on a hard bench. But they'll have to get used to it. Goalkeepers have always been in this position. The number two goalie can sit there literally for years doing nothing. Steve Harper spent five years at Newcastle waiting for his debut. Richard Wright, the top man at Ipswich, with England caps, could easily spend the next two years waiting for a game at Arsenal, if Seaman keeps taking the monkey glands. Done wonders for his hair and its sheen, so it must be working.

There's always something so touching about observing a goalie on the bench as opposed to an outfield player. Many of them sit with their gloves on — those weird, non-human, spaceman appendages — their eyes glazed, mouth set, waiting for a call to action, to go over the top from the trenches, but it never comes.

Goalkeepers are also going to find it harder in future now that clubs have so much money, such big benches. Gerard Houllier at Liverpool splashed out on the same day on not one, but two, top goalies. He must have got a discount. "OK then, wrap them up, I'll take both while I'm here, merci."

What is he going to do with them? I'll tell you. He's going to play them both together. After all, you are allowed two strikers or two central defenders. No laws against that. It will mean having only nine outfield players, but after Liverpool's 12 games so far without a clean sheet, he's worked out that two goalies between the sticks is his best way of not conceding any more goals.

Too much money in football, you see. In the end, it will turn everything into madness.

OK, SO I YAWNED DURING A MATCH, BUT IT WAS ONLY A VERY LITTLE ONE

1 OCTOBER 2001

"WHAT WAS THAT STRANGE NOISE?" ASKED MY WIFE, WHEN I eventually came to bed. Mice going walkabout, I suggested, a red squirrel snoring, Herdwicks coughing, a fox hunting, someone nicking the last of my apples, folks coming back late from the Kirkstile Inn? Could be anything, really.

"It was inside, coming from downstairs, a noise I've never heard before. It sounded like you yawning while watching football . . ." Ridiculous. Don't be potty, pet, I'd never do that, you're wandering, woman, go to sleep.

It had been a long, hard evening. By a sequence of events, forking out endless subscriptions, fiddling with lots of knobs, I'd been able to watch three live European matches — on BBC1, Sky and Channel 5. What a treat. They overlapped a bit, so I had to flick backward and forward, but it meant I had almost five hours of continuous football, with no pause for half-times. Isn't life grand?

It was during the Leeds game against Maritimo, which didn't start until 9.45pm, that I was aware of my first little yawn. Just slipped out. Followed by a lot of eye-rubbing, jaw-dropping, till, unbelievably, amazingly, the yawns got so bad that I gave up. I came to bed not knowing the score. Didn't find out for two days, because our copy of the *Independent* never carries late news. It was Postman Pete who told me.

Then, over the weekend, it happened again. I found myself wilting on Sunday afternoon with two live Premier games, one after the other, from two o'clock to six o'clock. But it's got to be done, I told myself. You're not meant always to enjoy yourself when you're enjoying yourself

Saturday had been even more knackering, what with *Football Focus* at lunchtime, Radio 5 Live in the afternoon, a live Scottish match at 5.35pm, the Premiership on ITV, then Spanish football on Sky. Can you have too much of a good thing? I used to think not. If it moves, I'll watch it. I could never knowingly, willingly, turn against footer. So what is going on?

I remember, a year or so ago, arguing with a friend who had taken a scunner against football after years of devotion. It depressed him — all the money, the mercenaries, the cynicism, the lack of loyalty. He wasn't going to go any more, it just wasn't the same. I maintained it had got better — thanks to all the money, all the foreign players. There was a stage in the 1970s when it was poor, the conditions appalling, crowds decreasing, but today I really do think the standard is terrific.

So why have I started yawning? Tiredness, trying to watch up to ten live games a week, at home and in Europe. That must be it. No need to panic. It is a particularly busy time of the season, with all our Brit clubs still alive, still kicking. When most get stuffed, as they certainly will, things won't be as hectic. It will sort itself out. No need for counselling. Or are we all reaching saturation point? Can one have too much football? Am I overdosing on pleasure?

While yawning that first evening, I was also thinking of the World Trade Center. Not like me. I do have my priorities. When they cancelled the European games the day after 11 September, I thought, bloody hell, what are they doing, it's not that serious, is it — though I didn't admit it, not out loud.

A day later, having lunch on my own in Cockermouth after my swim, I overheard six different conversations — and not one person was discussing America. At all the surrounding tables, they were talking about either their work or their families. I remarked on this to the waiter, and he said: "Oh, it's old hat, that's yesterday's news." I was quite shocked by their insularity. It was only when walking down Main Street that I heard an old woman say to a young boy, probably her grandson: "I do hope Bush doesn't do anything silly." Country folks do feel cut off, removed from the mainstream, but as the days have gone on I have found myself worrying less about Gazza growing grey, or even Michael Owen's poorly hamstring, than about Bush going ballistic. Is it at long last about to sink in that following football so fanatically is, well, pretty trivial? Then I think, steady on.

I was worried last week, for about ten minutes, when my younger daughter Flora said she thought she was going off shopping. She didn't seem to have the same enthusiasm for it any more, street markets no longer seemed exciting, she didn't know what was wrong with her. Oh, you'll get over it, I said. It's just a passing phase. Pull yourself together.

And that's what I'm going to do. I'm relying on football to keep me happy in the years ahead, when I'll have done working, done walking, and will merely get up each day and slump. Uncle Football will be there for me, wall to wall, morn till evening, the perfect opiate, from cradle to grave. I'm banking on it.

Then there's the immediate year ahead. Have I not spent a fortune on cable and Sky and pay-per-view nonsenses, £820 for my Spurs season ticket, my half a season ticket for Arsenal? I'm certainly not wasting all that just because of a passing spot of boredom, a bit of tiredness, some slight overdosing, a moment of illumination, or whatever it was. And it's World Cup year. So much to look forward to, with Sven's lads, and the Irish, and Scotland, possibly, maybe. Ingerland, Ingerland. I'm getting excited already. You misheard, pet. And even if you were right, it was only a very small yawn.

MY LIFE ON THE COMMITTEE FOR EVEN
MORE STUPID FOOTBALL STATISTICS

8 OCTOBER 2001

I'VE HAD A CALL FROM THE FOOTBALL ASSOCIATION. Someone at its office in Soho Square wants to know if I'll serve on the Dubious Fouls Committee. I have explained that I won't be back in London till next week, but they say that's no problem. They need some one with my football knowledge, expertise and wisdom, so they're prepared to wait till I return from Lakeland. They are also setting up a Dubious Throw-ins Committee and a Dubious Comers Committee. I can serve on one of those as well, if I like, but I think Dubious Fouls — or DFC, as they call it — sounds the more demanding and intellectual. I do like to help.

The DFC meets once a month in a safe room in Soho and watches videos of dubious fouls. There's a sifting process beforehand, so you don't have to sit through all the Premier League fouls from each month, as that would take for ever. You just watch the three-star, X-rated dubious fouls. The meetings last for no longer than an hour, so they say, for which you get £1,000, plus coffee and choccy bickies.

Yes, £1,000 sounds a lot for an hour's work. But don't forget that if you are an official in football these days — whether you work for the PFA, as Gordon Taylor does, or are the chairman of a Premiership club, even a failed one such as Coventry — you get at least f250,000 a year, plus perks. They have to pay the part-time advisers and consultants, such as *moi*, a commensurate amount, or it makes a nonsense of the big wads.

I'm a bit worried about the biscuits. The last time I helped out the FA, when it was still based at Lancaster Gate, we were served leftover World Cup Willy ginger nuts, which were, not to put too fine a point on it, decidedly mouldy.

We will operate much like the FA's Dubious Goals Committee, with our own secretariat, ties and blazers. As you have probably read, it has just adjudicated on Newcastle United's exciting 4–3 victory over Manchester United. At the time, the vital goal was awarded to Alan Shearer, but the Dubious Goals Committee, after a great deal of deliberation and a large quantity of biscuits, decided that the ball hit Wes Brown on its way into the net. Therefore, the official record now reads: "Brown, OG." That's how it will remain, till the last syllable of recorded time.

The reason for all these committees is the increased importance of football statistics, which, in the past five years, have become an industry, with around 3,000 people working full-time, totting up every incident and every move that takes place in every league game, plus details of everyone taking part, including the birth signs of strikers, the weights of referees, the heights of managers, the IQs of goalkeepers, the sexual preferences of supporters and the favourite angle of corner flags.

Everything is then put on a computer and analysed upside down, back to front, and poured into the sports pages of our national papers or shoved at the top of our TV screens. The media have so much space to fill each day that when they can't compete on the words or pictures, they battle it out graph to graph, fact to fact, stat to stat.

The *Times* has its Optrex list, which tells you how many players have been bathing their eyes each morning before training. The *Telegraph* has its Grecian list, which records the number of grey-haired midfield players making decisive tackles. A lot of these stats are now sponsored, or bought in, part of fantasy football games that people bet on. The poor old *Independent* can't afford to pay out money for stats, but it has now begun something called the Premiership Index. It looks official and awfully scientific, but in fact consists of the paper's football hacks sucking their pencils after a game and giving points out of ten to each player. Old technology, it's called, but bloody cheap.

At the other end of the market, those expensive and noisy TV commercials for the *Daily Star* and the *Express*, which I rely on to keep me awake when I'm watching Sky, now make a point of shouting out that their sports pages include stunning statistics. Who would have thought that boring old football facts would ever replace topless stunners?

The chairman of Bolton Wanderers was interviewed on *Football Focus* last week and was boasting that among the army of psychologists and dieticians Sam Allardyce has hired is a statistician. I should think so. No club, like no paper, can do without one. (Incidentally, close your eyes when next listening to Allardyce — which is hard, as his physiognomy is riveting — and he sounds just like David Blunkett.)

This obsession with stats has always been big in the United States, mainly because baseball, like cricket, is such a boring, slow game that they have to devise batting or bowling averages to keep the crowds awake. With the use of modern computers and action-replay machines, any old rubbishy facts can be analysed quickly. Because the technology is available, a use is found for it. That can be the only reason for shoving irrelevant and stupid stats at the top of the TV screen.

The FA, as lord of the universe, upholder of infinite justice, has to appoint these committees to arbitrate on any dubious football facts, such as who really scored. The chairman of the Dubious Fouls Committee will be Michael Knighton, much respected in football for his distinguished chairmanship of Carlisle United. The female member was going to be Mariella Frostrup, but she's still too exhausted after judging the Booker. The token woman is now Julie Burchill, biographer of Beckham. The lay member is A N Wilson. Should be fun. I'll report back.

LONDON IS AWFUL, HORRIBLE, BUT
THE FOOTBALL AIN'T TOO BAD

29 OCTOBER 2001

I DIDN'T REALLY WANT TO GO TO SEE SPURS ON MONDAY evening. The weather was wet and horrible, having to drag myself through north London was even more horrible, and because it was only Derby it was live on the telly, for which I've already paid, so why bother, what's the point'? But it was my first game of the season in the flesh — or what passes for flesh — so I had to go.

I always feel like this after five months away in Lakeland. London is so nasty, so brutish, that re-entry is culturally shocking. It's a foreign city, which is refreshing after five months of no black or brown faces, no foreign accents, no ethnic diversity. But at the same time, it is so filthy, so ugly — who wants to go anywhere?

It's a war zone out there, battling in the streets, aggression at every comer, people being horrible to each other. And nothing works, all services having collapsed. I rang my GP in Hampstead — don't ask why — and the first appointment was three weeks away. In Cockermouth, it was three days.

So that's how I felt when I arrived at White Hart Lane. I bought a programme: bloody hell, it's now £3, up 20 per cent from last season. Then a cup of tea: oh my God, that's now £1.20, also up 20 per cent. Is the service and quality 20 per cent better? Is it heckers, though they have painted the staircases and the lavs.

On the radio last week, I heard one of the new directors of Spurs saying that the club is a world-class brand that they are going to exploit properly — as if this was a new idea. For over 20 years they've been saying it, and doing it, alas. Not very difficult. All it means is launching even more merchandising nonsenses and creating further marketing cobblers.

They'll get away with it as long as Premiership football remains popular with the public. They will squeeze our pips and our bollocks, and we'll pay up, whether it's £850 for a season ticket or £3 for a programme. We're in a cycle where the stupid and the craven get taken to the cleaners. Player power is now so strong that an average team member can demand £20,000 a week, no problem.

I sat down and was convinced that my seat had become 20 per cent smaller since last season. There's no room to move, or to breathe. My son the barrister has been sitting in it while I've been away, so it hasn't been wasted. He rang me on his mobile at half-time during that Man Utd match to scream out the news that Spurs were three goals up. Lucky sod, being there, in my seat, for one of the games of the year, the decade, the century. I rushed in from the garden to switch on Radio 5 Live for the second half. And we all know what happened. Man U came back — and won.

Spurs started well against Derby, making lots of chances, which cheered up the crowd, who began singing: "If you hate Sol Campbell, clap your hands." Most of the crowd did, but I didn't, nor did the man next to me, a retired accountant who always brings his grandson. "I'm too old to hate," I said to him. "I'm too old to stand up," he replied.

Teddy Sheringham has made a difference. The crowd have quite forgotten how they stood up to hate him when he left Spurs for Man Utd. Now he's back, he seems better than ever. And quicker, which is weird. Perhaps it's in comparison with Poyet, who makes our tortoise look fast. But Poyet played well, as did Ziege, both confident, experienced players whom the younger players need around them. It was also my first sight of Dean Richards, this season's third new signing. He did OK, solid, no mistakes, and will probably be a more than adequate replacement for Sol. Over the past two years, Sol has been rubbish — well, not quite rubbish, but he didn't progress or develop, going backwards if anything. The crowd still love Rebrov, which surprised me. I hadn't picked that up from match reports or from watching Spurs on television. I think he has been a flop, apart from two or three early games. I'd get shot of him.

Most of all, the crowd loves Glenn. So nice to hear the Spurs manager being cheered by name, unlike this time last season. And he has improved the team. They are more fluent, more creative, more entertaining, even though they are no higher in the league than they were this time last season under wossisname.

It is a better team, and much better to watch. But are they 20 per cent better? Do they justify that extra 20p on a cup of tea and 50p on the programme? Hmm. Hard one, that. But as they won, easily, I came out thinking: I'm glad I went after all.

On the way home, London didn't look quite as menacing and scruffy and awful. It was either the win that did it or a sign that, after just one week, re-entry is complete. My Lakeland eyes have gone, green hills forgotten, pure air evaporated. I've been sucked in, joined the rat race, assumed my London mindset. I'm one of them now.

OK I HAVEN'T READ THE BOOK. BUT THEN, JULIE HASN'T BEEN TO A MATCH

12 NOVEMBER 2001

WHAT A SURPRISE I GOT WHEN I WENT OVER TO WATERSTONE'S in Hampstead last week. I don't usually go there. The staff are so snotty, so superior. I looked around for some of my own books, and found an excellent one about Eddie Stobart, which I immediately put in a better position, moving out of the way a little titchy book that I thought must be there by mistake, assuming it was for kiddies. Or perhaps it was a joke book, a Christmas stocking filler remaindered from last year, aimed at lads, as the cover shows the back of a naked body. Then I saw the title, *Burchill on Beckham*. Blow me. So it was true. And I thought I'd made it up.

About a year ago, I offered to be Old Ma Burchill's researcher, if she ever did a football book, willing to explain complicated, technical terms. We call them goals, Julie pet. And the round thing? That's a ball, my sweet.

I turned quickly to the end of the book to see if I'd got a mensh, as her researcher, but no. When I say 'quickly', I mean *instantly*. The book is so small, so skimpy, I turned instantly to the end. Only, 122 miniature pages. Can't be more than 18,000 words.

I thought about reading it, there and then, but I had to be somewhere in five minutes. It would have taken me, oooh, all of 12 minutes. I am a slow reader. But I did glance at the first page.

She starts with a story about Coutts, the Royal Bank, actively courting young footballers to open accounts with them. She thinks this is dead significant, the way that Coutts, the Royal Bank, as she keeps on repeating, want footballers. It shows, wait for it, that they are the new kings. Good one, Jules.

I can just see her little plump smile as she lay sprawled on her little plump sofa, someone having provided this cutting for her. I can use this, she smirks, this will give me an intro.

Quite unaware that Coutts, like all once exclusive banks, have for years been open to anyone with two bob in their pocket. I did a book about Lottery winners, back in 1995, and every posh bank was hounding them, hoping to grab their custom. As for young footballers being wealthy, that's been the case for about 20 years. Where has she been?

Nowhere, that must be the answer, staying plump on her sofa, living life at second hand, relying on the media to tell her what's going on outside. And that, apparently, is how this project all began. She'd picked up, out of the air, that Beckham was a baddy, a hate figure, booed and rubbished, who let the country down by being sent off in the World Cup, seen as petulant and silly and thick. So, naturally, Julie decided to praise him.

If she'd written this immediately, off the top of her pretty head, spinning it out in her *Guardian* column, doing it just to annoy, then it might have been a reasonable piece. But now, a year later, Beckham is no longer hated. He is a hero, an icon, endlessly praised, endlessly analysed. Her views on him are neither original, refreshing nor stimulating. They're clichés.

OK, so I haven't read the book — but then Julie hasn't been to a football match or met Bex, so I feel totally qualified in giving my opinion of her book, based on what I've picked up from the media. Just as she does.

She's made a big thing about footballers being wife-beaters, based on only two or three well-known examples, taken from the cuttings. She maintains that fans are closet homosexuals who secretly want to sleep with Bex, which is at least amusing, as we know she's saying it to tease. I heard her on *Woman's Hour* being asked about another of her contentions, that nine out of ten people who follow football are bad in bed. Asked where she'd got that from, she said she'd made it up. Brilliant.

No, really. I do admire her stuff. She writes so well, and keeps it lively, despite having only one trick — lifting something from the cuttings, then taking the contrary view. Yet she's managed to spin out this trick, mixed with a bit of rude-girl sex, for over 20 years now. Well done, gel. She hasn't actually held down the same column, in the same paper, for very long, but moved around, with the same sort of stuff. Which is even more admirable. And she earns a fortune. Excellent — I'm all for that.

I feel flattered, in a way, that she should now bother to come into football, giving us the benefit of her wisdom and insight. It makes football somehow more important, more worthwhile, just by her presence among us. Thanks, Jules.

I wonder what she got paid for the Bex book? It's priced at £10. It might be slim, based on a slim idea, but it's not a cheap project. I guess she got around a £50,000 advance from Yellow Jersey Press, whoever they are. Huge for most authors, but peanuts, really. For someone of her brilliance, stature, irritant power, she must be able to command £5,000 a piece, even at her age, from national news-papers. She's probably been doing us all a favour, bothering to knock out this football book over a long weekend instead of sticking to journalism. I do hope she's not been underpaid. (I know I got rejected as a researcher, alas, but how's about a bit of agenting, Jules?)

But I gather she's got even more for her next book, *Burchill on Ben*. This is said to be a brilliant analysis and explanation of that loveable, romantic, misunderstood, sexy old rogue, Osama Ben Laden. Her only problem will be to get it out sharpish, before we all come round to that opinion.

DOES WILLS CHEER FOR VILLA BECAUSE HIS NANNY CAME FROM BRUM?

19 NOVEMBER 2001

THERE ARE TWO QUESTIONS TO BE ANSWERED BEFORE WE progress any further with the season, three if you count Nobby Stiles's height loss. Did you see him before the England *v* Sweden game last Saturday, where he was guest of honour? I could have sworn he was normal size back in 1966. Now he's so titchy and weedy he makes Michael Owen look like a giant. Was he wearing high heels when he played? Or platform shoes?

It's the same with film stars. Their performance makes them bigger than they are. Watching little old Nobby, into my head came a forward flash of Roy Keane in 30 years time, once a colossus, turned into a midget man.

Now for the big questions. While visiting Latvia two weeks ago, Prince Charles was asked which teams his sons follow. He said that William supports Aston Villa, while Harry supports Arsenal. When asked why, he said: "I really don't know."

Not much of a dad. OK, he gets a point for getting his sons' teams right, well done, but ruins everything by not knowing the reasons. I don't know either, but here are a few educated guesses, from my educated left foot. First, William had a nanny who came from Birmingham, loved Villa and taught him to do the same. (That guess is based on how one of Tony Blair's sons came to follow Man Utd.) Second, William's mother, a well-known follower of fashion, decided that Villa's strip was the prettiest in England. She loved it, and so did William. (This is based on the huge sales of Villa shirts among well-bred Italians.) Third, perhaps William is in love with David Ginola, who is not fat, certainly not, and thinks it totally disgusting that John Gregory doesn't play him more often.

As for Harry, well, he couldn't follow the same team as his big brother. So he picked Arsenal. First, because someone gave him a free ticket. Second, he thinks it's a posh team, because the Hill-Woods (who have been directors for years) went to Eton. And third, it's got marble halls and reminds him of home. (If you know the real answers for William and Harry's loyalties, do share.)

But the big big question, being asked on back pages everywhere, concerns Manchester United—what's happened to them? Since March, they have been rubbish, by their standards, taking just 20 points from a possible 39, currently lying sixth in the league. It could be a mere blip, as their supporters maintain, or hope, the sort of marking-time period they have each season, from which they go on to win everything.

It looks more serious than that, judging by their recent ineffectual performances. Could it be caused by all the changes Fergie has made—upsetting the defence by getting shot of Jaap Stam, upsetting the midfield by buying Juan Veron, upsetting his attack by buying Ruud van Nistelrooy? Nothing wrong with those two new players. It's the effects they've had by having to be fitted in. It smacks of the conspicuous consumption syndrome. I can buy, therefore I will buy. A new player each season would have been better, not three in one go.

I think the most unsettling purchase has been the best one—Veron. He is much more valuable, desirable, would fetch more money than either Laurent Blanc or Nistelrooy, but Man Utd didn't need him, not as long as they had Keane. The fallout from having two such dominant players, playing almost the same role, in the same area, is that the roles of Paul Scholes and David Beckham have been diminished when playing for Man Utd. They now often look peripheral, confused, disheartened. We know from watching Beckham with England that he hasn't lost form, or his hunger. It's only when playing for Man Utd that he no longer knocks himself out.

Which is what Fergie has said, though without naming him. He clearly thinks several of his stars are not trying hard enough, have lost the will to win. Interestingly enough, few people have blamed all the money they now earn.

Could it be because Fergie has been there too long? That's another explanation being offered by everyone with a couch and a remote control. His players have heard all his pep talks before, know his tricks, his invective, his homespun philosophies.

They are probably doubting for the first time some of his decisions, such as letting Stam go, some of his formations, such as messing about with Scholes, and some of his pronouncements, such as saying earlier this season that Wes Brown was the best centre-back in the country. I thought that was a wind-up, to annoy Arsenal for buying Sol Campbell, but I think he meant it at the time, and probably now regrets it.

I don't actually believe he's been in the job too long. That's not the main problem. He is clearly as motivated, as determined and as mad and nasty as all successful managers have to be. His one big serious mistake was to let it be known, far too far ahead, that this is his last season. He should have reached agreement with the board, secretly, then lied to the players and the world, saying he hadn't made up his mind. It has done such psychological damage. When he starts ranting on, the players are not bothered much, saving themselves to impress the next gaffer.

Now back to William and Harry. Note their ages: 19 and 17. During the past ten years, Man U have been *numero uno*, followed by every middle-class kid in search of an acceptable team. You'd have expected them to do the same, especially with a non-footballing dad. Instead, they chose Arsenal and Aston Villa — each of which is currently higher in the league than Man Utd. They could both be ahead of the game, smarter than we all thought.

THE BEST WAY TO HUMILIATE A FOOTBALLER IS TO LAUGH AT HIM

26 NOVEMBER 2001

ONE OF THE ATTRACTIONS OF GOING TO FOOTBALL IS screaming and shouting, roaring on your team. Almost as enjoyable, for many people, is screaming and shouting abuse, usually at the other side, the other supporters, or the ref. And sometimes at your own players. These days, you can't make racial comments, and in Britain now people rarely do, but you can be as ageist, lookist or as sexually explicit as you like — something you can't do in normal life. Good old football. No wonder doctors recommend it for stress. Governments are grateful to it for relieving tensions.

All the same, I was a bit worried about going to Spurs last Saturday. Would the Spurs supporters be out of order, over the top, in their reaction to Sol Campbell on his return to White Hart Lane as an Arsenal player?

Surely it's happened before, said my dear wife. Players must have moved between the two clubs. Yes, but not very often. Pat Jennings did it, but near retirement, when it wasn't seen as desertion. The thing about Sol, dearly loved as a Spurs player, is that, right until the end, he seemed to be indicating that he wouldn't leave, far less go to Arsenal. Most TV commentators appear unaware of this — and that's the reason why so many Spurs fans decided to hate him.

Not that I'm bothered, personally. I think he made a mistake by going to Arsenal — but not because it's Arsenal. It shows a lack of ambition, a lack of confidence, to make a real change or face a proper challenge. If he had wanted to progress, both as a player and as a person, he should have gone to Spain.

He's also chosen Arsenal at a poor time, in a period of transition, and left Spurs when, at long last, they do seem to be moving forward. For the past year, he hasn't played well anyway, and, in Ledley King, Spurs have an excellent youngster who, if he continues to improve, could be better than Sol.

The rumour was that the crowd was going to stand in silence when he came on to the pitch, turning their backs on him. That would have been unusual, but I didn't believe it. British crowds love the crude, full-frontal, loud-mouth approach. Other nationalities do things differently. In that Iran *v* Republic of Ireland game a week or so ago, the home crowd showed their displeasure at their own team by burning their programmes and newspapers. Symbolic, but not much fun. I was once in Africa, watching a match in Cameroon, and the home crowd abused the other team not by swearing or jeering or booing—but by laughing, They waited for a mistake, then fell about, clutching their stomachs. For a player, being mocked is probably far more hurtful and humiliating than being sworn at.

When the players came out, the noise was deafening, so high-pitched, with all the whistling, that my ears blew, as if on a plane. First time it's ever happened to me at a match, but it could have been flu coming on. I've just had an anti-flu injection, which was daft, as for years and years I've never had flu anyway. I've felt rotten ever since I had it.

No one I saw turned his back, but about 4,000 white balloons were let loose bearing, the word "Judas", and then several thousand spectators each held up a white card bearing the same word. Presumably, Sol has gone for more money, as he is a professional, but it's hard to see how he can be described as a traitor. But when you're abusing, you don't worry much about logic.

Near the goalposts at the Park Lane end, two huge white notices were held up that read 'We don't need a queer. We've got Ledley King', which must have taken ages to paint or print. It could be taken to mean that Ledley King is queer, which I don't think was the intention. Interesting, though, that 'queer' is back in common usage.

When the game began, Sol was booed loudly every time he touched the ball, right to the very end, when at last Spurs got their well-deserved equaliser. Crowds often grow bored and forget whom they are booing or why. I can't believe it unsettles experienced players, though it perhaps makes them pass the ball more quickly. The crowd also had a go at Martin Keown when he went down, injured: "Get up, you're a monkey's head." No, this was not sexual. This is what we call lookist abuse.

Down below me, in front of the West Stand, I could see Glenn Hoddle standing for most of the second half, wringing his hands. He doesn't go in for screaming and shouting at his players. At derby games, they can't hear him anyway. And it's not waving, but sort of folding, jerking his hands, as if practising conjuring tricks, or dealing out imaginary cards. Garth Crooks does something similar when he's presenting on TV, talking as much with his hands as with his mouth, but he doesn't know he's doing it.

Hoddle is clearly trying to pass on some instructions, using his own form of hand language. I've got highlights from the match recorded on video, and when I'm really really bored over Christmas, as I always am, I plan to work out what he's saying. From some of his expressions, I suspect he was sometimes passing on more than instructions, especially when Arsenal got their goal out of the blue. What I think he was signalling was a bollocking to his defence.

If so, then there was, after all, some silent abuse at White Hart Lane last Saturday afternoon.

WHAT STRANGE BOOKS THEY HAVE IN OXFORD'S BODLEIAN LIBRARY

10 DECEMBER 2001

I GOT A CALL LAST WEEK FROM JIM WHITE, A FRIEND WHO works on the *Guardian*. He said he was acting as tutor to a bloke from New Zealand who was doing a PhD on football writing at Oxford. Could I spare some time to see him? It didn't somehow surprise me that someone might be doing research on football writing at Oxford. This is the modern world. Yes, I know it always is, but it's more modern than yesterday's, as it always is.

What surprised me was Jim acting as tutor.

"You should get on to it, Hunt. It's really well paid." Like how much? "Like £25 an hour." Our window cleaner gets more than that, I said. "Joke," replied Jim.

About 25 years ago, I got a call from London University asking if I'd act as an outside examiner for someone doing a PhD on the Beatles. Her thesis was on their lyrics as poetry. At the time, I thought it was a wind-up, unable to believe that one of our older universities was allowing such a project. Now it's commonplace. The other outside examiner was Wilfrid Mellers, professor of music at York. The student was Melodie Ziff. Brilliant name.

So Steve Braunias from New Zealand came to see me. Aged 40, rather dishevelled, very laid-back. He is doing a thesis on football writing, but it's not for a PhD. He's on something called a Reuters Foundation Scholarship at Green College. There are ten a year, for working journalists from all over the world. You did well to get it, Steve. "Not really," he said.

Most people put up boring topics, such as global warming or "whither the Euro?". He thinks he was the first to suggest a thesis on football writing. That's what probably did it.

And what's your angle then, Steve?

"Fucked if I know."

He discovered football when he was aged eight at his primary school in New Zealand, but not by playing it. You got the strap at his primers if you were caught with a soccer ball in the playground. It had to be rugby.

"We had art on Wednesday afternoons, which we did sitting on the floor. The teacher used to spread out old newspapers to save us making a mess. They happened to be four-month-old airmail copies of the *Daily Mirror*. As the harsh New Zealand light came through the window, and I was bending down on my bony New Zealand knees, I noticed a photograph of someone called George Best. Christ, I thought, he's cool."

From then on, Steve found out everything he could about football, which was hard, living in New Zealand in 1968, with no games on radio or TV. Mainly he read comics such as *Shoot!* and *Tiger* for *Roy of the Rovers*. "I still know the name of every player who played for Melchester Rovers for the next five years, and in my opinion, Vernon Eliot was the best left winger they ever had ..."

I thought he was fibbing, but he started reciting the teams till I stopped him. I was later showing him some of my priceless football treasures, such as my collection of England – Scotland programmes, and he was able to tell me all the scores, and scorers.

At 18, when girls and music came along, his obsession with football subsided. He didn't see his first proper game until 1990, when he came to London for five days as the escort of a handicapped girl who had won a competition in a magazine he was working on. "I parked her at the theatre to see a Lloyd Webber something, while I went to see QPR play Sheffield Wednesday. It was a religious experience.'"

This is only his second visit to the UK, but so far he's managed four games. It counts as research, funded by Reuters. He's been to West Ham and Southampton, loved both, and to Ipswich, which he didn't. "The ground was grubby, the people vile, the language appalling, all rancour and no wit. I also went to Edinburgh to watch Sunderland. That was excellent."

Hold on, Steve. Sunderland don't play in Edinburgh. "Yeah, so I found out. I was never good at geography. They looked quite near on the map, sitting in New Zealand. Luckily, I went the day before the match, so I got to Sunderland in time. I also met Princess Anne. She was sharp."

In Edinburgh or Sunderland? "No, Oxford. She came to open something at the Reuters Foundation. I was introduced to her, so I asked if she'd met David Beckham. 'Would that make me someone worth meeting?' she replied."

He's been going most days to the Bodleian Library, slowly working his way through its entire collection of football books, which comes to 237. "Their selection is strange. They've got only one volume of Gibson and Pickford's four-volume *Association Football and the Men Who Made It* from 1906, yet they've got *Ure's Truly*, Ian Ure's biography, which is awful."

I have all four 1906 volumes, bought at Sotheby's last year, which I was able to show him, but, alas, not the Ian Ure. But I do remember him. Steve tried to catch me out. These colonials.

He's loving Oxford. "It's so tender, as if it's built out of paper." But he is loving the football even more. He's noting down everything of interest, learning so much. Anthropology and linguistics, by the sound of it, rather than geography.

"My best overheard remark was at West Ham. 'I fink I dun it wrong, Ted.' I've been repeating it to myself ever since." He went off laughing, to get the train back to Oxford.

I'll think of Steve at matches to come. I like people who like football.

POETRY OR MUSIC NEED YOUTH,
BUT MANAGEMENT OR MEDICINE DON'T

18 FEBRUARY 2002

IN MUSTIQUE LAST MONTH, I HAD A DRINK WITH FELIX Dennis at his house, and he said something that has hung around in my mind ever since. We were not talking football, although he does own Man Utd, but talking about magazines, of which he owns many in the UK and the USA. Hold on, did I say he owns Man Utd? Yes, he does. His house in Mustique is called Mandalay, formerly owned by David Bowie, and has a full-time staff of 16. They have their own football team, Mandalay United, Man Utd for short.

I was saying to him there should be a proper, glossy magazine for oldies, for the over-fifties. After all, we own the world, run the world. There are 19 million of us in the UK today — a figure that will double in the next 30 years. Our disposable income is 30 per cent higher than the under-fifties. Most new cars are bought by us, most of the expensive holidays, we have more than 80 percent of the national wealth. Yet do the media give a damn about us? Do they heckers. Television and radio are obsessed by youth, and so are the newspapers. If I see another page of rubbish in the *Indy* about pop records I've never heard of, I'll scream.

Felix just sighed and ordered one of his staff to get us more drinks. Don't tell me, he said. I've looked at proposals for years, but there's not a chance. You won't get advertising unless you say your readers will be under 40.

Bloody hell, isn't that appalling, isn't that prejudiced, isn't that stupid, isn't that short-sighted? So hurrah for Bobby, Fergie and Graham and to the boards of Newcastle, Man Utd and Villa for seeing sense and having managers aged 68, 60 and 57.

If you're old enough, you're good enough. So they say. Age should not enter into it. So they also say. It's true about people in activities that depend on energy and enthusiasm. And also in the creative world. Poets, writers, artists and composers, on the whole, are better when younger. "The brisk intemperance of youth", as Edward Gibbon remarked. That's what's wanted in most physical and creative occupations.

But not in man management. A football manager, like a lawyer, GP, teacher or social worker, improves with age. You see the same tricks, strokes, ailments, nasty problems, dodgy characters recurring. First time round, you can get it wrong, get conned, but next time, you are ready, can read it better, deal with it better.

I can never understand why British football clubs so often promote a player overnight into management, just because he's been a famous, popular, successful player. How can they possibly cope? In Europe, it mostly can't happen, as you have to have the coaching badges. It's not just the problem of respect, having been one of the lads, then turning into the gaffer. It's lack of guile, lack of wisdom. You can teach knowledge. You can't teach experience.

If you start at the bottom in the Third Division or non-league, you do everything, see everything and have to manage on what you have. Making ordinary players play better, creating systems and tactics that work, has to be learnt by experience and in the end it's what you need most — at the top and at the bottom. We all know big cheques don't always work wonders.

Gianlucca Vialli, Bryan Robson and David Platt all appeared to do well at first, and might all come back and do much better, but they floundered by starting in management at the top. David O'Leary, after a brilliant beginning, now appears to be showing, his age — ie, his youth, naivety, inexperience and intemperance. This talk about Roy Keane taking over from Fergie is potty.

Kevin Keegan started in management at the top and blew out, lost it. Glenn Hoddle also began high, and got higher when given the England job, but he was too young, too foolish in what he said and did. Both Keegan and Hoddle are doing so much better, now they have matured, now they have seen so much, had the failures and flops. One of the best things about Sven Goran Eriksson is that he strikes you as a grown-up, fully formed, wise and mature.

With age there often does come weariness, cynicism. Enthusiasm fades, the pressures mount, bureaucracy gets burdensome. You think, is it worth it? GPs and teachers seem to suffer greatly from this. All my contemporaries who went into teaching or lecturing have long since given up, chucked in the chalk, many of them years ago, back in their early fifties.

This doesn't seem to happen in football management. Managers say all the time that it's an addiction, a drug; they are lost without it, don't know what to do with themselves. It's partly because it's all they know. I can't think of a manager who's retired at the top, the way players such as Cantona or Lineker have done. Fergie said he would, but didn't. Graham Taylor did, but not for long. Yes, Bill Shankly did then regretted it.

Football, unlike so many other walks of life, has realised that age counts, age is good, age has a lot to give. At the moment, anyway. Two years ago, there was a call to give young managers their head. In two years' time, or even two months, or even two minutes, we'll read that Fergie is past it, Bobby should take his pension, Graham Taylor is a has-been.

But for this week, at least, I'm saying: well done, football. You are showing a good lead. So bugger off, all the blinkered media. Up your bum, you advertisers. And on 18 February, happy 69th birthday, Bobby.

BACK TO THE DAYS OF NO LOGO AND
INCREDIBLY SHORT SHORTS

25 FEBRUARY 2002

I'VE HAD FLU ALL WEEK, DESPITE HAVING HAD AN ANTI-
flu jab, what a waste that was, and it's been so boring, staying inside
being sensible, overdosing on cough mixture, becoming addicted to
Lemsip, counting the hours till the next Strepsil. It always happens
after an expensive hol in the Caribbean. Oh, been away, have you,
say the neighbours, somewhere nice, you don't look it.

It's just men who have flu, according to the wife. Women simply
have a cold. But to cheer me up, distract me, she said why don't you
get out that video you got at Christmas from Caitlin, I'll watch it
with you, if you like.

"We might see you on it," she said, smirking, as she unwrapped
the 1966 World Cup Final, a BBC video of the full match, with original commentary by Kenneth Wolstenholme. No, I wasn't playing,
but I was there, as I've boasted for years, though I can't actually
remember the goals or any incidents. Just the atmosphere and
excitement, and, of course, England winning.

The first surprise was the quality of the film. Black and white, no
action replays or incredible close-ups, but you could see everything
clearly. And Wolstenholme's accent was not all that dated, no more
than Peter Drury's. No advertising hoardings except for *Radio
Times* on the scoreboard — no sponsors' logos on the players' shirts.
What an innocent, uncommercialised age it was. Every player had
the same hair, short back and sides, except for Bobby Charlton's
sweep-over. All shorts were incredibly short, almost up to their
bollocks. The crowd wore rosettes and did a lot of clapping, but very
limited singing, apart from "Oh when the reds go marching in", and
limited chanting, apart from "Ingland" or "Attack, Attack". No
obscenities. When the crowd didn't like the ref, they sang, "Oh, oh,
what a referee". Today it's "Who's that wanker in the black?".

In 1966, when the Germans chanted "Deutschland", we replied with "England". Today, it's more likely to be "You're gonna win fuck all".

It rained in the second half, yet in my mind the sun shone all day long and the Wembley pitch was perfect, as always. The England team are now all giants, but on the day they were so thin and wiry. Nobby Stiles looked malnourished and deprived. Must have been the war rations, observed my wife. He made Lee Bowyer look like Mr Universe. There was nobody in the England team who you would call big and strong, unlike Emile Heskey or Sol Campbell today. Jack Charlton was tall, but giraffe-like, awkward rather than hefty. You don't get such clumsy, awkward England players today, not since Carlton Palmer.

But they all looked incredibly fit, despite players' diets being rubbish in those days, so we are told, eating half a cow before kick-off. They did tire, though, and well before the end. With no subs, they were all knackered in extra time, except for Alan Ball. He was amazing, running non-stop.

There were no nasty tackles, no diving, no pretending, no push-ing and shoving, no arguing with the ref, and players helped each other up and shook hands. It was, after all, a World Cup Final. Players realised they were on show.

As for the skills, the passing, the control, the movements, I would say the quality of the England team today is not appreciably better than 36 years ago. Cruyff's swivel turn had not been invented, but almost all the other fancy bits were there, bringing the ball down on your instep, overlapping full-backs, clever side back heels. Our full-backs were poor, as they are today, with Ray Wilson giving away the first goal, but the rest of the team were excellent, not a weak link.

I interviewed Bobby Charlton last year, and his memory was of hardly being in the match. He and Beckenbauer had been detailed to mark each other, so cancelled each other out, but Bobby had a very good game. His passing was as good as Beckham's, but he could also shoot from any distance, which Becks doesn't. Bobby Moore was indeed elegant, but I'd forgotten his chest control, how it gave him so much space to come forward.

Germany had lots of possession, some good movement, but England took their chances and deserved to win. For the first time, I properly understood Wolstenholme's now famous words: "They think it's all over — it is now!" I was there, so didn't hear him say them. I'd assumed it referred to the ref blowing the final whistle, but he says the second part as Hurst scores — to make it 4 – 2.

I loved watching it; it took my mind off my aches, and I felt, well, uplifted. First, because my memory had not played tricks. The England team in 1966 were excellent. But also because I detect that Sven is slowly coming round to the belief that England should play as England have traditionally played.

We are not going to be able to pass or keep the ball as well as the Italians, French or the Argentinians. We are not suited to a slow build-up, passing our way intricately down the field. Such play can be good to watch, and frustrating for the opposition, but is ultimately pretty useless unless you have penetration at the end. Ideally, you want to be able to do both, but few teams ever manage that. France, the world champs, don't have it. The last ones were the Brazilians of the 1970s. In 1966, we had that penetration with Hurst. Today we have it with Owen. In 1966, there was no big belting of the ball from defence. Charlton, Ball and Peters moved the ball forward quickly from midfield, just as Becks, Gerrard and Scholes do so well today. Quick counter-attacking is what England are good at, were good at — not posing, endless passing, fannying around, getting nowhere,

England got somewhere in 1966. I am now feeling chirpier about WC 2002. My wife fell asleep.

THE MILLENNIUM STADIUM
BUGGERED MY MOBILE

4 MARCH 2002

WE SET OFF WITH SUCH ANTICIPATION AND EXCITEMENT
just before ten o'clock, Derek's car loaded with enough food and
drink and sweets and bickies to keep us going for a week. We
managed not to start eating and drinking, oh, till we were well
up Highgate West Hill. That's one street away.

There were five of us — me, my neighbours Derek and Sue, their
nephew Jim and niece Sita — all mad Spurs fans, all fully expecting
Spurs to stuff Blackburn Rovers. We were the favourites, the better
team, higher in the league, been playing so well, just think of how
we hammered Chelsea.

Sue, probably the most fanatical, insisted on having her Spurs
scarf trailing from the window. It's what you do, when going by car,
to a cup final. Derek was a bit worried. His car is an expensive
BMW and he didn't want any Blackburn hooligans taking a kick at
it. Derek, I said, we're in Bishops Avenue, Hampstead's millionaire's row. They wouldn't recognise a Spurs scarf if they met it in
their caviar.

I was so looking forward to the Millennium Stadium in Cardiff.
People have raved about it, said it's an experience in itself. It's good
that a national event should be spread around the nation, not limited to London.

On the M4, we played guessing games with points for spotting
Eddie Stobart lorries, Spurs scarves, stretch limos. We must have
passed about a dozen limos, mostly white, but some black, packed
with Spurs fans. Where do they get the money from? They looked
so sleek, immaculate, imposing, exclusive, except when they had a
piss-stop on the hard shoulder and all these scruffy Spurs fans stood
in a line hanging out their scruffy cocks. Didn't see anyone moon-
ing. We agreed that would be worth ten points.

Oh the camaraderie of going to a big match, for all classes, all ages, all sexes. It's what binds us together. Once we got near the Severn Bridge, we met the Blackburn hordes coming down the M5, then the traffic and rain got worse, but did we moan, did we heckers. We were going to witness a great victory, supporting our heroes in the flesh, into Europe, not like those pathetic stay-at-homes sitting by the telly.

We ignored the 'park and ride' directions, one for Spurs fans, one for Blackburn, reckoning it would take hours afterwards to queue for the bus, so we worked our way round Cardiff and parked just 15 minutes from the ground in a side street. We had our lunch, or what was left of it, in the car.

The first glimpse of the Millennium Stadium was most impressive, but then we got directed back across the river to the entrance for Spurs fans. One of the things about cup finals is the communal spirit, both sets of fans being so pleased to be there. Mingling happily, walking down Wembley Way, all together, concentrated the excitement, heightened the atmosphere. Here it was split, diffused.

Inside, the staircases and corridors were just as concretey and nasty and smelly as Wembley. I wasted half an hour queuing for a programme, as they ran out twice. Then the queues for the lav were enormous, with no proper system. The stadium itself was brilliant: uninterrupted views, lots of space, good seats at £39, cheaper than Wembley. The roof was closed, the noise deafening.

But the game, oh god, don't talk about it. Good to watch at home, I suppose, as there were lots of chances, but from the beginning, Spurs seemed out of sorts, lumpen, leaden, disorganised. Our so-called stars, such as Teddy Sheringliam and Darren Anderton, did nothing, couldn't even pass properly. We all groaned when we saw Ben Thatcher was playing, but he was our best defender. It was like going back two years, to George Graham's team. The fluency had gone. Was it over-confidence? More like worry, knowing how much it mattered. Hoddle had failed to relax them, and had passed on his own tension.

I tried to ring my son Jake at half-time on my mobile, just to show off that I was in the Millennium Stadium, but it said 'call barred'. It's true I haven't used it for a year, just as I never use my e-mail address or the internet, though I have both, somewhere in this house, so no one can say I'm out of touch.

The big screen in the stadium was useless, nowhere as good as the one at White Hart Lane. It was unable to give us any playbacks, so a black mark to the Millennium. Probably just as well. It would only have prolonged the agony.

It was hell coming back, so miserable, four hours of anti-climax. We listened to *606* on Radio 5 Live. Every Spurs fan rang in to say the same—"Gutted"—except for one who made it even clearer: "Me guts are hanging out."

Alan Green criticised the Spurs fans for leaving at once, before the medal ceremony, but he didn't know how let-down we felt. All that way, all that expense, all that rain, all that traffic, eating too much chocolate (which I hate), all that queuing (which I don't do in normal life), that lousy screen, crowded lavs, rotten Millennium Stadium, yes, I blame it for buggering up my mobile.

We didn't get back till ten at night. A whole day out of my life, 12 hours bloody wasted, down the drain. Bring back Wembley. At least that got the agony over with quickly.

WHEN I GROW UP, I WANT TO BE SVEN, WITH THE BEST SEAT AND A NICE RUG

11 MARCH 2002

THE COMMENTATOR WAS GOING ON ABOUT SVEN, HOW HARD he works, he's here, there and everywhere, never misses a match, whether in the UK or Europe, look, there he is again, in the directors' box, can you see him, it wouldn't be a proper game without Sven, they don't kick off till they check he's arrived, ha ha, what a treasure, what devotion, what a worker. Which made me think, yeh, I wouldn't mind some of that sort of work.

When I grow up, I'd quite like to be Sven. No need to send for tickets or hang on the line for hours and then get charged extra for having the impudence to expect to buy a ticket by phone. Free parking, with lackeys to do the parking. Drinkiepoos before, during and after. Best seat in the house. Tartan blanket on your lap, if it's parky. I wonder when he last bought a programme? Never, I bet. Or a pen. I've still to see him write down a word, yet he's supposed to be working. A hidden assistant probably makes notes for him. Lazy sod. And every penny he does have to pay, he can charge for, as a legitimate expense, which football fans can't.

Plus, he does get a million a year. Hard job? On your nelly.

When I was 11, I was asked by the headmaster of my secondary mod what I'd like to do in life, and I said be a footballer. At the age of 16, on arriving at Carlisle Grammar School, I changed it to teacher, dunno why, except to please my mum. At 21, on leaving Durham, I said to the appointments people I wanted to be a journalist and they said no chance, we haven't heard of anyone doing that, why don't you try to get on a management training scheme with Benzole. I thought they'd made it up, or it was a vulgar joke. She was only a garage mechanic's daughter, but she liked the smell of Benzole. But it was a real firm. And they turned me down.

Oh, if only I could have become a footballer, how life would be so different today. Probably be dead, or crippled by arthritis, or an alcoholic, or bankrupt, though I might have been prudent and bought a newsagent's shop.

Starting again now, which footballer would I like to be? Whose skills would I like to have? I'd have to take their character as well, such as it is, such as we all perceive it, which could be a problem.

It would have to be someone with sublime talent, otherwise what's the point. Not Becks. You'd have to be married to Posh and she's too thin, spends too much. You'd also get followed everywhere. Roy Keane, what a player, but what a miserable looking bloke. Always seems to be moaning. Paul Scholes, I do like his talent, but his hair, ugh, and he does have asthma. I've got that already, so why should I be him?

Steve Gerrard, he's ace, but he looks stupid and is always being injured, throwing himself around like a daft hap'orth. I'm not doing all that. Robbie Fowler, he doesn't knock himself out, does a lot of standing around, looks a soft job, being Robbie Fowler, but he's also got awful hair. And I wouldn't like to play for Leeds.

Michael Owen? He's every boy's hero, admired by Boy Scouts everywhere, clean in word and deed, no filthy habits — but come on, it must be pretty dull being Michael Owen.

Teddy Sheringham, he's one of my heroes. I like the way he passes the ball around, brings other people into play, does intelligent things. Shame about his age. He hasn't played so well the past two weeks. I suspect it could be downhill from now on. I also sense his time at Man Utd wasn't happy. So, on consideration, no, I wouldn't like to be him.

Two years ago, it would have been good being Dwight Yorke, playing with a smile on my face, so effortless, scoring all those goals, winning all those medals. I couldn't have lived alone the way he does, in such a big house, that would have been a drag, and having to put up with the tabloids writing rubbish about my sex life. But now, alas, his career is collapsing.

Thinking carefully, looking at our top players, at this moment in time, I can think of two I envy, whose skills and career I'd like to have, and whose personalities appear attractive. First, Steve McManaman. I like it that he's not big and muscle-bound, doesn't look like a footballer. I admired him going off to Real Madrid, showing the sort of enterprise and ambition that someone like Sol Campbell clearly lacks. If you call yourself a footballer, you want to have played with the best. His girlfriend is a barrister, another plus. I do like clever women. But he's not currently in the first team. That is a problem.

So, I'm going to be Thierry Henry, another weedy-looking player, who floats but stings. I'd like to be from Guadeloupe, have a World Cup winner's medal, with another WC to look forward to this summer, not be flash and overexcited when I score, be cool and put my finger up in the air, have got better and better every season, defying all my critics. I'd like to have foreigners chanting my name, Tee-Eree Onree, Tee Erce Onree, and getting it almost right. Having to play for Arsenal, hmm, could I really manage that? Plus this summer, all the heavies in the world will be trying to kick me.

On reflection, perhaps it is best to stick to being Sven. Then I'll never get injured. Unless I fall off my blanket.

FOOTBALLERS ARE ADMIRED FOR THEIR EXCESSES, NOT FOR GOOD BEHAVIOUR

25 MARCH 2002

I USED TO HAVE DISCUSSIONS WITH THE BEATLES ABOUT being role models. There was, and is, a section of society which says that if you are rich and famous, doing a job that millions of others would like to do, then you have a duty to set a good example. This varies from generation to generation. Having long hair, swearing, being rude to elders, chewing gum, eating in the street — those were seen as hanging offences not long ago.

Taking drugs, wrecking hotel bedrooms, sleeping around — that was considered awfully bad until, well, quite recently. It really pissed the Beatles off when they were reprimanded and criticised by various politicians and churchmen of the time for not behaving as they wanted them to behave. They didn't set themselves up as models of behaviour, so they said. They didn't ask anyone to copy them, they moaned. They just sang and played the guitar. Gawd, it seems centuries ago that such an archaic conversation ever took place.

But blow me, it's happened again. The Lord Chief Justice, Lord Woolf, has come out with a load of claptrap that I thought I would never hear again, this side of Mary Whitehouse. It's all about this Premiership footballer, still unnamed, who's been having it off with two women. A newspaper wanted to reveal all, but was stopped by a High Court judge who said that the footballer was entitled to his privacy. Lord Woolf was quoted as saying, among other things, that 'footballers are role models for young people and undesirable behaviour on their part can set an unfortunate example'.

I'm not here to argue about rights of privacy. I don't actually care whether the footballer is exposed or not. What a lie. I do. I'll read every word. Why should his dressing room have all the fun? His fans pay his wages. They deserve every sordid detail. And the rival fans are going to love it. They'll chant his name like mad next time he tries to score, ha ha.

It's that one remark I object to. Politicians, or people who stand for election, asking the public for approval, have got to set good examples, or at least not get caught setting a bad example. Clerics and moralisers, who tell the rest of us off, they, too, have to behave.

On the whole, the worse examples footballers are, the more we like them. Footballers are admired for their excesses, not for good behaviour. Half of Gazza's attraction, even now, is his stupid behaviour. George Best is still a hero, remembered as much for his excesses as for his successes. Bad boys don't even get ticked off by their management, if they're good enough. Arsène Wenger never admonishes his players for red cards. Fergie stood by Cantona when we all saw him kicking the shit out of someone.

Lord Woolf was right in one sense. Footballers are role models to the young — because they fantasise about emulating the roles they play. Having all these dopey girls queuing up for you. Driving £150,000 Ferraris far too fast. Smashing up hotel bars. Not having to pay for anything, getting money for doing bugger all, never having to say sorry. As long as you are still in the team, doing the business.

I bet most of today's footballers had such fantasies in their heads when they were young. They dreamt about stepping out at Wembley, but just as often they were stepping out with a lap-dancer, driving her too fast, or sleeping with a blonde Ferrari.

Famous footballers should not be expected to behave any better than the rest of us. They are not modelling roles, just rolling a ball. Their behaviour off the pitch is irrelevant, unless it affects their performance on the park.

Except in one way. It's an interesting sign of the times, not the moral times, but the commercial times, in which our millionaire footballers now live. Suppose that a footballer has a million-a-year deal with a cornflakes firm that uses him and his lovely family in its wholesome advertising, showing him having a lovely breakfast, eating his lovely cornflakes with his lovely children. And the next day, in the Sunday papers, some lap-dancing blonde nursery teacher describes his sexual inadequacies in brilliant, sorry, disgusting detail. End of contract.

Your role as a model person will be over for purely commercial reasons. Nothing at all to do with being ticked off by the Mary Whitehouses or Lord Woolfs of this world.

HOW I NEARLY GOT KEN LOACH AND
RICHARD LITTLEJOHN IN THE SAME TEAM

1 APRIL 2002

I THINK I'LL GIVE UP FOLLOWING FOOTBALL, OR AT LEAST give up telling people I follow football. Last week I was so shanned. That's a Carlisle expression, one I've never heard used elsewhere. It means ashamed, shown up, embarrassed, and can be active or passive, transitive or intransitive, not that I know the difference. So an embarrassing situation will be a 'queer shan', and you yourself will be 'shanned to deeth'.

Months ago, I had my arm twisted to take part in a Barnardo's football quiz. It's an annual event, apparently, very popular, raises lots of money for Barnardo's, usually around £20,000, and is good fun all round, allegedly. This year, it was taking place at White Hart Lane, home of the famous Spurs. I didn't really know what it meant, though I do know about Barnardo's, which 98 per cent of the population don't. In the 1930s, there were 188 Barnardo's homes. Now there are how many? Go on, guess. The answer is none. Barnardo's today is huge, with 5,000 full-time staff, but they're into projects not homes.

Then I forgot about it, thinking 21 March would never come. About a month ago, I was reminded that I'd promised not just to take part, but to raise a team of five people who like football. Oh no. Who do I know? Where do I go? So I sat down, sucked my pencil.

I wrote to eight people, hoping four would sign up. There was Alastair Campbell, who's always going on about Burnley, and Melvyn Bragg, my Cumbrian chum, who supports Arsenal. Then Richard Littlejohn of the *Sun* and Matthew Norman of the *Guardian*, who both support Spurs. Then Brian Viner of the *Independent*, who's an Everton fan, and Jim White of the *Guardian*, who supports Man Utd. I also asked my neighbour Ken Loach, the film-maker, who's been a director of Bath City. We live in back-to-back houses. I use his outside lav and he keeps his coal in my bath. No, I mean his lovely house backs on to my lovely house.

I also wrote to Pat Jennings, thinking I needed a real celeb. Melvyn said sorry, he'd be away on holiday in Egypt with his wife. That was interesting. He doesn't normally like going on foreign hols. Alastair Campbell and Matthew Norman never replied — but I'm not fingering them, they probably never got the letter, as they do lead such busy lives. The other five all said yes, at once, which was good. When I told Ken Loach, he said he wasn't all that keen to meet Littlejohn, not caring for some of his political views. I said Littlejohn's a nice bloke, got a lovely wife. Then, fortunately, Littlejohn decided he liked the idea of the quiz so much that he'd set up his own team.

I gave Ken a lift to Spurs and learnt that his latest film, *Sweet Sixteen*, which he's now dubbing, has a foolball connection. It's about a boy of 10 in Greenock with a mum in prison. All the people in the film are real people, with no acting experience. By chance, the boy they looked at for the lead part was also applying for something else at the same time — to be a professional footballer. And got both. He now plays for Greenock Morton, and stars in the film. Martin Compston, he's called. If he does well at both, I wonder which he'll choose in the years ahead.

We got to Spurs, to one of their hospitality places, and it was heaving with about 200 people. I'd expected sweaty England shirts, big beer bellies, but they were mostly office types, many from the City, who'd got together an office team. The team at the next table to us was called Baddiel Utd, featuring David Baddiel and Frank Skinner. The latter did the auction at half-time, and was excellent, funny without ever being rude or obscene. What an achievement. There was utter concentration as Eleanor Oldroyd of BBC Radio started to read out the questions. I was convinced I'd do well, having spent half my life watching football.

"*I was born on 11 September 1945 and first played for my country in*

1965 — who am I?" That question earned five points, if you got it right, without any other clues. Bloody hell. Who can possibly know that? The answer was Franz Beckenbauer.

There was another equally hard one. *"I was born in Sacriston in 1933 and my first team was Langley Park."* The answer was Bobby Robson. Ken got that right, amazingly. Back in 1973, he shot a film, *Days of Hope*, in Langley Park, and Bobby Robson's father had a part.

"Steve Hodge has kept it in a bank vault for many years and it is now worth £100,000 — what is it?" The answer was Maradona's Hand of God shirt, which both Brian Viner and Jim White knew. Well, their brains are young. Thanks to them, our team did quite well, coming about halfway, but I was hopeless.

Though I cheered up when there was a 1966 World Cup Final question. *"Hurst got his hat-trick with his right foot, his left foot and his head, true or false?"* I'll answer this, I said, no probs, I was there, wasn't I, and I also watched a film of the match only the other week. Trust me. I could see in my mind two of his shots, but I couldn't remember his header, so I wrote down "False". And got it wrong. Oh gawd. What a shan.

Pat Jennings didn't turn up in the end, though he sent a pair of his gloves, which were auctioned for £250. I'd boasted that he was coming, so people kept coming to our table for his autograph, which was a bit embarrassing. What with that and my appalling ignorance, I'd have to say the evening was a big success for Barnardo's, but for me I'd have to call it a double shan.

THESE ARMBANDS AND ONE-MINUTE
SILENCES HAVE GOT OUT OF HAND

15 APRIL 2002

THERE WAS A CALL FOR ONE MINUTE'S SILENCE FOR THE Queen Mother at the Arsenal–Spurs match on 6 April. As there was everywhere. I turned and made a face at my neighbour in the next seat in the West Stand at Highbury. "Didn't know she was an Arsenal fan," I said. He didn't smile. But then it was a pretty silly remark. He was young, shaven-headed, hung-over looking, one shaky thumb on his mobile.

Over the tannoy came the voice of the Arsenal tannoy voice. A voice I have grown to hate. Nothing to do with being a Spurs fan. It's his phoney, mid-Atlantic DJ accent. "The Queen Mother," he sonorously intoned, "was a much-loved figure around the world."

"In China?" I muttered to my young friend. "In Russia?" He just looked at me. After the one-minute silence, which seemed to last about ten minutes, there was the sound of a scratchy gramophone rendition of the National Anthem.

"Bring back the police," I said. It did look this time as if he might duff me up, should I make any more inane comments. I wasn't thinking of Sting and the Police, but thinking back to 30 years ago, when one of the highlights of going to Highbury was the police band, which played before every game. I did enjoy them. You can't beat live music.

During the one minute for the Queen Mum, I watched all the Arsenal players being dutifully silent—and during the dreadful recording of the British National Anthem, players such as Vieira, Henry, Ljungberg, Edu, Wiltord, Luzhny, Lauren, Bergkamp, all born within the sound of Bow Bells, well, give or take a 10,000-mile radius. They do have good hearing, these modern players. It's the diet that does it.

Did they know what was going on? Would they have recognised

the Queen Mum if they'd met her in the wine queue at Safeway? Can they tell *God Save the Queen* from *Good King Wenceslas*? This passion for armbands and one-minute silences is getting out of hand. It was a whole week, after all, since the Queen Mum had died. Is it because it's football? In that case, why didn't the ref and linesmen have armbands, or Arsène Wenger, or the ball boys, or everyone in the crowd? Is it because they were working in front of the public? In that case, did all the West End actors act in armbands all week, or bus drivers, or policemen, or traffic wardens?

I can't remember when this began. In 1952, on the death of George VI, did all footballers wear armbands as a mark of respect? Do tell. They would at least have all been Brit-born players. It seems to happen all the time these days at football grounds—not just remembering national figures, but some obscure football official. At Spurs this season, we all stood for one minute's silence for Glenn Hoddle's dad.

Before the match, I went to lunch again with my Arsenal chums, determined to keep my opinions to myself, not get involved in silly arguments, assuming I'd be the only Spurs fan. I found myself beside Melvyn Bragg, so that was safe because, deep down, our first love is Carlisle Utd and I know how he got into following Arsenal (through his son Tom). Beyond him was Simon Schama, the eminent professor, man of parts, most of them dead clever, and he whispered that he'd followed Spurs since he was a boy. That was reassuring.

You have to be clever to follow football these days. I don't understand why it's not a mainstream university subject. There are courses and degrees in pop music or cooking or gardening. Why not football? It should be taught from the beginning in primary schools. It might attract the interest and attention of all those boys who give up on learning at an early age.

Years later, out in the world, many of them become football anoraks, stars of pub quizzes, brainboxes at football facts and figures, yet at school they wouldn't learn nuffink. Any subject is worth learning, for the sake of learning. Football is just as worthy of study as Latin. It has a history, a grammar, a discipline, set texts. Think about it, Estelle Morris.

During the game, I was able to help my young Arsenal friend with a few translations. I could clearly hear the Spurs crowd to my right, tucked into a corner of the Clock End, singing what appeared to be the Arsenal song about Vieira. You know the one. "Vee-ehra, ahh hah ha ha, Vee-ehra. He comes from Seny-gall. He plays for Arsen-all." Sung to the tune of *Volare*.

At first, the Arsenal crowd were confounded, trying to work out why Spurs fans were singing their song. The Spurs version is rather vulgar, so look away, if you don't want to know the score.

> Vee-ehra, ahh ha ha ha,
> Vee-ehra, ahh ha ha ha
> He wants to leave the scum
> Cos Campbell wants his bum.
> Veer-ehra …

No, don't go away. For GCSE students of semantics, the word *scum* is interesting, used by both sides about each other. Football scholars who have done their homework will know that there have been reports all season about Vieira leaving. As for Campbell, not true, I'm sure: students of international football can compare and contrast, as the same form of sexual abuse is used throughout the known world at every football ground.

Spurs got beaten, by the way. End of story. End of season. Roll on the World Cup.

BECKHAM IS BANDY-LEGGED —
BUT ONLY FROM THE KNEES DOWN

22 APRIL 2002

I'VE BEEN WEARING A GREY ARMBAND ALL WEEK, SHOWING respex for Bex. I am so worried about him. And about my friend Rupert and his wife Sal. All three have been awaiting medical reports, not knowing what was going to happen next.

I don't understand people mocking the attention Beckham has received. Tony Blair was spot on to express concern at a Cabinet meeting. It was right that he featured in a *Thought for the Day* on the *Today* programme, and it was only proper that *The Sun* (or was it *The Mirror?*) showed his foot on its front page and asked the nation to lay their hands on the photograph and pray. It didn't matter that the same papers ridiculed Hoddle for having faith in a faithhealer. We're not talking logic and consistency here. This was a national emergency, though many have wondered whether, if Bex had had a groin strain, *The Sun* would have printed a full-page photo of his injured parts and asked us all to lay our hands on it.

Which brings us to my friend Rupert. He developed a nasty skin rash on his private part, so his GP referred him to the Whittington Hospital. Meanwhile, his wife, Sal, started having pains in her chest. Tests showed that her blood pressure was very high, yet she's a fit woman and plays tennis all the time.

Awful, isn't it, all this worry and concern over health. Once you get over 50, that's what happens. I myself, perfect specimen though I am, had my eyes tested last week by Dollond & Aitchison. All perfect, but Ms Dollond, or it might have been Mrs Aitchison, asked in passing if I'd had my blood pressure done recently. I rushed over to Hampstead to see the nurse at our general practice. She told me I was 140 over 80. You what? It means excellent, she said.

I walked back over the Heath singing "Tot-ing-ham, Tot-ing-ham". This is part of our family myth. Our son Jake, as a little boy, always sang this when he was in a good mood. I then rang my friend Sal to say that, in my will, I was leaving her my blood pressure. It's just so obvious, leaving your kidneys to help the human race. Everyone does that. It did cheer her up.

I tried to ring Tony Stevens, who is Beckham's agent, and also Owen's, Shearer's and Dwight Yorke's, to ask if Bex might like one of my toes, but he was engaged. If it's going to take eight weeks for his broken metatarsal to heal, a toe transplant might be much quicker. I'm hardly using mine at present, since I gave up Sunday football.

If I was Fergie, worrying about my two major invalids, I'd want Roy Keane fit first. He is far more important and valuable to Man Utd than Bex, who this season has often been peripheral. But for England, Bex has become our leader, inspiration, talisman. Who would have thought it, just a year ago? That's why a nation has been mourning. A nation does not get these things wrong.

A lot of people did go tut tut, ridiculous, what is the world coming to, when the news of Bex's foot got precedence in the headlines over the Israeli-Palestinian conflict. This is to misunderstand the nature of headlines. Like is not being compared with like. Newness matters most. Whatever is the very latest drama jumps ahead of the running story.

Second, headline writers know that we all know Bex, a topic we all share, all have an opinion on, all can rubbish, even if we know bugger all about football. Bex's toe might have been bad news in one sense, but it's linked up with a feel-good event, one that makes us cheerful and happy. Until, that is, it happens.

Afterwards, 31 out of the 32 nations will be decidedly unhappy. We need Bex, not just for his footballing skills, for his contributions to our knowledge of anatomy, but for his haircuts. I bet he's got one up his sleeve, or wherever he keeps it, ready to surprise and amuse us all. There is no one in the England squad so concerned about his appearance, which is fortunate for us. When things get boring, as they will in that first game against Sweden, with nothing much happening, we can enjoy close-ups and speculate about his eyebrows, the colour of his roots, the patterns on his bonce, the amount of gunge on his hair.

Or his legs. I've always been fascinated by them. At first glance, when you observe him walking, you think he's bandy-legged, bowed like a jockey. Study them closely next time you have a chance, which, dear God, we all pray is soon. He is bandylegged — but only from the knees down. This is most unusual. Bandy-calfed, so they call it in medical circles. Above the knee, his legs and thighs go straight up and are what we call normal. But below the knees, each leg is curved inwards like a boomerang. Very weird. This abnormality explains how he can bend the ball when taking corners and free kicks.

I do fear for him in the years to come, as he's bound to get appalling arthritis, but for now, at his age, it's not a disability but a gift, sent from heaven. Naturally, David has had to work at it, as we all have, with whatever modest gifts God has given us, and all of us, friends, have been given gifts that we have to work on. How many words did you say for *Thought for the Day*? What? Forget it. I'm not doing one. Back to Rupert.

It's turned out to be good news. He went private, not being prepared to wait 15 months, and paid to go to the King Edward vii Hospital for Sick Officers. He had a biopsy, and there is no sign of skin cancer. "I've been told I've got a hearty dick," so he told me when he and Sal came for lunch last week.

Not such good news for Sal. "I've been told I've got a dicky heart."

Please note, all medical references are true. Bex is a real person. So are my friends. I have made up nothing. Not even the quotes.

GEORGE BEST'S GLAMOROUS YOUNG WIFE WAS AMAZED TO READ WHAT I HAD WRITTEN ABOUT HER HUSBAND IN 1965. COULD HE EVER HAVE BEEN SO SHY, SO NAÏVE, SO NON-DRINKING?

6 MAY 2002

I SPENT AN AFTERNOON WITH GEORGE BEST LAST WEEK. The appointment was in an Italian restaurant in Chelsea and I was there early, just in case he arrived early. Fat chance, though his agent had assured me that George is a reformed man, now he's given up drink, always punctual, not like the old days.

I first interviewed him in 1965. I was doing the Atticus column on the *Sunday Times*, just at that moment in time when the world changed, or at least my world changed: the Sixties had arrived and I was at last able to stop interviewing boring bishops and masters of Oxbridge colleges and talk to real people, like northern novelists, pop stars and footballers.

George was aged 19, a naïve young lad with a strong Belfast accent and Beatles haircut. He was in the first team at Man Utd, but still living in digs, polite and deferential, worried that the older players in the dressing room would tease him about his haircut and the flash new jacket he'd just bought. He had arrived at Old Trafford aged 15, then run away, homesick, to Belfast. "I thought I'd never make the grade. It was my father who talked me into coming back." He still seemed a bit in awe of senior players such as Denis Law and Bobby Charlton, whom he had hero-worshipped as a kid.

At the age of 19, he didn't drink or smoke, so he told me, and I believed him. "Well, perhaps on rare occasions I might have a lager. Then it gets back to the boss, Mr Busby, that you're drunk. I would like to have a flat of my own, but the boss thinks there might be temptation. Perhaps, when I'm 21. I've no complaints. I like my landlady."

By 1968, when he was 22, it had all changed. Man Utd had won the European Cup and George had been made European Footballer of the Year and England's Footballer of the Year.

He'd also become a household name, a household face. I went to interview him again that year, this time for Granada TV. George had agreed to see us, but having waited outside his house for hours, there was no sign of him. We went to the training ground, but he wasn't there. We went round some nightclubs, but couldn't find him. I rang the producer of the programme back in London, John Birt, with whom I used to play football, and said it's all a nonsense. I'm packing up. John said no, hang on, stay overnight.

We were kept hanging around Manchester for another day before George finally emerged from some drunken, sexual or similar exploit and agreed to see us. And he was good: fluent and amusing. One thing people forget about George is that he is clever — the only one in his class to pass the 11-Plus and go on to grammar school.

It was strange, waiting to interview him again after a gap of more than 30 years. I knew he wouldn't know me from Adam, or Tony Adams, why should he? He's been interviewed a trillion times since then, but I have watched him from afar, seen his career end too early, his body collapse too fast.

He arrived just 15 minutes late, with his glamorous, blonde wife Alex. He seemed to stagger a bit at first, but was fine when he sat down, clutching a box of pills. The appointment was to talk about the World Cup for a *Mail on Sunday* piece, which we did, and when it was finished, I pulled out my faded 1965 cutting and gave him a copy. He read it slowly, as if reading about a total stranger, which in a way it was. Then Alex, his young wife who has only ever known him as a middle-aged man, often drunk, read it as well, in quiet amazement. Could he ever have been so shy, so naive, so non-drinking?

No need to feel sorry for him financially. They live in some style in Surrey and Chelsea. At 55, he is better off than he was ten, 20 years ago. The older he has grown, the more of an icon he has become. There is also far more money floating around in football today, fromTV and publishing. His last biography, the fifth by my reckoning, sold 300,000 in hardback. I couldn't believe it. He said he, too, was amazed when his royalty cheque came in. Now he's working on another.

Today's middle classes follow football in large numbers and buy lots of footer books. Anoraks, who had not even been born when George played, know everything about him. They are even bringing out a George Best boot, 20 years after he last played (for Bournemouth in 1983).

In 1968, his best year as a player, his total income was £30,000 — from football, plus commercial stuff. This past year, he must have earned ten times that, if the sales of his book are correct. Who would begrudge him? In my lifetime, there has not been a British player more touched with footballing genius.

But he may not live long enough to reap the benefits. He's on a bleeper, waiting for the call to be rushed into hospital for a liver transplant. It will be a seven-hour operation, three weeks in hospital, then recuperation, if all goes well. Don't you regret it now, George, all those years of drink?

"Not at all. I regret nothing. I have a great lifestyle — and hope to continue to have one, after the operation."

IN THE MORNINGS, I USE THE SAME BATHWATER AS MY WIFE. SO FOR THE WORLD CUP, SHE WILL HAVE TO SHARPEN UP HER ACT, GETTING OUT OF IT THE SECOND THE HALF-TIME WHISTLE BLOWS

3 JUNE 2002

IS 12.30PM A LUNCHTIME TIME OR MIDNIGHT TIME? THAT was the first problem I had to overcome in my World Cup preparations. My mummy, or it may have been my wife, taught me the difference between am and pm by saying that am comes before pm because a is before p in the alphabet. So I filled in my diary accordingly, telling myself to stay up late to watch the France–Senegal opening game, only to see that the highlights were being shown five hours earlier. You what? Must be the stupid *Indy*, always getting things wrong. It had two different kick-off times for England against Cameroon.

My silly mistake, of course. And what a mess my diary now looks, with all the crossings-out. Buggered it up before a ball has been kicked.

Apart from that, preparations have been going well. The England–Cameroon game provided a perfect wet run for the real test of this year's World Cup. How to get up in the morning.

I have gone through life taking two hours each morning to greet the new day. My dear wife wakes me at 7am with a cup of tea and the *Indy*, pulls the curtains, switches on the wireless (as I just have no strength at that time of the day), then closes the bedroom door, very quietly. I eventually get up and into her bath. After her. She is very clean. It's not meanness, though I do get pleasure out of thinking how much money I'm saving. It's mainly that I hate running my own bath. What a waste of time. I lie there until *Thought for the Day*, when I have a sudden energy burst—enough to turn it off .

So how am I going to manage to sustain this ritual during the next four weeks? Fifa has been so thoughtless, letting the World Cup be played in such inconvenient time zones as Japan and Korea. Last Sunday, for the trial run, I set the alarm for 6.30am and bounded up. I watched the first half in my jamas and then, at half-time, ran like hell upstairs, dived into the bath, shaved and dressed in 15 minutes flat. A world record. The bath was unoccupied, fortunately, but the water was lukewarm. I've told her straight, she'll have to sharpen up her act in the next four weeks. She must time her bath exactly, getting out of it the second the half-time whistle blows. No excuses about injury time or delays. You've got to cope. We all have to, in these unusual times.

What's going to be weird these next few weeks is eating muesli all the way through a game. And drinking endless cups of coffee. My alcohol intake will fall dramatically — which is good, I suppose. I don't think I can manage a bottle of Beaujolais at 8am. At 12.30pm or even 12.30am, whenever that is, I should be able to manage a stab at normal life.

Facts-wise, I'm up to scratch. Got almost a roomful of World Cup supplements, pull-outs, posters. And I've done my homework. I spent a whole morning analysing the 32 squads and worked out that there are 112 British-based players in this year's World Cup. So whatever happens, as the WC progresses, we should have some players to cheer. The most English-based squad is Ireland's. Yup, all 23 play in England (now 22, since Keane left). All 22 out of the English squad play in England.

I've also worked out who is the real winner of the World Cup so far — Slovenia. Their population is only 1.9 million, the smallest country in the WC, so they have done brilliantly just to be there. After them comes Uruguay, 3.4 million, then Costa Rica and Ireland, joint third on 3.8 million. I plan to award points based on how each country progresses in relation to its population. If I don't fall asleep. I know before we start that China, at 1.3 billion, will be bottom.

I'm so looking forward to watching the co-hosts play. The Japs and Koreans are so smart, modern, up to date — and that's just the haircuts. It must take triple strength bleach to turn their hair a lighter shade of pitch black. Their fans are equally clued up, with their English-style shirts and English football chants. Their passion for Beckham is so touching. I bet Posh has a lump in her throat, not just her tum. The crowds appear to be younger than in England, and with more women. Very modern. Their football is also surprisingly good, judging by the Korean performance against France — fast, clever, skillful. All they lack is finishing. England's football in the final two warm-ups was normal. Lumpen, leaden, dull, unimaginative. All they lack is, well, everything really, thanks partly to the injuries. Their second-string players have been embarrassing, while the so-called best 11 look mediocre. But, I still expect them to struggle out of their group, finishing second behind Argentina, and reach the second stage. And they'd better. I've got in double muesli supplies for the next three weeks.

WHY DO FAIR-HAIRED FOOTBALLERS NEVER DYE THEIR HAIR BLACK? IF BECKS WERE REALLY A TRENDSETTER HE'D HAVE GOT OUT THE BOOT POLISH BY NOW

24 JUNE 2002

AT HALF-TIME DURING THE ENGLAND–DENMARK GAME, MY daughter Caitlin rang from Botswana. She was watching with her friend Beauty and her family. On the way to Beauty's house, her car had got stuck in the sand, this part of Botswana being near the Kalahari Desert. By the time she'd been pulled out, she was five minutes late and missed the first goal.

I was able to tell her what had happened, about Ferdinand's jammy goal, not that she had heard of him. She's not really a football fan, but it's England, innit, and you're ten million miles from home. Her Botswana friends watching with her, all women and children, were well clued up, explaining the offside rule to her and what a yellow card means. One of them was puzzled by all the black players in the England team: "Do they come from Africa?" Caitlin had to explain our West Indian connections. They were rather contemptuous of the England supporters monotonously singing the same old chant, Inger-land, Inger-land. "Why can't white people sing properly?" They were supporting England, partly because they didn't know where Denmark is. Caitlin had to tell them. At the end, they all jumped up and cheered our lads.

After the USA–Mexico game, I decided to ring my friend Dr John Davies in California. He's a nuclear chemist, a friend of mine from Durham days. I got him just getting into bed, having watched the USA live, thumping Mexico, well pleased, of course, but a bit saddened for Mexico. It would have done so much to their self-esteem to beat Big Brother. We agreed we would both miss Blanco from now on, the Mexican with the humpy back and the white boots, what a good player. I was a bit worried saying humpy backed, but John said that in Mexico the fans call him the hunchback.

I asked if he'd seen the Ireland–Spain game. Poor old Ireland, they deserved better. Spain were so fortunate. He hadn't stayed up for it but watched it later on video — except for the penalty shoot-out. His bloody tape ran out at the vital moment.

So it goes, all round the globe, where eight out of ten of the human population will have tuned in at some time between now and the final, so Fifa says. As I sit on my own in my little room in Lakeland, bog-eyed now, limbs weary, I do like to think that I'm in communion with trillions of others, excited or worried by our own team, asking the same sort of questions in our heads.

The Japanese and Korean fans who support foreign teams, how do they decide? Is it on a whim, do they draw lots or get ordered by the local authorities? YOU, you and you, no arguing, you will follow England, yes you may fall asleep, yes you could go through agony, yes it will be a frightening sight if ever Keown comes on, but the minute you see the camera, smile.

The Japanese players' hair, that's another puzzle. Why is everyone a blond, except for the redhead? One starts and they all copy. But why, then, do fair-haired footballers never dye their hair black? If Becks was really a trend-setter, he'd have got out the black boot polish. He's had that soppy, semi-bleached, grown-out Mohican for, oh, it must be minutes now.

Why does Motty keep on clearing his throat? Is it to let us know he thinks he's made a joke? Why does Graham Taylor say "very much so" all the time? "It's hot this evening, Graham." "Yes, very much so," he replies. "Would you like a slap round the chops, Graham?" "Very much so." "Who's your man of the match, Graham?" "Velly Much Soo, Korea's exciting number nine shirt." He got you there. He's not stupid, our Graham.

Why is they playing like they is? I'm sure that's a question which has been asked by supporters everywhere. Each country puts its fans through it, even the best, playing havoc with our nervous systems.

Perhaps it's all in the eye of the beholder. And as beholders of England, we are all too close, like knowing your own family only too well. When your children start to speak, managing to form a whole sentence, you think, amazing, how did they do that? You know where they've come from, all about them, so you get carried away and go around saying, "Heh, we've got a genius on our hands." Then, later, when they do something really, really stupid, you despair, wonder what's gone wrong. By being so close, you get their bad days out of proportion, just as you did with the good days. The truth is that most children, like most of the England team, are pretty average performers. But they can have very good days. Will England against Brazil be one of them? By the time you read this, you'll probably know. I just hope that, if Becks doesn't get us into the semi-finals, then at least he will have been at the boot polish and given us all something to talk about afterwards on the telephone.

I'VE BEEN SITTING IN FRONT OF THE TELLY FOR WEEKS, STUFFING MYSELF WITH CRISPS AND CHEAP WHITE WINE. AND NOW I GET A LETTER SAYING I'VE HAD A HEART ATTACK. OR SIMILAR

1 JULY 2002

THE POSTMAN CAME JUST AFTER ENGLAND WAS KNOCKED out by Brazil, while I was still moaning at Sven for sitting there, rubbing his nose, doing nothing. I was also still groaning at our lads, especially the three subs who'd come on, supposedly fresh, who looked as tired as the whole team, yet they'd had five whole days to recover and been given so many advantages—Owen's early if rather jammy goal, Brazil down to ten men, Ronaldo being taken off, France, Argentina and Italy knocked out early doors, England, it's going your way, if you can't get to the final this year, you never will, so what are yous playing at, you plonkers…

So, I was still in a bit of a state, as I opened the post. To find I'd had a heart attack. Or similar. My London GP was instructing me to attend a chronic disease clinic, because 'you suffer from heart disease'—and enclosed a pathology test form to take at once to the Royal Free Hospital.

Gawd, that was quick, I thought. I know I've been sitting in front of the telly for weeks, if not centuries, going through endless stress, not to mention stuffing myself with crisps and cheap white wine, the stuff with plastic corks, now that is stressful. How I hate them, agony to get out of the bottle, further agony to get out of the corkscrew, then impossible to get in the bottle again, should you want to save whatever's left, which has not happened, during this World Cup.

We are 300 miles away in Lakeland. I haven't seen my GP for ages, so I rang to say I'd received this frightening letter.

"Threatening letter?" asked the receptionist. She laughed,

ghoulishly, when I explained, but said she'd investigate. I'm assuming it's a mistake. Countless other things wrong with me, from rheumatoid arthritis to cut fingers through trying to shave plastic corks, but so far, the old ticker is fine. And with England out, I've been able to relax, think about other people's problems, such as underarm sweat. The managers of Spain and Mexico will have learnt many lessons from this World Cup, one of which is not to wear a blue shirt.

The Italian team have learnt that their especially tight, natty, sexy shirts, meant to restrict the chance of shirt-pulling, did them no bloody good, har har. We've learnt that one verse of our national anthem is quite sufficient, thank you, how kind, but please, please, no more.

Now we're down to just two teams, I'm missing so many familiar faces, players and managers who became part of the family these past four weeks. Blanco, will I ever see your sloping shoulders again? That bloke beside the Japanese manager, will he still have that stupid middle parting? I had my own little domestic routine, which had grown up around the games. Gone for another four years. Though I will not miss getting up for 7.30am kick-offs. That was knackering.

Football-wise, we haven't learnt much. No new systems, no new tricks, no new stars, while the old stars like Bex, Owen, Zidane, Thierry Henry, Batistuta, Raul, Totti, Hakan Sukur, Roy Keane, either disappointed, got injured, were sent off or went absent.

Was it fair? There were some dodgy decisions, which, in the future, technology should eliminate, but no, it wasn't fair. My wife came in from time to time, gave her informed opinion on who was clearly the better team, with the better players, having more of the ball, and said surely, they will win. It doesn't work that way, pet, I sighed. Football is not fair. No more than life. Now, close the door.

What we have had are new teams emerging, countries hardly rated who surprised us all, but I doubt if the old world order is over.

In Germany in 2006, I don't expect an African or Asian country to win it, but this time, Senegal, Japan and South Korea did excellently.

Most of all, it's been South Korea's World Cup. They've given most pleasure, most joy, as have their fans. That sea of red will stay in my mind for oh, perhaps till August and the new season. Communism imposed regimentation, uniformity and patriotism, but never managed much joy, unlike football, which can do all of that, with no force, no bloodshed. Hurrah for footie.

And hurrah for Sven? Yes, he got us there, when all seemed lost, then got us further than most expected. Yet at the same time, he left us disappointed. He didn't help our cause when it mattered most, failed to rejuvenate them, which should be part of his job. But on reflection, I don't think, if he'd jumped up and down, screamed at them, that it would have made much difference. We were revealed to be a pretty average team, as we already knew, deep down.

So who's going to win the final on Sunday? Probably a slightly better but still average team, performing well on the day, being lucky with dodgy decisions, not making too many silly mistakes. My head fears Germany, but my heart says ... yes just checked it, it's still there ... that Brazil will do it.

2002–03 SEASON

Football memorabilia, Sir Bobby and Wayne Rooney

I'VE FOUND SOMETHING BRILLIANT. HONEST, I REALLY HAVE

23 SEPTEMBER 2002

UNTIL LAST WEEK, I'D BEEN TO PRESTON ONLY THREE times in my fun-filled life. In the late Fifties, I spent a long weekend there in order to graduate as a Ribble bus conductor. I was nervous about the exams but I got through, phew, and attended a passing-out parade, holding my ticket machine and leather money bag. Oh, if only I had a photograph. My children, when I moaned at them as students for not having proper holiday jobs, never believed me.

In the Nineties I went twice, working on books. I interviewed the staff of a chemist's shop who had won half a million each on the Lottery. Then, for a book about people born in 1900, I went to see a local GP, then aged 96. What took me there this time? The National Football Museum, of course. It opened last year, but I've been saving it up till now, a treat for myself. Only an hour and a half down the motorway from where we are in Lakeland, so I was there before it opened, hammering to be let in. I spent five hours, dazed by all the wonders, and can't wait to go again. It's brilliant. I do overuse that word, like the kid in *The Fast Show*, but I honestly, sincerely think it's amazing.

You have to be interested in football history to appreciate the 1,000 items on show, such as an England shirt worn in 1872 against Scotland in the world's first international. Or the 20,000 objects behind the scenes and available to researchers, such as the museum's 1585 copy of a book, in Italian, about the Calcio [Italian for 'football']—probably the world's oldest book on football. Such excitement as I put on white gloves to inspect it. (Second time in a week. At the Armitt Museum in Ambleside, I was white-gloved to look at a first edition of Peter Rabbit, the self-published one, worth about £55,000.)

The organisers have nicely combined the educational side, putting football in a social context, showing the Dick Kerr women's team of the Twenties against suffragette images, and with lots of fun stuff, such as interactive displays and games on TV. There's even an indoor football pitch where you can take shots at goal and have a computer score your speed and accuracy.

It cost £15m in all (thanks to Lottery money), and is in spanking new premises, under the stand at Deepdale. It's the only national football museum in the world, apart from Scotland's. So far, Preston has had visits from football officials in Brazil, Germany and Norway, each of which is now planning its own version. The museum had hoped for 80,000 visitors in this first year—but, alas, has managed only 40,000. If it's so brilliant, as I maintain, and if football is so successful, rich and popular with millions, why have people not been queueing all the way along the M6? I wish I could answer that.

I asked Hugh Hornby, one of the curators. He thought one problem was lack of money for publicity and marketing. It did cost a fortune to create, but is now running on a very small budget, so not enough people know it exists.

Inside, it is huge and spectacular, but from the outside it looks nondescript, more like a shop, and the 'FM' logo is too cute and gets lost. That may deter people. So might being in Preston. Football-wise, as all football historians know, being in Preston is justified, but perhaps not otherwise. Who wants to go there? I've had specific reasons for four visits in 40-odd years, but I wouldn't have gone otherwise.

Perhaps the real problem is the football psyche. Becks has not been there, nor any present-day national football star, but Bobby Charlton and all the 1966 team have. Today's players think only of today, not where they and football have come from.

Most football fans, especially new ones, are the same. It takes time for them to realise that there is a past. It's great that our National Football Museum exists but, like Martin Peters, it could well be ten years ahead of itself.

I TRIED TO WATCH THE MATCH IN THE PUB, BUT MY NECK ACHED AND MY EYES HURT

21 OCTOBER 2002

COMING BACK TO LONDON, AFTER FIVE MONTHS OF Lakeland life, it's such a social and cultural shock, seeing the strange-looking people, funny clothes, foreign voices. Which of course is part of why we come back. Gets so boring, living in a nice green pleasant place, waking up each day and saying oh no, not another lovely view.

It takes over a week before I remember how urban things work. This year it's happened much quicker than normal. On the second day, I sat down in front of the telly, drinks ready treats, lined up, but couldn't find Sky Sports. Who's been at the telly, the one I keep in my room, specially for football? Someone's buggered up the channels. Let me see, it has to go on number 5 first, or is it 39, then I set it to AV, whatever that is. Still no picture. I must be going senile. Then I remembered. Just before we left in May, ITV Digital went bust.

I rang Sky about their special deal of £30 for connection, including a dish, agreeing to pay £37 a month for their top package, which means all their rubbish channels, but after a month, I can dump the rubbish and just have sports. Don't they make it so complicated. Aren't we daft to accept it.

The dish got put up, nicely hidden, the digital box connected — but no sign of the card. After three days I was screaming at them, so they posted another. Still hasn't arrived. So last Monday, in desperation, I went to the pub.

I don't usually go to pubs, certainly not London ones. And I don't watch telly football with other people. I find human beings so irritating, with their stupid remarks, idiotic reactions. I have enough of my own.

The pub was called the Duke of York, last time I looked. It's now gone upmarket with a poncey name. I thought that's good, bound to be nice and quiet, no noisy lads. And it was. Very quiet. Practically empty.

I picked a comfy couch in front of the huge screen, put my jacket on it, and went to the bar for a drink of er, I dunno, what do I drink in pubs? I'd had my supper, drunk most of a bottle of Beaujolais. I don't drink after a meal, so I tell myself. Then I saw a cappuccino machine.

I took my coffee to my couch — and found two girls sitting on it. They budged up a bit, reluctantly. "Are you going to smoke?" I asked them. Quite politely, so I thought. "Piss off," they said.

I moved to a wooden seat, very hard and uncomfortable, much closer to the screen than I wanted. My neck was soon aching, having to stare up, my eyes hurt, my ears were battered by all the noise as the pub filled up.

To my left was a pool table where a couple of teenage waifs were playing. She was pale, deathly looking. He looked like Lee Bowyer, or perhaps Jeffers of Arsenal, if not quite as deprived.

Behind me, the two girls were indeed smoking, while each was busy on their mobile phone at the top of their voice, fucking this, pissing that, ha ha ha. They showed no apparent interest in the game. What were they doing here? On my couch. Which I'd bagged. At the bar, about a dozen lads stood half-watching the game, but mainly talking, smoking and laughing as they supped their pints, pausing only to give an ironic cheer when any Man United player made a mistake. It was Man Utd – Everton. Not that anyone seemed to care, except me.

I came home absolutely knackered and went straight to bed. Hello, London. Goodness, how I've missed you.

I DREAM OF SCORING FOR SPURS, WHICH
SURELY BEATS SCORING WITH THE QUEEN

ONE OF THE GOOD OR AT LEAST INTERESTING EFFECTS OF SO
many league clubs being heavily in debt is that they are being forced
to think of new ways of making money. For almost a hundred years,
supporters' clubs rallied round, held raffles, ran competitions, sold
badges and gave the profits to the club, who were usually totally
ungrateful and continued to treat them like dirt. For the past 30
years, clubs themselves have made money by selling their souls to
shirt sponsors.

This season, something new has been happening—clubs are
starting to sell places in their squad. A 42-year-old salesman has
paid £2,000 for Colchester United's number 71 shirt. At Preston
North End, a 34-year-old businessman has paid £4,100 to be named
as number 64 in their squad—a privilege he secured at an auction.
At Notts County, a 53-year-old university worker has bought a
squad place for £2,500. What fans get for their money varies, but the
squad places are official, with non-contract Football League forms
being signed, the player issued with his kit, his name in the
programme, allowed to come out with the team and take part in
the warm-up.

What fun, what joy. All these years, only child mascots have
been allowed to get so close to their heroes. (It's not widely realised
that most of the mascots have, in fact, paid a large amount for
the honour.)

So far, none of the squad-place purchasers has come on and
played. But then, most clubs have squad players who never appear.
Leeds has a squad with numbers going up to 50. Newcastle has 45,
Man Utd 42, Bolton 41, Fulham 40, Chelsea 39. I look down their
squad lists, and they're full of names who might be anybody. Hold
on. At number 31 in the Chelsea squad has been lurking Mark

Bosnich. Hasn't played for a year, yet must be on £2 million. Now wouldn't it be more sensible to sell these spots and make money?

It will happen soon that one of these fans in the squad will actually come on. A sum of £5,000 will probably do it, if just for five minutes at the end. Or, in the case of Carlisle United, 5p might be enough.

For many years, I had a dream where I was at a Spurs match when they were one man short and I came on. And scored. I can't understand these people who dream about being in bed with the Queen. Pathetic. They should grow up.

My knees are not up to it now, I mean for Spurs, not the Queen, but I'd be willing to pay good money to be manager for one match. No club seems to have thought of this yet, though Burnley have got near. When their manager, Stan Ternent, got banned from the touchline, they auctioned his seat on the bench, which went to a fan for £561. It could have been Alastair Campbell. He's daft enough.

It would cost a bit more actually to be manager for the day, to pick the team, give the team talk, bollock them at half-time, throw a few teacups, then give the press interviews afterwards. You could do that. Our tortoise could do that. And by the law of averages, half the time you'd do as well as the professional manager.

This idea could spread to other fields, such as £10,000 to take part in a cabinet meeting. Better, cleaner way of making money than selling honours to dodgy businessmen. Singing on *Top of the Pops*? Who would ever know the difference? Being a guest on *Have I Got News For You*? That must be cheap, as guests never get a word in.

But let's not get carried away. Let's stick to football, where fantasies are already being fulfilled. The ultimate dream of any true football fan is to appear here, shooting his or her mouth off. What am I bid for this space next week? Come on, £100? OK then, £10. Right, let's see your washers.

THE LATEST GOSSIP FROM PARIS IS THAT ARSÈNE WENGER 'FEELS' HIS PLAYERS

25 NOVEMBER 2002

I DIDN'T HAVE A TICKET FOR ARSENAL – SPURS, AS THE HALF season ticket for Highbury I had for a few years has been reclaimed. I hate football-less Saturday afternoons, so I sat listening to the game on the radio while watching the rugby on television while making tea for the builders doing damp-proofing work downstairs. I always believe someone who can do three things at the same time can easily do a fourth, so the moment Arsenal went a goal up I thought, oh God, it's going to be a hammering, I know, I'll fax my friend Pierre in Paris, see if he can give me any dirt on that bastard Wenger.

Pierre Merle is a French writer who happens to share two of my interests, football and the Beatles, and has written books on each subject. Clearly a talented, intelligent, admirable person.

Mon cher Pierre, I wrote, right, that's enough French for one fax, could you please answer some questions for me? I know Wenger sounds German, presumably because he comes from Alsace-Lorraine, but what sort of first name is Arsène? Pretty poncy, if you ask me. And what do French fans think of him?

'*Dear Hunter,*' replied Pierre, '*Wenger began as what we call 'entraîneur adjoint' — second manager — in a town called Nancy, in Lorraine, in the east of France, which is where he originated. The name Arsène is not very common in France, old-fashioned, I would say, but everyone knows it in France because of Arsène Lupin, the gentleman burglar, a hero, of the French novelist Maurice Leblanc (1864–1941).*

"*French fans like him because they remember how well he did at Monaco. They say over here that he 'feels' his players.*

"*By the way, I seem to remember some English press when he came to Arsenals saying Arsène who?' Now they have the answer…*"

OK, Pierre, calm down. Why are French league clubs so rubbish in Europe?

"Because English clubs steal all our players, particularly you know who..."

What do French fans think of English players generally?

"We know Beckham and Owen and think they are good, just like Ronaldo and Zidane, but no more, no less. I think G Neville is good. We see English football as strong, spectacular, with lots of goals and lots of heads, that is, goals from headers."

Gary Neville? You taking the *pissoir*? I personally think the Spanish league is the best, and I'm sure most Brit fans would agree.

"I think most French fans prefer the Argentinian and Italian way of playing."

Sven and Ulrika, did their affair make the papers in France?

"In France, we make love, not gossip. Seriously. I've never heard of Ulrika. Who is she?"

History, history, so let's look forward. Who's going to win the Euro nations championships in 2004?

"Germany, Spain, Portugal and Netherlands. I don't think Italy, France or England will make it."

Sending faxes to Pierre took my mind off listening to Spurs, which was just as well, as they got stuffed 3–0 by Arsenal. I went down to tell the damp-proof men the score. One didn't understand, being from Kosovo, but the other cheered, so I presumed he must be an Arsenal fan. Turned out to be a West Ham fan who has always hated Spurs.

The rugby in the end was very exciting, England beating Australia, thank goodness we are good at something, and it was interesting to see a new development since I last watched a rugby game. Rugby players are now wearing gloves, fingerless ones, like tarts. So, it wasn't totally a wasted afternoon. And I now know a lot more about Arsène, who is not a bastard, the bastard.

THE JUDGE PUT SOMETHING ON HIS HEAD.
BUT IT WAS A POM-POM HAT, NOT A WIG

9 DECEMBER 2002

GOING TO SPURS THE OTHER WEEK, I WAS STRUCK BY ALL the shirts. Not the cheapo Spurs T-shirts on the street stalls with the rude words, though I did write them down, as a matter of sociological research. "You can stick your Double up your Arse," said one T-shirt. "Support the Scum — I'd rather rod my dog," said another. Who writes them, I wonder. Who then decides to manufacture them, convinced they're on to a winner.

No, what surprised me was the vast number of fans wearing the brand new, up-to-date, official Spurs shirts, the ones with the Thomson logo and the silly face. They had all obviously splashed out once again, spending £35 or so on this season's latest. Where do they get the money from.?

Same at Arsenal. I went there a week ago, with my friend who is a judge. He has three tickets for his family but one person couldn't make it so he rang up and invited me, so kind. As the match began, he started pulling this horrible old thing out of his pocket and proceeded to put it on his head. Oh no, I thought, it's his wig. Turned out to be his ancient Arsenal red-and-white wooly hat. So embarrassing. Least he wasn't in an Arsenal shirt, this season's new one, with the stupid O_2 on. I still don't know what it means. Some sort of bottled water? But all the Arsenal fans are now wearing it.

Arsenal are doing brillo, so their present loyalty and love is understandable, but throughout the Premier League, even down in the depths, there are full houses, with fans buying all the club tat and souvenir rubbish, despite the disappointments. That's what supporters do. Despite everything. They support. And yet there are so many new despites, unknown in ye old old days. Despite, for example, that match fixtures are being mucked around even more than ever. I can't now remember the last time Spurs had a Saturday afternoon home game. It's been on a Sunday five times in succession. Yet still they come, despite the fact that on Sundays you can stay at home and watch live Premiership games on Sky.

It was thought when radio and TV coverage began that the fans would stop coming. That's what the FA and Football League assumed. In the Thirties, the FL banned live radio reports, which led to the BBC covering games at Arsenal by having a relay team of runners who every 15 minutes would race out of the ground and bring the latest information to a commentator, crouching in the street with his mike and machinery.

Eventually, live radio reports were allowed, and the gates, surprisingly, did not drop. Same with live TV. So far, it appears that fans still want to see a game in the flesh, to turn up and support their team, despite all the other attractions.

A week ago, with Man United, Arsenal, Fulham, Liverpool all abroad in Europe, playing midweek games at really awkward times in really awkward places, we still saw large huddles of their supporters who had managed to get away to cheer them on.

Amazing, where do they get the, etc. And amazing, when you think their teams are no longer English, the majority of them foreigners, mercenaries who just happen to have fetched up on these shores, passing through, only temporarily wearing the famous shirt, knowing nothing of its history.

The fans should have the real shirts, for free. They have put their money where their heart is. The players should be forced to buy the rip-off, phoney replicas.

It's potty, dopey, the devotion of fans. But will it last? That's what the clubs assume. Yet football collapsed during the Seventies and Eighties. Gates dropped from 41 million in 1949 to 16 million in 1986.

Fans can be pushed too far. Oh yes. One day they may wake up and decide they'd rather rod the dog.

24 FEBRUARY 2003

SVEN, LIKE TONY BLAIR, MUST ALWAYS HAVE KNOWN IT WAS coming. Our hero, our saviour, what a great victory over Germany/the Tories, can do no wrong, kissy kissy, we love you we do, the greatest manager/PM in the history of blah blah, followed by what a load of rubbish, how were we taken in, he's weak and useless, a poodle, pathetic, he's shite, get him off.

I haven't actually gone off Blair yet, he'll be pleased to hear, but Eriksson is certainly no longer flavour of my month, or even the half-time break, especially the one against Australia. But he still has one thing going for him, unlike Blair — Sven has no natural, obvious, likely successor. That's what everyone agrees. Except me. I know the man for the job. Oh yes.

Peter Taylor, he was being touted not long ago, but now you can't even remember him; and Bryan Robson, John Gregory, where have they gone? Steve McClaren was also a favourite; but he doesn't get tipped any more. David Moyes has been this season's taste thrill, but he's too young and inexperienced, and he's Scottish. Our two most successful managers, Fergie and Wenger, wouldn't take it if asked, why should they, it would be like demotion.

I didn't mind Sven having it off with Ulrika. Time does hang heavily for England managers. When scouting, Sven always leaves games ten minutes early, so he has to go somewhere to park his shoes. Being found out and ridiculed, that was bad, showed lack of planning and cunning, but nah, didn't really bother me. Cashing in on his position, promoting other stuff, when he's on £2m a year, that was poor, but what do you expect, they're all so greedy. Apart from Wenger.

It's his football management that's let him down. Or lack of it. In the World Cup game against Brazil, he sat there like a stuffed dummy, unable to move, summon any emotion. Now It's true we've suffered from over-emotional England managers, like Kevin Keegan and Graham Taylor, working themselves into a lather, losing the plot. There's a lot to be said for staying cool, calm and detached. But there are also times you have to give them a bollocking, stand up and shout. At least show you care.

I forgave him then, for he told us later they were knackered, had given their all. He must know them better than we do. But then it happened again in the Oz match. Like a trapped rabbit this time, stunned, unable to move, apart from the odd twitch at the corner of his tight little mouth. He did nothing to ruffle the course of the game or the feathers of his players.

So who should take over? I bet when he does go, it won't be another foreigner. When things haven't worked out, appointments people always like to go for a different solution, to ring the changes. Which was how Sven got it last time.

That will mean an Englishman. David Platt is still being heavily tipped, but he's done nothing. Alan Curbishley, I'd have him, but not yet—too early. Venables will never return but Hoddle could one day come back. For his Second Coming, of course. It's only really a part-time job, managing England. No need for all that rushing around. Perfect for someone elderly, a senior citizen who has seen it all, is wise and sensible, knows when to smile and when to scream, but is still full of energy. Step forward, Sir Bobby Robson. But steady, mind how you go.

Being 70 means he won't be distracted by the Ulrikas of this world. Even at his age, I'm sure he can still give a girl a good time, but it's no longer one of his priorities. In bed, he'll be up for it. Getting into bed, and out of bed, that will be the hard bit. At 70, he now knows how to conserve his strength for the real tasks. Sven has watched trillions of League games, which did unearth Chris Powell of Charlton, overlooked by all the experts, but then he dropped him. As he has done with many others.

Robson knows the field already. And is decisive. But it's his passion for the game that's so remarkable. He might give Newcastle another season, but after that, he'll be perfect for England. He's got his knighthood already, so no need for arse-licking. He's the most loved and respected football manager in England, so has more chance than Sven in dealing with the Premiership pigs. All I am saying is give age a chance.

TO SOME, ROONEY MAY SEEM A THUG, A THICKO, A FIVE BELLIES IN THE MAKING

14 APRIL 2003

I WAS OPENING THE 'NEW STATESMAN' LAST WEEK. OUR copy comes by post in one of those stupid shrink-wrapped things. Got the cellophane off, put my hand in to pull out the mag, and some little bugger crouching inside bit me. That was my first thought. Then I saw blood on my finger. I'd cut myself on the cover. I put TCP on it, as Mummy always said, then completely forgot about it. Two days later, it started to swell. In four days I was in agony. My GP's given me penicillin, but it's still sore.

I've rung my son the barrister to see if I can sue. He doesn't think I have much of a case; anyway it's not his field, he doesn't do personal injury. Typical. People with doctors in the family say the same. The minute you have something wrong, you ask your daughter or uncle who's a doctor and they say, "Sorry, it's not my line, I don't do cuts, ring me when you've got VD."

So I'm finding it hard to concentrate on anything, except watching football. That's very efficacious. Doctors recommend it. But my mind did start wandering while watching Everton beat Newcastle. Why isn't Wayne Rooney playing for Ireland? Or Danny Murphy, Martin Keown, Kieron Dyer? Michael Owen, he should really be playing for Wales, Scholes and Butt for Germany, the Nevilles for France, Ferdinand for Spain. Beck-ham, now that sounds genuine Old English. I'm sure Mr Blunkett will let him keep his passport.

Lucky for Everton and England that Rooney is English not Irish. A kid like that doesn't come along very often. I got him wrong at first. I thought all he had was premature physical maturity, which is not unusual. We can all remember lads at school aged 13 with deep voices, pubic hair, monster willies and their own razor, but who never grew much bigger.

Rooney is clearly mature as a footballer, as mature as footballers ever get. This is not a sneer. You don't want them too clever, too wise, or they'd never put up with all the shit from coaches in their early years. He's mature in the sense of knowing what to do on the field, where to run, where to pass, and mature in his confidence, in his own ability, not fazed by responsibility or all this expectation and fawning. So far.

Many know-alls have been comparing him with Gazza, saying look at Gazza now, gone to fat. Which happens to be wrong. Gazza is as thin as a rake, the lightest he's been for years. Gazza's not the player he was, but he hasn't gone to seed physically. But looking at Rooney's build, you can sense there might be a weight problem, if he ever gets an awful injury, then sits around stuffing his face.

He doesn't have the twitches, display the nervous tensions, get himself overhyped as the young Gazza did, which is fortunate. His humours appear well balanced, his character phlegmatic. And I do like his girlfriend being 16, from the street next to his, still at school, still wearing ankle socks and her school clothes. She missed his England starting debut as she was in a school play. So sweet, having a Premiership player going out with a schoolgirl, rather than models or lap dancers.

What will happen to Rooney? Will he be self-indulgent? Will events ruin it for him? Will he fade and become as boring a player as Robbie Fowler, a young Scouser once tipped for glory?

Stanley Matthews, Bobby Charlton, Gary Lineker, paragons of all the known football and human virtues, always looked like goody-goodies, healthy in mind and body, took care of themselves, natural Boy Scouts. And Gary did have such a lovely smile. Rooney's looks work against him, as if he's not the part, a throwback to the olden days. I can show you lots of bull-like Rooneys in my collection of Thirties' ciggie cards. Come up and see them some time. These days, forwards are built more like Thierry Henry, Francis Jeffers or Steve McManaman.

His narrow eyes, mean mouth, pasty complexion, boxer's body, chewing gum in his only public appearance, might give some the impression he's a thug, a thicko, a five bellies in the making. Pure class prejudice, of course, and clearly wrong.

He does seem like a good lad, as a player and a person. I've got my fingers crossed for him. Oh no. Now it's agony again.

A MOMENT'S SILENCE, PLEASE, FOR ALL THOSE WHO DIE OF STRESS ON THE TERRACES

5 MAY 2003

OF COURSE, WE'RE SORRY FOR GLENN ROEDER, AND ALL managers with heart problems who collapse under the strain (and there have been some dramatic ones over the years), but come on, managers are not the only ones in football under stress. It's easy to think footballers don't feel such pressures. They are on long contracts, big money, able to switch off after each game and think more about their hearty dicks than their dicky hearts, but they suffer, oh yes, they do. In three ways.

When they are new to a club, at whatever age, they find it very hard to adjust to new colleagues, new systems, perhaps a new language and culture. Young ones can get depressed, give up and go home, as George Best and Graeme Souness both did as teenagers. Older, so-called established players, who come for big money, can feel equally nervous and isolated. I remember Ralph Coates, a big signing at Spurs, coming out in a rash with the worry of it all.

Being injured, that's another terrible time for them, fearing their career might be over, or someone will get their place. And while injured, it's as if they don't exist, become non-persons. Managers can be pigs when a player is out, treating the injured as if it's his fault, while the first-team squad think only of themselves.

Being dropped, stuck on the bench, that's also hell. Beckham has done so well, taking it, not moaning, not giving in to paranoia. It's no use saying he's got all that money, all that fame and his own hair. Nothing makes up for not being picked, especially at his age. He's 28 on 2 May — happy birthday, Bex. For a footballer, he's at the height of his powers. Next stage, it's downhill.

However, save your sympathy, hold back the tears. The people who really suffer in football are the fans. No commentator puts on his caring voice, the one used for poorly managers, to express their sorrow. Dead players from long ago, chairmen you've never heard of, get one minute's silence before a match and black armbands, but I've never heard a crowd being asked to stand in memory of a fan who's had a heart attack at a game. Yet it happens all the time. I've seen them being carried out.

There's a young bloke, slightly over-weight, shaven head, who sits in front of me at Arsenal who works himself into a total rage each week. I can't see him making 40. Arsenal, in theory, should be an easy club to support, as they have been so successful, yet they are putting their supporters through agonies at present.

Even if Man Utd win the league, they have also given their fans some awful moments, humiliated by Real Madrid, failing once again in Europe. The higher you go, the worse the disappointment can be. At the bottom of the leagues, for supporters of Sunderland, West Ham, Sheffield Wednesday, Brighton, Northampton, Carlisle United, Shrewsbury, Exeter, oh and loads more, the whole season has been one of pain and agony and constant stress.

I used to get hellish earache when watching Spurs, from grinding my teeth and clenching my jaw. It also happened when I got in a panic over work, doing too much, or in a state in traffic jams. Stupid really, but it went on for years, and endless dental surgeons buggered around with complicated solutions and plates to wear in my mouth. In the end, I taught myself to relax when I felt it coming on. And if that failed, I used a hot-water bottle on my ear, a little one, which I now always carry when travelling. Works a treat. That will be five guineas.

Now at Spurs, I sit with my jaw open, a forced smile on my face, making myself relax, while all around are losing their heads, moaning and groaning, frothing at the mouth.

So don't say fans aren't under stress. But there is one vital difference between managers and players suffering and supporters suffering. They get paid for their pains, handsomely, and in the Premiership, all managers and players are now millionaires. We pay to suffer. Spending a thousand or so each season. And we don't have to do it. Nobody forces us. Which makes it worse. Madness. So before turning to the next page, please, a moment of silence for all fans. Respect.

SIXTY JIMMY SAVILE LOOKALIKES FROM LEEDS AND OTHER AWARD-WINNERS

12 MAY 2003

ANOTHER SEASON, ANOTHER REASON FOR MAKING "WHO HE?" —which is what rival supporters shout when Beckham prepares to take a corner. So let's start with him in the annual awards.

Alice Band of the Year. No competition, really.

Horrible Hair of the Year. Freddie Ljungberg. After several seasons of dyeing it red, he's given up and we can see the reason why he did it. He's got really nasty, thin, weedy hair.

Phrases of the Year. The most frequently used has been "I've seen them given", which does not refer to the Newcastle goalie but a penalty claim or a similar so-called talking point, which is another over-used phrase. But the winner is, "He's been a good servant to the club." It suggests the player in question has played for nothing, as opposed to being paid a fortune. If he'd been any good, not so dozy, he'd have gone elsewhere like a shot, and not given a bugger about being a loyal servant.

Chant of the Year. "All you need is Duff", sung by Blackburn Rovers supporters.

Wigs of the Year. At Arsenal–Leeds, I came across a gaggle of Leeds fans in long white wigs. Could it be an allusion to Alan Smith, who has short, bleached hair? But he wasn't playing. Excuse me, sirs, I said, why the wigs? "Now then, young man, young man, now then." They were Jimmy Savile impersonators. Sixty of them had dressed up for their trip to London to cheer themselves up, as they were sure they were going down. I bet the TV men did close-ups, but did they know the reason?

Crowd of the Year. Man Utd, for clapping Ronaldo off the pitch after he'd scored a hat-trick against them for Real Madrid.

New pronunciation. Jermaine 'Jeenas' of Newcastle, who until halfway through the season was 'Janus'.

TV Image. Beckham blowing kisses during the England–Turkey game. The cameraman caught it, but it didn't make sense until later, when it turned out that some Turkish players had been trying to wind up Bex by making suggestions about his sexuality. Some brutes will stop at nothing.

Real Image. Still in my mind's eye, an incident from the Arsenal–Man Utd game when Campbell elbowed Solskjaer. The referee and linesmen conferred, holding their hands to their mouths so cameras across the pitch could not read their lips—but unknown to them, a Sky cameraman was running like hell from the corner flag, where he usually stands, his camera hung over his belly. He got right up behind them and caught every word.

Bye-Byes of the Year. Peter Ridsdale, Michael Knighton, Sergei Rebrov, Terry Venables. Where is Tel, by the way? Sulking in Spain?

Hellos of the Year. Wayne Rooney got all the attention, and deservedly, but for my money, John O'Shea is the most valuable young player.

Mad Money. That £30m paid for Rio Ferdinand. Probably now worth £13m. Not just because he's done little, but because such fees are from another era. Since Alf Common went for £1,000 to 'Boro in 1905, which shock-horrored the football world, transfers have inexorably kept climbing. This season, for the first time, they look like going backwards. Hurrah for that.

Commentator of the Year. You would have thought the success of the Spanish and Italian teams in Europe, and the rubbish performances by Man U and Arsenal, would have made our TV commentators stop boasting that the Premiership is the world's best. Yet Andy Gray is still saying it—on the basis that our games are 'unpredictable', with lowly teams always liable to win. It happens everywhere. Such as last week: Real Madrid getting beaten 5–1 by

Mallorca. Get a grip, Gray.

So the award goes to Big Ron. Earlier in the season, his co-commentator observed that a player "has had some big misses over the years". Back came Ron, like a flash. "I didn't know you knew about his wives…"

Disappointment of the Year. Spurs, of course. I told myself I would not renew my season ticket unless they finished higher than last season. They won't. But I will, being stupid.

See yous next season.

POMONA BOOKS

POMONA'S AIM IS TO PRODUCE A CLASSIC BRANDING OF TITLES, each of them beautifully presented and immediately identifiable to readers. We will publish the work of stimulating and talented authors. Our website is www.pomonasounds.co.uk.

Also available:

FOOTNOTE*
by Boff Whalley

ISBN 1-904590-00-4

FOOTNOTE IS CLEVER, FUNNY AND IRREVERENT — A STORY ABOUT A boy from the redbrick clichés of smalltown England reconciling Mormonism and punk rock, industrial courtesy and political insurrection.

He finds a guitar, anarchism and art terrorism and, after years (and years and years) of earnest, determined, honest-to-goodness slogging, his pop group† makes it big; that's BIG with a megaphone actually. They write a song that has the whole world singing and, funnily enough, it's an admirable summary of a life well lived — about getting knocked down and getting back up again.

Meanwhile, there's a whole world still happening: authentic lives carefully drawn, emotional but not sentimental and always with a writer's eye for detail. *Footnote* is not another plodding rock memoir but a compassionate, critical and sometimes cynical account of a life steeped in pop culture, lower division football and putting the world to rights.

---

* See page 293 of Boff Whalley's book.
† Boff Whalley is a member of Chumbawamba.

RULE OF NIGHT
by Trevor Hoyle

ISBN 1-904590-01-2

IF THE SIXTIES WERE SWINGING, THE SEVENTIES WERE THE HANG-over — darker, nastier, uglier — especially if you lived on a council estate in the north of England.

Rule of Night was first published in 1975 and has since become a cult classic. It pre-dates the current vogue for 'hard men' and 'football hoolie' books by 25 years.

It is, however, much more than this. Trevor Hoyle creates a chillingly detailed world, where teenagers prowl rainy fluorescent-lit streets dressed as their *Clockwork Orange* anti-heroes. The backdrop is provided by Ford Cortinas, Players No.6, the factory, the relentless struggle to maintain hope.

Hoyle, who has since been published by John Calder (home to Samuel Beckett and William S. Burroughs), has added a fascinating afterword to his original book which has been out of print and highly sought-after for many years.

LOVE SONGS
by Crass

ISBN 1-904590-03-9

CRASS: A LONDON-BASED COLLECTIVE FORMED IN 1977 OF A diverse and eclectic group of individuals who operated for several years using art, literature, film and music as vehicles to share information and ideas. They also wanted to change the world.

This is a collection of words spanning those seven short years; a book of shock slogans and mindless token tantrums. An anthology of passionate love songs that sought to inspire a generation.

> *Our love of life is total,*
> *everything we do is an expression of that,*
> *everything that we write is a love song.*

> –Penny Rimbaud
> *Yes Sir, I Will,* 1983.

.   .   .

To be published 14th February 2004

The perfect Valentine's gift, for those who love life.

WARNING:
CONTAINS SOME CHOICE LANGUAGE.

POMONA SOUNDS

POMONA SOUNDS IS OUR AFFILIATED RECORD LABEL.
The following CD albums will enhance your life:

PS-001	The Rosenbergs *Ameripop*
PS-002	Black September *Black September*
PS-003	Mudskipper *Eggshells*
PS-004	The Monkey Run *Escape From The Rake*
PS-005	Crass *You'll Ruin It For Everyone*
PS-006	Killing Stars *When The Light First Fell*
PS-007	Black September *You Can Do Anything If You Set Your Mind To It*

These should be available through your friendly local record store.
If yours isn't so friendly, they can be bought at:

www.pomonasounds.co.uk